"*Losing My Country, Keeping My Soul* is Allan Glass's insightful memoir of escaping to Canada to avoid the Vietnam draft...The writing is evocative, whether Glass is describing carefree days surfing, scuba diving, and crabbing in crystal-clear bays, or hearing Walter Cronkite's authoritative voice describe the Tet Offensive. It brings beach bonfires to life and sheds light on the narrator's inner psychological turmoil; he cannot reconcile himself to killing or being killed. Glass captures his feelings of confusion over the war and his fears about landing in jail...Dialogue is recreated in exacting, believable detail that has the ring of truth."
—*Foreword* Clarion Reviews

"Glass skillfully captures the tense mood among forced recruits, watching those who resisted get dragged away. He also explores abuse at the Presidio with great care, narrating a near uprising among soldiers."
—*Kirkus Reviews*

Losing
my Country,

Keeping
my Soul

allan glass

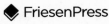 FriesenPress

Suite 300 - 990 Fort St
Victoria, BC, V8V 3K2
Canada

www.friesenpress.com

Barbed wire, rifle and Canadian flag vector by Vecteezy.com

ISBN
978-1-5255-2733-3 (Hardcover)
978-1-5255-2734-0 (Paperback)
978-1-5255-2735-7 (eBook)

1. BIOGRAPHY & AUTOBIOGRAPHY, PERSONAL MEMOIRS

Distributed to the trade by The Ingram Book Company

Table of Contents

Dedication

I dedicate this book
to all of the people who helped
make this journey a successful one.
To my parents, whose support
gave me the courage to continue.
To Tom, wherever you are.
And last but not least, to Keith,
the brother I never had.

Preface

In 1965, everything began to change, both for myself and the world. I had just graduated from high school in May and I had turned eighteen in June.

At the same time, the Vietnam War was beginning in Southeast Asia.

I enrolled at Miami-Dade Junior College, which gave me a deferment from military service.

After the first year, I was ready to begin my second and final year, but other forces took over, and I ended up going on a roller-coaster ride that lasted for two years. It included love, despair, and murder. This story is an actual account of those two years, from fun, fun, fun, to guns, guns, guns, to run, run, run—losing my country, but keeping my soul.

PART I:

Fun, Fun, Fun

Chapter 1
THE BEGINNING

It was mid-May, 1967, a typical hot and humid day in south Florida, when I got a call from my best friend, Keith.

"Let's go to the beach," he said. "I just talked to Donny and he told me the waves are starting to build." Donny was a fellow surfing buddy whose father was a senior lifeguard at one of our favorite beaches, so Donny would get up-to-the-minute information on the surfing conditions each day.

As I had done so many times before, I said, "Sure, I'll be right over," and rushed out to load my board onto my car. My mother was used to this scenario, so she didn't need any explanation as to where I was going or when I would be back.

I was twenty years old, attending Miami-Dade Junior College, working part time at a super market, and driving a beautiful 1965 Malibu Super Sport. My father was away in Europe, working for Pan American Airways, and my three older sisters were all married. Keith was nineteen and attended the same junior college as I.

I picked Keith up and we headed for South Beach. Upon arriving, we could see that there wasn't anybody else around. Three-foot waves with a slight offshore breeze made the conditions perfect, so we unloaded our boards and went in. After an hour, we decided to take a break and head to the nearest food shack.

While we were waiting for our order of hot dogs and shakes, I brought up the idea of going somewhere else to surf.

"We've been doing the same old thing now for two years," I said. "Wouldn't it be great to expand our travels and drive further up the coast of Florida? Maybe even to Georgia and South Carolina?"

"I recently read in a magazine article," Keith replied, "that said there are places in South Carolina that are really good for surfing."

After tossing the idea around, we went back to the beach and resumed surfing.

It didn't take long for me to fall off my board, and as I swam to retrieve it, I felt a tingling sensation around my ankle. As I kept on swimming, the tingling progressed up my leg, around my waist, and over my back. It traveled up around my shoulder and neck, and it was becoming apparent that I was having some difficulty treading water. Soon, I became numb all over, and I looked for Keith. He was busy catching a wave, and didn't notice my predicament.

I was now panicking, and was barely able to keep my head above water. I yelled out, but Keith didn't hear me. I tried a few more times until he finally noticed me and paddled over.

"What's wrong, Allan? Where is your board?"

"I'm paralyzed, and it stings all over my body," I said.

"There must be a Portuguese man o' war jelly fish around here," Keith said. "Come on, I'll help you get onto my board."

I struggled to climb on, and Keith paddled us to the shore.

"We should go up to where the fresh water showers are," Keith said. "Can you walk?"

I could hardly stand up by myself, so Keith helped me to the showers and once we got there he started rubbing sand over my legs and back.

"This might relieve some of the stinging caused by the jellyfish poison," he said. "I learned this from Donny's father."

"It seems to be helping," I said, "but my whole body still feels weird."

Keith continued rubbing for ten more minutes and then I said, "It's okay now, just let me sit down for a while."

As I rested, I explained to Keith how it felt as the poison entered my body.

"At first I felt a stinging sensation like being stung by bees, and as it went up my leg and around my waist, it started to paralyze my muscles, and I could barely move my arms."

"You're lucky that we practice the buddy system," Keith said. "If you were here alone, you might have drowned."

The thought of that sent shivers down my back. "We should tell those guys over there," I said, pointing to some new arrivals that were getting their boards ready.

"I'll go and tell them," Keith said. "I'll be right back."

When Keith came back, we decided that we had had enough excitement for the day, and headed home.

Keith took my keys and said, "I'll drive. You might still have a reaction on the way home."

On the way home, we joked about the other close calls we've had; surfing with three-foot sharks at Cocoa Beach, scuba diving with stingrays and barracudas, and of course the oncoming storms brought on by hurricanes.

It was this feeling of being dependent on one another that strengthened our bond of friendship after each incident.

After we arrived at Keith's house, I told him I felt good enough to drive myself home.

"All right," Keith said. "I'll phone Donny, and tell him to call his dad and let him know about the presence of the jellyfish."

I drove home, and as soon as I walked in the phone rang.

"It's me," Keith said. "I just got off the phone with Donny and he told me that there had been another jelly fish attack at his father's beach, and that the people were taken to the hospital. How are you feeling?"

"I'm fine," I said, "but it sounds as though there isn't going to be any surfing for a few days, until they're gone."

"I'm working tomorrow at the gas station, so I'll talk to you later," Keith said.

Chapter 2
A MAJOR CHANGE

The month went by quickly, and even though we still had three more months of summer, I began thinking about going back to school. I was majoring in business and bookkeeping accounting, but the classroom was slowly giving way to my outdoor activities. I now wanted to change my outlook on life, so I went to see my sister, Pam. She and her husband were into their careers: Pam was a nurse, and John was working for an underwater-communications company, who were involved with the US Navy.

"You like the ocean a lot," John said, "so why not seek a career that is related to it?"

"As long as it's not a military job," I said, "I'm open to suggestions."

We tossed a few ideas around, and we came to the conclusion that I might like to become a professional diver. The fact was that John could get me a job working with his company, but that I would first have to obtain a minimum two-year degree in marine biology.

I told John that sounded great. John then insisted that we go out to the swimming pool for a test. He grabbed a pair of swimming trunks from his bedroom and handed them to me. I followed him to a storage shed, and he showed me some diving gear. He grabbed a scuba tank and mask, and said, "Follow me."

We went to another shed, one used for changing, and he told me to put the trunks on. I then followed him to the shallow end of the pool where he started to instruct me on how to put the mask on, turn the air on, and clear the mask of water. I told him that I knew all of that, but before I could say anything else, he threw everything in the water. I looked at him and asked, "What am I supposed to do now?"

"Dive in," he said, "and put everything on while you are underwater."

I repeated in my mind the steps that John had told me, and dove in.

First, I put the mouthpiece in, then turned on the air and put the mask on. Then, using the bubbles coming from my mouthpiece, I tilted my head to one side and allowed them to clear as much water from my mask as possible. Once this was done and my breathing was under control, I strapped on the tank and began swimming. I went around the pool once, and then surfaced.

I looked at John, who was clapping his hands.

"Congratulations," he said, "you just passed the Navy's preliminary dive test, the shortened version of course."

"Very good Allan," Pam said, "I knew you could do it."

I got out of the pool and went back to the shed to change, feeling very proud of myself. After changing, I thanked my sister and John for everything, and told them that I would let the college know right away of my wish to change courses.

I called the school the next day and was told to come in right away to see a counselor.

After telling the counselor about my wish to change my major from business to marine biology, he said, "That's quite a change. Looking at your high school record, it shows your only science is grade 10 biology; you never took chemistry or physics."

"I just want to become a professional diver," I said, "not a chemist. Is this going to keep me from taking this course?"

"No, it isn't," he said, "but you should let the teacher know."

He proceeded with the required paperwork and I was officially enrolled in my new courses. Now it was time to get back to having fun again. I called Keith and told him of my plans for the upcoming school year, and how I felt good about my future. Keith was a year younger than me. He had always been mechanically inclined, so working at a gas station was his way of going to school, and learning how to fix cars. He lived with his mother, Maria, and his cousin, Johnny, and had no contact with his father, who was somewhere in California.

"So, what are we going to do today?" I asked.

"Let's go over to Naples on the west coast," he said. "We'll fish and set our crab traps."

"That sounds great; I'll be right over."

I grabbed my fishing and scuba gear, loaded them into my car, and took off.

Keith was ready to go, and loaded a couple of small crab traps into the car.

On the way, we started talking about our dream of going up the east coast on a "surfing safari" trip.

Keith had brought a map and a couple of magazines, and he started telling me about different places that he had found to be excellent for surfing.

After discussing a few options, I asked, "Whose vehicle are we going take?"

"Why yours," Keith said. "My VW is too old. Yours is practically brand new."

"I wish we had something big enough to sleep in," I said. "Then it wouldn't cost so much for motels."

"Yes, you're right about that," Keith answered, "but we could sleep on the beach, it is summertime."

"We could," I said, "but it would be better if we had something that we knew we could sleep in, just in case it rains."

"Yeah, I guess you're right," Keith said. "We can look for something when we get back."

When we arrived in Naples, we went straight to our favourite area for crabbing, a small bay with crystal clear, shallow water. We put on our masks and snorkels, and took our traps out far enough to where the crabs hung out. The coral reefs were also the perfect refuge for lobsters, a prized catch on our previous trips. After setting the traps, we swam back to shore and hoped that our baited traps would soon lure them out.

The famous Naples fishing pier was nearby and we were soon greeted by the locals.

"How's the fishing today?" I asked.

"It's been real good," one of them said, "plenty of mackerel."

After we fished for a few hours, we gave our catch away and went to check on our crab traps. We were delighted to see that we had about six large blue crabs in each trap, but all of the bait had been eaten, so we brought the crabs back and put them into our holding tank, a five-gallon bucket. We baited the traps again and put them out in a different spot.

"Do you want to fish some more?" I asked.

"No," Keith said, "I'm getting hungry. Let's go and get something to eat."

We ended up at our favourite hamburger joint and began talking to the locals.

We asked them if they knew of any surfing spots on the west coast of Florida, but they didn't know of any. After telling them of our plans to go up the east coast, we took off to get our fishing gear. We fished for another hour before Keith told me that he was ready to call it quits, so we grabbed our gear and left to check on the traps. We were blessed with another dozen crabs, and decided that we had enough.

"Let's go home," Keith said. "I'm excited about our trip and looking for a vehicle to go in."

When we arrived at Keith's house, his mother had a large pot of hot water waiting for us. She always knew that we would come back with enough crabs for a feast. She called up Donny and his parents, who lived next door, to come over and take part.

"Why don't you call your mother," Maria said, "and get her to come over?"

"My mother doesn't go anywhere," I said. "She is content to stay at home and watch TV."

"Oh well," Maria said, "the more for us."

Donny and his parents came right over. Soon, the water was boiling and eight crabs were dumped in. Everyone helped in setting the table, with a dozen or so lemons cut and ready to add to the meal. After ten minutes, the first batch was ready, and the second batch of eight was placed into the boiling water.

"There are twenty-four of these critters," I said. "That's enough for four each."

"I can tell that you're doing well in school," Maria said. "Aren't you taking accounting or something like that?"

"Yes," I replied, "but I'm thinking of changing to a marine biology degree."

"Why are you changing?" Donny asked.

"I'm getting bored with bookkeeping," I said, "and because I like being near the ocean so much. I am going to become a professional diver and work with John, my brother-in-law."

"That's a big change," Donny's father said. "But as long as you stay in school, you don't have to worry about what's going on in Vietnam."

"Yes," I said, "I haven't really thought about that. It's been two years since it started, so I'm sure that it will be over soon."

"Yeah," he replied, "it shouldn't take too long to put those communists in their place."

After the last batch of crabs was cooked, Maria said, "Let's eat," and everyone started to devour their crab. After hearing the word

Vietnam, I decided to change the subject, and began talking about the trip that Keith and I were planning.

"So, Keith, where should we go on our surfing trip?" I asked.

Keith looked at his mother, and waited for her reaction. When he saw that she was waiting for his answer to my question, he said, "I think we should stay on the east coast and head for South Carolina, maybe even up to Virginia Beach."

"So that's why you were so interested in my magazines," Maria said. "You should have told me what you were planning."

"I was going to," Keith said, "but we aren't sure of which vehicle to take."

Donny's father laughed and told us that my car would be too expensive for gas, and that Keith's was too old. "Besides that," he said, "where would you sleep, and take a shower?"

"You kids are nuts," Donny's mother said.

Maria asked about our jobs. Keith explained that he could probably get his back when we returned. I told them that my job in the supermarket was getting boring, and that I was going to look for something else that related to my new choice of careers, diving.

"I think a bit of traveling is a good idea," Donny's father said, "as long as you have the proper vehicle to do it in."

Keith's mother just sat there, staring at the two of us. "It's up to the two of you, since you have been doing everything else together."

I looked at Donny and asked, "What about you, Donny, want to come?"

"No way," Donny's mother blurted, "he's staying right here."

We went back to finishing our meal in relative silence, and after cleaning up the mess we had made, Keith and I decided to leave and plan on how we were going to travel up the coast.

Chapter 3
THE HEARSE

As Keith and I were driving around town, we both agreed with what Donny's father had told us about getting a proper vehicle in which to travel. Suddenly I spotted a large black vehicle, and something told me that we had to go back and check it out.

"Slow down!" I said, "We have to turn around."

"What is it?" Keith asked.

"That car lot we just passed," I said. "I saw a big black truck or something like that. Trust me, we have to turn around and go back."

Keith found a side street and turned into it, then swung around and headed back to where I saw the truck. He pulled into the lot and parked. We got out and stood there, gazing at the vehicle, our mouths open. Just then, a salesman came out and saw us staring at the truck.

"Hello, boys," he said, "I'm Carl. Isn't she a beauty?"

"Yes," I said, "what is it, and is it for sale?"

"Why, it's a hearse," he answered. "Are you interested in it?"

"Yes, we are, how much?"

"Well," he said, "before we get into that, why don't you take a closer look at it?"

Keith and I could not believe our eyes. Each side had three incredible-looking church-style-shaped windows with carved figurines.

"This is like a panel truck," I said, "but it's like no other one that I've seen."

"You got that right," Carl said. "It's a one of a kind vehicle. Here, let me show you the inside."

He walked to the rear of the vehicle and opened the back door.

"This is a 1941 Cadillac hearse," he said, "complete with a coffin in the back."

"This is unbelievable!" I said, "It's huge, creepy, and really neat."

"There is more to this than meets the eye," Carl added, "but I'll tell you more about it inside my office if you're really interested in buying it."

Keith and I kept walking around the vehicle, totally in awe of it.

"It runs good?" Keith asked.

"Yes, it does," Carl stated with pride. "Wait here and I'll go get the keys."

When he returned, he handed me the keys and told me to start it up.

"If you want to, you can take it for a spin around the block."

I looked at Keith, who was trying to find out how to open the hood.

"Hey Keith," I called, "we can take it around the block! Do you want to?"

"Yes, I would!" he said. "You drive."

"Now remember," Carl said, "this vehicle is much larger than your ordinary truck. Are you sure you can handle the extra length and width?"

"Yes," I said, "I'll drive slowly." I hopped in and started it up. The motor sounded really good and Keith gave me the thumbs up signal.

"Now remember," Carl said, "just around the block; I don't want you to be stopped by the police."

"Don't worry," Keith said, "we'll just go around the block."

I pulled out of the parking lot, and turned right down the first side street. As I turned and began to straighten out, I felt the rear wheels of the hearse hop over the curb.

Keith started laughing. "Way to go, Allan, you just ran over the sidewalk."

"Wow," I said, "this is different than anything else I've driven, but it's so cool."

The interior of the hearse was in excellent condition.

"I guess this thing hasn't been driven too many times," I joked. "No wonder it's in good shape."

"Here's the next turn," Keith said. "Remember to take it a little wider this time."

I slowed down and made sure there was no one coming as I went into my turn.

"That's more like it," Keith said. "Now back to the car lot."

I pulled into the lot and asked Keith if he thought we should buy it.

"That depends on how much this guy wants," Keith said. "It's in such good condition, but I hope we can afford it."

Carl was there waiting for us. I got out and handed him the keys.

"So, what do you think of it?" he asked. "Did you have any problems?"

"No, I didn't," I said.

"Would you like to come into my office?" he asked.

"Yeah," I said. "Let's go to your office."

The three of us sat down and Carl reached into his desk drawer and took a large newspaper clipping out, and placed it in front of me.

"The vehicle that you just drove," he explained, "is the one pictured here. The same one that carried Al Capone's body to the cemetery."

Keith and I looked at the clipping, which in fact had a picture of the hearse, and the heading was "Al Capone Buried Today."

"Wow," I said, 'you're kidding, right?"

"No, I am not kidding," he said. "You have a chance at owning a piece of history."

I sat back in my chair and asked, "How much?"

"First of all," Carl said, "I'd like to know why you want it."

I told him about our surfing safari trip, and he just laughed and said, "That's wonderful. I wish I were your age to be able to do something like that. Alright then, I'll take four hundred dollars for it, and that includes the coffin."

Keith and I looked at each other, as neither one of us could say whether or not it was a fair price.

To buy some time, I insisted that he tell us the truth about the newspaper clipping, and added that it didn't matter to us who it had carried.

"Look boys," Carl said, "the article came with the vehicle. That's all I know."

"Alright then," I said, looking at Keith, "we'll buy it."

"How soon can you get the money?" the salesman asked bluntly.

"Well," I said, "I need to go to the bank, so how about tomorrow?"

"Alright then," Carl said, "see you tomorrow."

The three of us shook hands and Keith and I left.

On the way home, we traded ideas on what we were going to do with it, and Keith suggested that we first bring it to his gas station and check everything out.

"That sounds like a good idea," I said. "See you tomorrow."

The next day, Keith picked me up in his VW and we went to my bank.

On the way to the car lot, I asked Keith about Carl mentioning the fact that this vehicle qualifies as an antique, and that we could get a cheaper insurance rate, as well as a special antique license plate.

"Yes," Keith said, "he did say something about that, but I'm sure you will have to apply for one, and who knows how long that will take."

"Who cares?" I said. "We've got ourselves a very cool truck."

I had told my mother about buying the truck, but I didn't tell her that it was a hearse. She just told me that since it was my money, I could buy whatever I wanted.

When we arrived at the car lot, I couldn't take my eyes off the hearse.

Carl came out and shook my hand. "I finished the paper work, he said, and now all that remains is your signature and of course the cash."

We followed him into his office and sat down. I took my wallet out and proudly slapped the money on top of his desk.

He grabbed it, counted it, and said, "Sign here and here, and it's yours."

It only took a few minutes to close the deal and then he gave me the keys.

"Oh yes," he said, "one more thing. I got you a temporary insurance sticker, at no extra cost, that will allow you to drive it from here to your home."

"Thank you very much," I said. "I forgot about that."

"Most people do," Carl said as he placed the sticker on the windshield. "There you go. Now you are officially legal to drive her away."

We shook hands and I hopped into the driver's seat.

"I'll see you later," I said to Keith. "You should follow me just in case something happens."

"No problem," Keith said, as he got into his VW.

The drive home was a bit nerve-racking as the larger-than-life hearse rumbled down the road. I began to notice people were staring at me as I drove by them. At a traffic light, I saw a police car behind me and I began to get really nervous. As I took off, I was hoping that he would turn, but instead he turned on his red and blues, and I pulled over to the curb.

He walked up to my window and asked me for my driver's license and registration.

"Here you are," I said. "What did I do wrong?"

"Oh, nothing," he said with a smile. "I just wanted to take a look at this vehicle, because it looks like a hearse."

I smiled and said, "Yes, it is a hearse. I just bought it from the used car lot only a few blocks back."

He returned my license and registration to me and proceeded to walk around the hearse.

"What's inside, a coffin?" he asked jokingly.

"Why, yes," I said. "Would you like to see it?"

"No, that's okay. You can go now, and drive carefully."

I thanked him and drove off. I could see that Keith had stopped a little way up the road and was waiting for me.

I took a direct route home. Keith pulled in and the two of us just stood there and stared at the hearse, as we were still in awe over the whole ordeal.

I looked at the front window of my house and saw my mother standing there, looking out.

"Come on," I said, "let's tell my mother what we did."

We went in and my mother asked, "What is that, and who does it belong to?"

"It belongs to the both of us," I said. "We are going to use it to go on a surfing trip up the east coast."

"It looks like a hearse," she said, smiling. "Is it?"

"Yes, it is, Mom, and the salesman told us that it is the same one that carried Al Capone."

She just laughed at that remark. "I think he told you that just so you'd buy it."

"Well Mom," I said, "it doesn't matter to us who it carried, we just needed something big enough to take us surfing."

"When do you plan on going on this trip?" she asked.

"Soon," I said. "Keith is going to check it out at the gas station, and then we will be ready to go."

"Well," she said, "at least I won't have to look at that ugly thing for too long."

"No Mom, you won't. Now just relax and don't worry about it."

I grabbed Keith's arm and said, "Come on, let's go take the coffin out and put it on the trash pile."

I could see my mother watching us take the coffin out of the hearse and place it on the pile that would be picked up in the morning.

"She's definitely going to be worried about this," Keith said, "I sure hope the garbage men take it."

"Why wouldn't they?" I asked. "It's garbage now."

After removing the coffin, I said, "I'll take my car and follow you to your house. I can't wait to tell Donny about the hearse."

We arrived at Keith's house and told everyone about the hearse.

"It sounds really neat," Donny said. "How's your mother taking it?"

"She's okay with it for now," I said. "We'll be leaving soon, so she won't have to look at it."

The next day, I drove the hearse a short distance to the garage where Keith was working. Bob, the owner of the garage, took one look at the hearse and said, "We might have a problem here, as my hydraulic lifts are only wide enough for normal-sized cars and pickups, and this definitely looks to be wider. Anyway, pull up to them and we'll see."

He was right. It was wider than the lifts were so Bob told me to pull over into the next bay, as it had a pit. A worker could jump down into an area that was beneath the vehicle, rather than lift the vehicle up. This enabled Bob and Keith to inspect the undercarriage.

"Whoever had this vehicle before," Bob said, "did a really good job of maintaining everything."

"That's good to hear," I said, "because I don't know where we would even get parts, or the money for that matter."

Keith said it was time to have a look under the hood. They climbed out of the pit and raised the hood.

"Oh yes," Bob said on seeing the motor, "it's a straight eight, which they don't make anymore. I take it you're happy with the power and the way it sounds, so let's check the oil.

"The oil still looks pretty good, and I didn't see any smoke coming from the tailpipe when you drove in, so that's another good sign. I would have to say that you boys have yourself a pretty rare vehicle, even if the parts are going to be hard or impossible to get."

"Oh well," Keith said, "we'll cross that bridge when we come to it."

As Bob walked around one more time, he noticed that there wasn't any license plate.

"Hey, where's the license plate for this thing?"

"Oh," I answered, "it's an antique so I'm going to apply for one today."

"That's fine," Bob said, "but how are you going to go anywhere until you get it?"

I looked around the garage and saw some empty cardboard boxes, so I walked over and grabbed one. I tore a rectangular piece off, and asked the owner if he had a felt marking pen.

"Why yes, I do," he said, "there's one in the office."

Keith went and got the marker and handed it to me.

"What are you going to do with it?" he asked.

I thought for a moment then wrote "TAG APPLIED FOR," and looked for an appropriate place to put it.

"Here," Bob said, "this is where the plate should go. I'll get a piece of plywood and some new nuts and bolts and we'll make a place to put your sign."

After fastening it down, we stood back and had a good laugh.

"I don't even want to think of what a police officer is going to say when he sees that," Bob said.

"I'll just tell him that I've applied for an antique tag, and that it's being processed and I should have it any day now."

After we were done, I told Keith that I was going to take it back home and I would call him later on that night.

When I got home, my mother told me that a man had phoned. "He wanted to speak to you about a surfing trip that he had heard about, something about going to California. You never told me anything about going to California, did you?"

"No Mother," I said, "I never mentioned anything to anyone about going all the way to California, but it would be quite the trip."

"Now don't you start getting crazy ideas," she said, "I don't mind you going a ways up the coast, but clear across the United States, that would be out of the question."

"We're not going to California, Mom, so don't worry about that."

I went to my room wondering who it was that would phone with such an incredible story. An hour later the phone rang.

"It's for you, son," Mom said, "it's the same man that phoned earlier."

"Hello," I said, "who is this?"

"My name is Wayne and I'm a writer with the Miami *Herald*. I heard that you and some friends are planning a trip out west, and you are going to live in your hearse, is that true?"

"Well no, we're not planning on going west, but we are planning a trip up the east coast. How did you hear about this?"

"I'm a newsman," he said, "I hear about these things; it's my job. Anyway, I'd like to do a story about it. I'll send a photographer out and to get some pictures, what do you say to that?"

I was so stunned that I could not speak.

"Are you still there?" he asked.

"Oh yes, I am, uh sure, that would be great, when do you want to do it?"

"How about tomorrow?" he asked. "and could you also get your friends to come out and bring their surfboards too?"

"Yes, I could do that. What time would he be here?"

"Say, one o'clock; the sun would be at the right height for picture-taking. Is that okay with you?"

"Sounds good to me! I'll see you and the photographer tomorrow; thank you."

"I'm pretty busy here at the newspaper," he said, "so just give all of the details of your trip to wherever you are going to the photographer. Thank you. Bye."

After I hung up I called Keith right away.

"Hey Keith, I just talked to a Miami *Herald* reporter and he wants to do a story on our trip, complete with pictures."

At first Keith thought I was joking but after a few minutes he agreed to come over the next day, and he told me that a guy who lived down the road from him, Dennis, had shown up at his house and wanted to go surfing with us.

"He seems like a nice guy, can I bring him along or what?"

"Sure," I said, "the more the merrier. And why don't you try and get Donny and Frank too?"

"I think Frank has gone on a vacation," Keith said, "but I'll ask Donny. See you tomorrow."

The next day arrived, a warm sunny day that would be perfect for taking pictures. Keith and Dennis arrived around noon and we went over our story of where we were going on our trip.

"I think the California trip sounds a lot better than just going up the coast," Keith said. Dennis also agreed to the California idea.

"I'd really like to come along," Dennis said, and he tried his best to become a part of our plan. We told him we would think about it.

At one o'clock, a large station wagon turned onto my street and stopped in front of the hearse. The photographer smiled as he got out and came over to where we were standing.

"Hello boys," he said, "my name is Albert, and I'm a photographer with the *Herald*. Which one of you is Allan?"

"I am," I said, shaking his hand.

"Well now," Albert said, "you spoke with Wayne, who told me that you are going to California in this hearse, is that right?"

"Yes, we are going to California in this hearse." A white lie indeed, but I figured it wouldn't hurt anyone. Keith and Dennis played along, as the photographer was writing in his notebook everything that I was saying.

"What are you going to do on this trip?" he asked, "It's a long way to California, you know?"

"We plan on sleeping in the hearse," I said, "to save money on motels. We can also look for work if we have to, but we should have enough money to at least get us there."

"Have you ever been away from Miami?" he asked.

"No," I said, looking at the others, "not really. It will be the trip of a lifetime."

"Yes," he said, "I'm sure it will be. Oh yes, one more question, Allan. How much did you pay for the hearse?"

"It was four hundred dollars, and that included the coffin, which is still over there in the trash pile. They didn't take it for some reason."

"All right then," Albert said, "it's picture time. I'll set up my stepladder on the road, that way I'll get a better angle. You boys grab your surfboards and stand behind the hearse."

We did as he told us to do, and after he set up his ladder, he asked one of us to climb on top of the hearse and make like the other two were handing their boards up. I quickly climbed up on top, and placed one of the boards on the rack. Dennis and Keith grabbed another board and placed the nose of the board into the back of the hearse.

The photographer started taking pictures, with Dennis and Keith in different positions, while I stayed on top. Once he had enough, he came down off the ladder and put it into the back of the station wagon.

"There now," he said, "that should do it. Thank you very much." We shook hands again and I asked him if he knew when it would appear in the paper.

"Oh probably in a couple of days," he said. "It's up to the editors now, but it shouldn't take too long. Anyway, take care, and I hope you have a very rewarding and safe trip. Maybe we'll do another story when you get back."

"That would be great," I said.

After he drove off, Dennis said that he had to get going, something about working in a mall at a clothing store. After Dennis had left, Keith and I both agreed that we didn't want him going with us on our trip.

"He's a little weird," Keith said, "but I don't blame him for wanting to go with us. Just look at this beauty."

Keith and I were still in awe of our find, and with so many possibilities, we got into the hearse and began thinking of where we really wanted to go.

"I'm beginning to think that California is too far to take this hearse," I said. "We'd better stick to our original plan of going up the coast; this way, if something happens to it or us, we won't be far away from home." Keith started laughing at my indecision and paranoia.

"Yeah, I guess you're right," Keith said. "At least we'll get away from here, meet other people, and have a lot of fun doing it."

For the next couple of days, I kept checking the newspaper for our story. On the third day, I saw it. I called Keith and told him to look in today's paper.

"It says the three of us are going to California! We're famous now."

I could hear Keith drop the phone as he went to get the morning paper.

"Wow," he said, "this is really cool."

Surf's Hearse

Three Hialeah youths try their surfboards for size in the hearse that will hopefully take them to California

—Herald Staff Photo by ALBERT COYA

where the surf's really up. Allan Glass, Dennis and Keith (l-r), will leave June 12 and sleep aboard their boards in the back of the hearse to cut down expenses. Allan bought the hearse and the youths refurbished it at his home, 610 NE First Pl.

Here is the actual photograph used in the Miami Herald. Later, I received another version of the story, but with the same photograph. Although I forgot to take the newspaper article from Carl, which claimed the hearse to be the one that was used to bury Al Capone, I have since found archived evidence that tells me that my hearse could be the actual one.

After the *Herald* ran the article, Keith and I dismissed the idea of going to California.

In the meantime, a girl whom I had met a month ago while she was visiting her grandmother next door, showed up. I saw her go into her grandmother's house so I waited for a few minutes, then I called.

"Hello," I said, "is this Jody?"

"Yes, it is," she said. "Who is this?"

"It's Allan. Do you want to come over and see my new hearse?"

She laughed as she said, "Okay, I'll be over in a minute."

I grabbed the newspaper article and went out to wait for her.

"Where and when did you get this?" she asked when she came over.

"A few days ago," I said. "And we have even made the newspaper."

"Wow, look at you," she said. "And who are those two guys?"

"This one here," I said, pointing to Keith, "is my closest friend, Keith, and Dennis is someone we just met."

She read the article and asked, "Are you really going to California?"

I told her the truth about it being just a dream, and that we were really going to go up the east coast.

"I've got a friend who is in the Navy," Jody said, "and he is in California right now."

"Oh really?" I said. "Is he a relative or just a friend?"

"Well," she stammered, "he's kind of like my boyfriend, but it's nothing serious. We just met six months ago, and then he had to go to California."

"I see, so you are just finishing high school, or what?"

"Yes, I am finally graduating, and our senior prom is coming up."

"Wow. I guess you already have a date for it, don't you?"

"Actually no, I don't. I was waiting to see if Dan was going to be back in time for it, but I guess that isn't going to happen."

"When exactly is it?" I asked.

"June 10," she said. "Only a week from now."

"Well," I said, "I could take you in the hearse, if that is alright with you."

She laughed at that idea, and then she got serious and said, "That would be something else; all of my friends would be surprised to see us coming in this.

"I'll have to think about it. I should go back to my grandmother; she'll be wondering where I am. Talk to you tomorrow."

"Where will you be tomorrow?" I asked.

"I'm staying here overnight," she said.

"Alright," I said, "I'll see you tomorrow."

I called Keith and told him of my impending date.

"On the tenth," he said, "That's when we are supposed to leave for our trip."

"It's going to have to wait," I said, "besides, she's really cute, and I think I like her."

"Does she surf?" Keith asked. "How did you meet her?"

I explained to him how I had seen her run in and out of the house next door for the last couple of months and had wanted to get to know her.

"She doesn't surf. Her grandmother told me one time that she was seeing someone, but I had never seen him, and now I know why."

"Why?" Keith asked.

"He's in the Navy and he got sent to California six months ago."

"Oh," Keith said, "one of those kinds of relationships. Well buddy, good luck on this one."

After talking to Keith, I began thinking of what I would do if Jody said yes to my idea of taking her to her prom. It was possible that she would want me to take her, but not in the hearse. I was okay with taking my car, but the idea of taking the hearse would be so much more exciting.

I wanted to call Jody first thing in the morning, but I decided to wait for her to call me. It wasn't until noon that the phone rang.

"I've decided to let you take me to the prom," Jody said, "and I'll leave the choice of vehicles up to you. My grandmother thinks the hearse will be dirty inside, and that I would have to put a clean sheet on the seat to make sure I don't get my dress ... well you know what I mean."

"Yes, I know, that's great; I think we'll take the hearse, and don't worry, I'll make sure it is spotless inside."

I found out the details of the prom and what time I would have to get her back home. I asked her if her parents wanted to meet me before the prom, but she told me that her grandmother had vouched for my moral character. I hoped the arrival of the hearse would not create doubts of my character.

The day came and I had everything ready to go, including the clean sheet and her corsage. I drove to her parents' house and anxiously went inside.

Her father had seen the hearse and said, "You'll have to show me that hearse, it looks real interesting."

They were appreciative that their daughter had a date, knowing that her boyfriend was still in California.

"You bring her back before midnight," her father said.

We left the house and drove directly to the prom. We got to the parking lot and within minutes, we were surrounded by her friends. I showed them the interior and one of them insisted we take them for a ride.

"Maybe later," I said, "after the dance."

The prom was strange to me because I didn't know anyone there, and they were all a couple of years younger than I was. Jody introduced me to some of them, and the only thing they wanted to talk about was the hearse.

We danced and drank a mild punch that someone said was spiked with alcohol, but nobody believed him.

While we were sitting with some of Jody's friends, one guy brought up the idea of joining the Army and going to Vietnam. I asked him why he wanted to do that, and his answer was, "My dad says that we have to stop Communism from taking over the world."

"Oh," I replied, like Hitler tried to do in World War II."

"Yeah," he said enthusiastically, "but this time it isn't the Germans, it's those Chinese communists that are doing it."

I realized nothing I could say would change his mind, so I changed the subject to surfing and going to college, instead of war. All of the others said that they were going to stay in school. It was the only way to get a better job and not have to go to war.

The prom ended around eleven o'clock, and a few of Jody's friends asked me to take them for a ride.

I looked at Jody who said, "It's up to you, Allan, we do have an hour before I have to be back home."

I said, "Alright, let's go."

As soon as we got to the hearse I tried to count the number of people that wanted to go. I opened the back doors and like Noah's ark, they went in two by two. As the hearse filled up fast and the last two got in, I saw one more couple running to join us. I closed the doors and told them they could ride with us up front. Once we were all in, I slid open the Plexiglas window, which separated the front seat from the rest of the hearse.

"How's everybody doing back there, are you ready to go?" A cheer went up from the group and off we went. I didn't want to go too far from the parking lot and I certainly didn't want to go on any major streets, so I stuck to the back roads and like everyone else, settled in for what was to become the ride of a lifetime for them, as well as Jody and me. No sooner had I made a couple of turns, than a police siren sounded and the familiar blue and red lights were indeed meant for us. As I pulled over, I could hear the cheers turned to moans and someone said, "What's going on? Why are we stopping?"

The police officer came up to my window.

"License and registration please," he said.

"Here you are, officer," I said. "Did I do anything wrong?"

"Oh no," he said, "I just spotted your strange looking vehicle. Is this a hearse?" "Yes, it is," I said. "They just finished their high school prom dance and I'm taking a few people for a ride."

"How many people do you have in the back?" he asked as he handed me back the papers.

"I don't know," I said. "is there a law against it?"

"No, not really," he answered with a smile, "but could you open up the back for me?"

Allan Glass

I got out and opened the back door. Looking inside, the officer and I stood there dumbfounded, as it was too crowded to see just how many people were in there. "If they get out," I said, "they might not all fit in again. We wouldn't want that now would we?"

"No," he laughed, "I guess not. Alright, you can go, just make sure you stay on the back roads."

"Thank you, officer," I said politely. "Have a good night."

We took off and we all started laughing at our run-in with the law.

"I'm surprised he didn't say anything about my 'Tag Applied For' sign," I said. "It seems that they are more interested in the vehicle's appearance than with the legality of it."

"I'm sure glad he didn't arrest us," Jody said. "My parents would be so mad at me!"

"This is the second time I've been pulled over," I said. "I'm starting to think that the police don't care about the fake license tag, they just want to look at a one-of-a-kind vehicle."

"Well," Jody said, looking at her watch, "we'd better get back to the parking lot."

"That's exactly where I'm heading right now," I said.

When we arrived back at the parking lot, I opened the back doors and I counted the people as they came out. I was amazed to see that there were ten couples that stumbled out, and all of them thanked me for the short but eventful ride.

After Jody said goodbye to her friends, I drove her home, this time without getting stopped.

I walked her to the front door. The porch light was on, but I could not see her parents.

Jody reached out to give me a kiss on the cheek.

"That was a wonderful evening," she said. "Thank you very much."

I agreed with her, and tried to kiss her again, but she held up her hand and said that we shouldn't.

"I had better go in," she said. "Goodnight, Allan."

On the drive home I had a big smile on my face. I knew that even though I was attracted to her, and could have easily fallen in love with her, it was the innocence of the whole thing that made me feel good.

The next day, Jody called me and told me that her boyfriend was coming home and that she was ready to resume her relationship with him. I thanked her for her honesty and told her that I was happy for her. Whether or not she believed me was another matter.

That same day, Keith phoned and said, "My friends in college are holding an outdoor barbecue and dance tonight. It would be great to take the hearse there and show it to everyone."

"Sure," I said, "What time?"

"If you want to have some of the barbecue, we should be there around six-thirty."

"Alright, I'll pick you up around six."

"No need to," he said. "I'm taking my car. You never know what will happen after the dance..."

"Oh, well then, I'll see you at the party."

I hung up and thought, *Oh no, there's sure to be cops at this thing, I'd better go and make a new sign for the hearse.* I found a better-looking piece of cardboard and replaced the old sign with a new one.

I cleaned out the inside of the hearse and told my mother what was happening.

She just shrugged her shoulders and said, "Have a good time."

The dance was being held at one of the many baseball fields in the area, and there was plenty of space for an outdoor party. When I arrived, I could hear a live band playing music.

I parked the hearse, and Keith showed up with his arm around a girl's shoulder.

He introduced me to her, and proceeded to show her the hearse.

"She saw the picture of us in the paper," Keith said, "and now she really likes me."

I laughed at that one, and a crowd started to form around the hearse.

"This is the coolest thing I've ever seen," said one guy. "Where did you get it?"

After telling the story numerous times, we heard someone shout, "barbecue is ready!"

Everybody ran back to enjoy the food, and while we were eating I had more than one request for a ride in the hearse.

"Later," I said, "for now let's just enjoy the food and the music."

For the next couple of hours, I found myself dancing with a different girl each time the song changed. Keith's girlfriend made sure that I knew who was single and who was not.

Finally the band took a break, and everyone who knew Keith started asking him for a ride.

"Hey Al," Keith said, "how about it?"

"Sure," I said, "We'll take as many as we can cram in."

As soon as I said this, a bunch of people started to run toward the hearse. It was on a first come, first served basis as the hoard got to the hearse and they started to jump in. When I arrived, I could hear them laughing and saying things like, "get off me!" and "you're squishing me!"

"How many are in there?" I asked. I heard different answers like, "there must be at least twenty!" and "too many!"

There were another dozen or so people waiting to get in, but I finally had to say, "Look, there are enough people in there now. I'll take them around the block and come back for you."

I secured the back doors and jumped into the driver's seat, along with Keith and his girlfriend.

As I drove away, the people who were left standing there went back to the field. I spotted a police car parked on the other side of the field, and thought, *oh no, here we go again*. I drove in the other direction and turned down the first side street. After five minutes, I looked in my side mirrors, expecting to see the cop, but he wasn't there. I relaxed as we went down the road, and the people in the back started singing a song.

Keith had brought along a flask of his favourite drink, gin and purple Kool-Aid. He handed it to his girlfriend, who took a sip, and then handed it to me. I looked at it and said, "No thanks, I'm a whiskey and ginger ale man."

I took the hearse as far as the road went and then it came to a turnaround.

"Well," I said, "that's far enough. Let's head back to the party."

We got back to the parking lot, and saw that everyone else was still at the field, dancing, singing and having a good time. I got out and released everyone from the hearse.

"That was so cool," they said. "Can we do it some other time?"

"Maybe the next party," I said.

Keith and his girlfriend stayed with me while the others went back.

I could tell that Keith was beginning to feel the effects of the booze, so I asked him if they needed a ride home.

"No thanks, Al," Keith said. "She can drive if I can't."

I looked at her, and she told me that she wasn't going to be drinking anymore and that she was sober enough to drive.

I looked at my watch, and told Keith that I was going home.

"You didn't find anyone here that you liked, did you?" he asked.

"Of course I did," I said holding up a piece of paper. "I got a couple of phone numbers."

"I told you he was single and looking," Keith said to his girlfriend

"You two take it easy," I said. "Talk to you tomorrow." I got into the hearse and left.

Chapter 4

A CHANGE OF PLANS
AND VEHICLES

I called Keith the next day, and his mother answered.

"Hi Allan, Keith isn't home. He didn't come back last night; I'll tell him you phoned."

I went out and started up the hearse to see how much gas was left. After driving it for a few days, I noticed it was using a lot, and I thought there might be a leak somewhere. The gauge read almost empty and I knew that there was at least a half a tank before going to the party last night.

I got out and looked underneath to see if I could see a leak or at least smell it, but I could not find either. I knew that an eight-cylinder vehicle uses more gas than a six- or a four-cylinder, but it was obvious that this one was using even more than my Malibu Super Sport, which had a bigger engine than the hearse.

I shut the motor off and realized that in order to take this on any extended trip, I would need a lot of money just for gas. I felt depressed at the thought of this, and went back inside my house.

Just then, Keith called, and after finding out what happened after I left the party, I told him the news about the amount of gas that the hearse was using.

"I knew it would use a lot of gas," he said, "and I agree, it might change our plans for a vehicle to use on our trip. But hey, it's still the coolest vehicle around and I wouldn't get rid of it just yet."

"I'm not going to sell it that's for sure," I said, "but I do think we should think about taking a more gas efficient vehicle, like your VW."

"You know my bug is too old for something like that," Keith said. "We'll just have to think of something else, or stay here for the summer."

"That doesn't sound great to me," I said, "but what else can we do?"

"Let me take care of it," Keith said. "I'll think of something."

We spent most of the month of June using our vehicles to go surfing, and each day went by without a solution to our dilemma.

I was home watching TV with my mother when I got a call from Keith.

"Come on over," Keith said, "I think I have the answer to our problem."

I left immediately, as the tone of his voice sounded serious.

When I arrived, he came out to my car and got in.

"What's that you got in your hands?" I asked.

In one hand, he had a bottle of gin, and in the other hand, some wires with alligator clips attached.

"What are those for?" I asked innocently.

"You'll see. Just drive north on 16ᵗʰ Avenue until I tell you to turn."

I kept on driving, and finally Keith let me know his plan.

"We need a new, gas efficient vehicle to go on our trip, right?"

"Yes," I said reluctantly, "but ..."

"Well, I know exactly where and how we are going to get it. Turn here."

I turned the corner and he told me to pull over and shut the motor off.

"Now what?" I asked, as I was getting a bit worried.

"It's my girlfriend," Keith said. "She gave the idea last night."

"What idea?" I asked. "What are you talking about?"

Keith drank his gin, and then told me of his plan to steal a brand-new VW.

"I don't know about this," I said. "Where is this VW?"

"It's on the next block over. Come on, let's do this while I still have the nerve to do it."

We got out and walked to the next block, and there it was, sitting all by itself, one street lamp shining brightly on it. The house that we presumed the owners of the VW lived in was on the corner of the block, and we could see that there were no lights on.

We approached the car, and Keith got the small front-side window open, reached in, and opened the door.

"Okay," he whispered, "get in."

I got in the passenger side and he got in the driver's side, and within a few minutes, after attaching the wires and alligator clips to the wires under the dashboard, the motor started.

While he was doing this, I opened the glove box and took out the insurance and registration papers.

"Look at this," I said, "it's covered for theft, and it is owned by a Cuban."

My heart was racing as Keith put the vehicle in gear and drove back to where I had parked my car.

"I'll take it back to my place," Keith said. "Don't follow me."

"Don't worry," I said, "I won't."

I left him and drove home, in a quandary about what had just happened.

When I went in, my mother asked me where I had been.

"Oh, nowhere," I said, "just to Keith's and Donny's."

I couldn't sleep that night, and I lay wondering about what we were going to do with a stolen car. I felt sad because of who we took it from. Probably some poor Cuban, I thought, who finally could afford a new car, and now he'll wake up and find it gone. Then I remembered the insurance papers stating that it was insured for theft and I smiled, thinking, *He'll probably get a new one. Yes, that's what will happen. A mere justification for auto theft, maybe, but it would have to do for now.*

The next day I took my car over to Keith's. His mother told me that he was next door at Donny's. I went over and saw Keith and Donny in the backyard, alongside the new VW.

Keith saw me and shouted, "Hey Al, isn't it great that your sister is lending you her car for our trip?"

I looked at the two of them, and understood what Keith was trying to do, so I went along with his story.

"Yeah, isn't it great," I said.

"How come it's here in my back yard?" Donny asked suspiciously.

"Allan doesn't have room at his place to keep it," Keith said, "and you know I don't have any room at my place. Do you think your dad will mind if we keep it here until we leave?"

"I guess not," Donny said, as his father came out to see what the fuss was all about.

"Who does this belong to?" he asked.

"It's my sister's," I said, kicking the dirt, "and she is going to let us use it for our trip."

"Oh I see," Donny's father said. "Is it a brand new one?"

"Yes," I answered, "and it's really different than Keith's 1961."

"Yes, it is," Donny's father said as he walked around it. "Very different indeed."

I sensed that Donny's father wasn't buying our story, as he clapped his hands and went back inside the house.

Meanwhile, Donny, Keith, and I also went inside the house and into Donny's bedroom. Soon, there was a knock on Donny's bedroom door.

"Come on in," he said, "it's not locked."

There, standing in the doorway, was Donny's father.

"The next time you 'borrow' a car," he said, smiling, "remember to take these out." He held up the wires with the alligator clips still attached, and tossed them at Keith.

My heart started pounding. At least he was smiling, and didn't look too mad at the idea of having a stolen vehicle in his backyard.

"Get that vehicle out of my backyard now," he said, "before the missus finds out. I have to go to work now, and it better be gone by the time I get back."

"Yes, sir," Keith said. "Right now."

After Donny's father left, we all gave a huge sigh of relief and then we started laughing.

"You guys are crazy," Donny said, "and you're lucky that my dad is very understanding."

"I'll agree to that," I said. "Come on, we'd better find a place to put it."

"We can keep it at my cousin Johnny's," Keith said. "He has a garage that's empty and he also has the equipment that we need to paint it."

Donny stayed at his house while Keith drove the VW over to his cousin's place, and I followed him in my car.

When we arrived, Keith told me to wait outside. A few minutes later Keith and his cousin came out of the house.

"A fucking VW?" Johnny shouted. "Why the hell did you steal a VW?"

"Never mind that Johnny," Keith said. "We need you to set up your garage so we can paint it."

"You can clean it out yourself," Johnny shot back. "And I'll make sure my spray painter is cleaned and working. Oh yes, and one more thing, you can buy the paint and do the work yourselves."

I looked at Keith and thought, *We've never done anything like this before, the painting that is, and now we have to rely on this idiot.*

"Come on," Keith said to me, "let's get started on making room for the car."

"I'm glad we didn't take a Cadillac; we'd be here all day making room."

After moving a few things around, Keith went out and drove the car into the garage.

Johnny came out and said, "Go to the backyard and grab the large tarp that's there and nail it up so that it covers the entrance. That way nobody can see the car from the sidewalk."

"Good idea," I said. "I'll get the tarp."

Once everything was in its place, Keith asked Johnny how long would it take to paint the car.

"Not long," he said. "A couple of hours, but you should then wait twenty-four hours before you put a second coat on. Make sure you get the right paint; you don't want it to come off in a rain now do you?"

We laughed at Johnny's sense of humour, and then we told him we would get the paint tomorrow and drop it off, just to make sure we got the right kind.

The next day, Keith drove over to his garage and got some tips from his boss on which paint he should buy, telling him that he was helping a friend paint his old car.

From there he went to an auto body shop, and purchased a five-gallon can of paint, which they told him was on sale. Keith didn't care what colour it was, as long as it saved him some money. After buying it, he picked me up and we went to Johnny's. When we opened the can, we were horrified to see that the paint was a bright canary yellow.

Johnny started laughing when he saw it. "Wow, they are going to see you guys coming a mile away. Are you sure you want this colour?"

"Why not?" I said. "I've seen other cars this colour. Not many cars, but ..."

Keith interrupted me and said, "Let's use it; who cares?"

Johnny prepared his spray painter, attaching it to the top of the can, and after a quick inspection of the car for dirt and dust, started up his compressor.

Johnny had on his protective mask and breathing apparatus, and began spraying.

Keith and I stayed outside, taking the occasional peek inside.

After an hour, we heard the compressor shut off, so we went in, wearing handkerchiefs over our faces.

As we looked at the first coat, we heard a sound from underneath the car.

Out from under the car, came Johnny's dog. A dark brown Labrador, he now had a bright yellow tail.

"Screwball!" Johnny shrieked, "What the fuck are you doing under there?"

Keith and I started laughing as we led the dog out of the garage to get some fresh air. Johnny came out and looked his pet over, and then told him to go and lie down.

"I never saw him come in, did you?" he asked.

"No Johnny," Keith said, "we would have said something if we knew."

We went back in and had a closer look.

"Well," Johnny said, "aren't I the greatest auto painter in the world?"

"Yeah Johnny," Keith said sarcastically, "you're the greatest."

"Come on," Johnny said, "let's go have a beer."

Johnny wanted to know more about our scheme involving the car, but Keith kept the details to himself.

"Well," Johnny said, "tomorrow I'll put the final coat on, and that should be good enough."

We thanked him, and as we were leaving, he told us that we owed him one.

On the way home, I asked Keith what would happen if we ever got stopped by the police and asked for license and registration.

"First of all," Keith said, "we will change license plates, and second, I have a valid registration for a VW, so I could just show the cop that one. I'm sure he wouldn't catch the difference."

"There's a big difference between a '61 and a '67 bug," I said.

"It's the only thing we can do," Keith said. "Besides, we won't get stopped driving a brand new car, would we?"

The rest of the ride home was done in silence.

The next day we went back to Johnny's to make sure he was going to finish the job. When we arrived, Johnny was already in the garage, and getting ready to start spraying the second coat. I looked under the car to make sure his dog wasn't there.

"He's not there," Johnny said. "I made sure he stayed in the house."

When Johnny started spraying, Keith and I went back outside the garage.

"Did you see the differences in the two VWs?" I asked.

"Yes, of course I did," Keith said. "We can put some surfing decals on the rear side window and on the bumpers, or just change the bumpers altogether."

"Now you're being ridiculous," I said. "Why don't we just change the whole body? Take the new one off and replace it with the old one."

"Now who's being ridiculous?" Keith shot back. "But maybe it would work. I'll have to ask Johnny about that."

Once Johnny was finished, Keith asked him about the change in bodies.

"No way," he said. "I just finished a brilliant paint job. Why would you want to put your old body on a nice new one?"

"I agree with Johnny," I said. "Let's just go with what we've done and leave it at that. Who knows, we might even return it to the guy we took it from once we're back from our trip."

Keith looked at Johnny and the two of them started laughing at my idea.

"You're kidding, right?" Keith said.

"Well, why not? I kind of feel bad for taking it in the first place, so if we just put it back when we are finished, everybody will feel better."

"I can just see the guy's face," Johnny said, "when he wakes up and sees a bright yellow VW parked outside."

"It would be an ironic twist to this whole situation," I added. "Like the saying goes, all's well that ends well."

"Alright you two, stop it. There are a few more things you have to take care of before you take this car anywhere."

"What's that?" Keith asked.

"Well, for one, I'll have to rig up a starter switch to replace the two wires that are at present hanging down under the dash. Any cop who sees that will know right away that it's a stolen vehicle. Second, you don't have any key for locking the doors at night, but there's nothing really that can fix that. So, Keith, do you want me to install the switch?"

"Can you do it?" Keith asked. "Do you have all the parts?"

"Yes, I do," Johnny said. "Have you set a date on when you are going to go?"

"No, not really," Keith said, "but we want to leave pretty soon."

On the ride home, I said, "It's going to be a long week; do we really want to wait that long?"

"Well," Keith said, "not really, I just have to tell my mother, my boss and my girlfriend. What do you have to do?"

"I also have to tell my mother and my boss, and go to the bank and get some cash."

"So," Keith said, "we could leave in a couple of days, right?"

"Yes," I said, "let's do it."

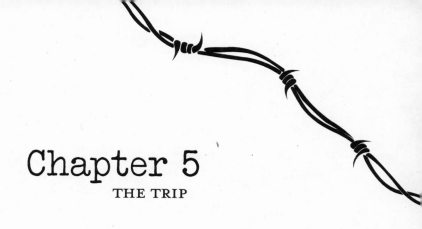

Chapter 5
THE TRIP

Finally, on July 10, we were ready to take off on our long-awaited trip. Johnny had set up the new ignition switch, and we were all set to go.

My mother, with tears in her eyes, wished me luck, and told me to call her if there were ever any problems. I was packed and waiting for Keith to come over and get me.

Soon, my mother yelled out, "There's a car outside, a little yellow car, is that Keith's new one you were talking about?"

"Yes, Mom," I said, "that's him. I'll be home before you know it; I love you; bye!"

My surfboard had been put on the day before so I grabbed my bags and left.

"Alright!" I shouted, "I can't believe we are finally going!"

"This car really has a lot more power than my old one," Keith said, "and it's bigger inside too."

As we drove along, we started passing places that used to be the end of our short trips up the Florida coast. I waved ceremoniously as we passed them, and sat back to enjoy the ride.

I looked at our map and found Cocoa Beach.

"Hey Keith, you remember surfing with the sharks at Cocoa Beach?"

"I sure do; I'll never forget that experience."

"Well," I said, "Daytona Beach is next; it's only another fifty or sixty miles from Cocoa."

"That's where they have a famous car race," Keith said. "Do you want to stop there for anything?"

"We'll see," I said. "I'm more excited than hungry right now."

As we arrived in Daytona, I looked at the map again and saw the town of St. Augustine, one of the oldest towns in America, followed by Jacksonville, the largest city in Florida.

"So," Keith said, "now do you want to stop for lunch, or keep going?"

I looked around for a clue as to whether or not they had any surf shops or something that would tell us if they even had any beaches to surf at.

"I don't see any vehicles with boards on top," I said, "so, let's keep on going."

We made it to Jacksonville, and decided to stop and get something to eat at one of the local hangouts, a burger shack right on the beach.

"This looks like a familiar place to eat," I said.

We noticed a few vehicles with boards on top, and once we parked, we saw another couple of surfers heading in the same direction.

"Hi, are you guys from here?" I asked.

"Yes, where are you from?"

"Miami," I said. "We're on our way up the coast, and this is our first stop."

The four of us put our order in and sat down at one of the tables.

"Are you staying overnight?" one of them asked. "There isn't much to see north of here, except Fernandina Beach, which can sometimes have good waves."

"Yes," I said, "we are staying here overnight. Do you know if there would be a problem if we spent the night on the beach?"

"No problem," they said, "it's summer break around here, and the cops don't mind it as long as you don't do anything illegal."

"That's great," I said, "then that is what we'll do."

"There isn't anything happening tonight, being the middle of the week," they said, "so it should be pretty quiet."

We took their advice and found a spot where we couldn't be seen from the road, and settled in to sleep. In the morning, we got up early and took off.

We passed the border and I drove into the state of Georgia. The map showed the coastline dotted with small islands, with the largest city of Savannah about sixty miles north. There were lots of "private property" and "private beach" signs, so we kept on driving.

"This is crazy," I said, "it has been hours now and there don't seem to be any places that allow surfing."

Keith was trying to be positive about our predicament, so he told me to keep on driving while he looked at the map.

"No turning back now," Keith said, smiling. "Things will get better."

He then reminded me about a place that he had read about in a magazine.

"Myrtle Beach," he said pointing at the map. "It's at the north end of South Carolina, so let's just enjoy the scenery until we get there. I'll take over driving; you need a rest."

After passing through Savannah, Georgia, we headed for Charleston, South Carolina.

"I'm tired of all this traveling," I said, "and we could both use a hot shower."

"Alright," Keith said, "we'll stop at the first motel we see."

Driving through Charleston, with its southern-style buildings and homes, made us feel like we were in another country. On the outskirts of the city, we found a motel and got a room. We each had a long, hot shower and then went for dinner at a quaint little restaurant nearby. Our waitress was a cute southern belle, and Keith and I both agreed that we were in love with her, overwhelmed with her southern accent.

After a good night's sleep in a real bed, we took off at sunrise, and headed for Myrtle Beach.

"I hope you're right about the surfing at Myrtle Beach," I said. "This is supposed to be a surfing trip, isn't it?"

"Relax," Keith said, "we'll find our perfect waves eventually."

Once we passed a city called Georgetown, the coastline opened up, the map showing two smaller towns, Garden City Beach and Surfside Beach.

"With names like that," I said, "we should check them out."

It was just what we were looking for. Beautiful beaches, with small but adequate waves rolling in, came into view. A few surfers were already out, enjoying the action, which was indeed a sight for sore eyes.

After parking the VW, we unloaded our boards and raced down to the shoreline. Soon, we were alongside the others and introducing ourselves. Inevitably, their response was one that we would continue to hear throughout our trip.

"You're from Miami! Wow, we've never met anyone from there."

Keith and I explained our trip to them, and how we wanted to go as far as our money would take us. They welcomed us to their little beach, and asked us about Miami, and if there were any special places to surf. After naming a few spots, we asked them about Myrtle Beach, which was only ten miles away.

"Yes," they said, "and we do go there sometimes, but it's a lot bigger and a lot more crowded than here, you'll see, too many tourists, especially at this time of the year."

"On the weekends there are too many people at some of the beaches in Miami," I said, "so that's when we head up the coast to the less crowded places."

We continued surfing and talking about the similarities that surfers had, and then decided to go to the local hangout and have lunch, and afterwards we went back and enjoyed another couple of hours of surfing. We asked them if there was anywhere on the beach that would be okay for spending the night.

"Just about anywhere," they said. "You shouldn't get hassled by anyone."

After dinner, a few people started a bonfire, so we decided to join them. Keith and I were offered beer and wine, and we thankfully accepted.

Soon, there were about twenty people sitting around the bonfire, drinking, playing music, and singing. A warm summer breeze gave it the perfect atmosphere,

and it made Keith and me feel pretty good about our trip. As the evening came to a close, the bonfire died down, and everyone left.

Keith and I spent the night with no one bothering us, and we awoke to another beautiful sunrise. With no one around, we decided to go surfing, making it double as an early morning shower. Finally, some of the locals whom we had met the night before showed up. We thanked them for their hospitality, and told them we were continuing our journey up the coast to Myrtle Beach.

It didn't take too long to arrive at Myrtle Beach, and it was obvious that there were going to be a lot more people there. The beaches were filling up with tourists, and we wondered where the locals were.

"It's the same as South Miami," I said, "the locals aren't here because there are too many people."

We found a burger joint, had a bite to eat, and took off. Looking over the map, I told Keith that there was only one small town left, North Myrtle Beach.

"We might as well stop to see what it's like," Keith said.

Once we arrived, there wasn't much to see, so we kept on going north, into North Carolina. Driving along the coastline, we found a lot of small towns, but the beaches were not made for surfing or tourism, as they were mainly fishing villages located on the edges of swampy, wet ground.

We stopped for lunch midway through North Carolina, and headed for Virginia Beach, located just across the border.

We stopped in the middle of town, and saw a few local surfers sitting at a nearby café. They told us that today's conditions were flat, meaning no waves, so we talked for a while and then decided to spend the night and see if the conditions improved the next day. We got a room this time, and in the morning, went for breakfast. We got the weather forecast from one of the locals, and again, no wind, no waves. We thanked everyone and took off.

The scenic coastline was now changing to a more industrialized part of the state, with large fishing vessels, oil tankers, and farming being more visible than ever.

As we continued northward, we began to feel like fish out of water. Our bright yellow VW with surfboards on top probably looked more like a UFO to these people than a simple car loaded for fun at the beach.

"Maybe we should go back," Keith said. "It's beginning to look like there aren't any more places to go surfing, and it's certainly getting more crowded."

"I know what you mean," I said, "but let's keep on going."

We followed the coastline of Chesapeake Bay up to where the Potomac River emptied into it, then followed the river up to Washington, D. C. We drove past a few famous landmarks, and stopped for lunch.

"Where to next?" Keith asked.

"Well," I said, looking at the map, "I think we should head north to Baltimore. We're still east of the Chesapeake Bay."

"That's why we haven't seen any surfboards," Keith said sarcastically. "We're miles away from the ocean."

We kept heading north until we saw signs pointing to Philadelphia, Pennsylvania and Wilmington, Delaware.

"Let's head for Wilmington," Keith said, as I had taken over the driving.

As time passed, I said, "We should have been in Wilmington by now. Are you sure we are on the right freeway?"

"Good question," Keith said, looking at the map.

We drove along, not knowing where we were, and then I spotted a large sign,

"Philadelphia, 10 miles, next right." For some reason, I panicked and took the exit, as Keith yelled out, "Where are you going?" Soon we found ourselves driving around in an all-black neighbourhood.

"Oh great," Keith said, "now where are we?"

"You've got the map," I said, as I began going in circles, looking for a sign to point us back onto the freeway.

After failing to find the way back to the freeway, I stopped the car and asked a man who was walking by for directions. He had a quizzical look on his face as he stared at our surfboards.

"What are those?" he asked.

We could hardly understand him, so we asked him again. "How do we get back onto the freeway?"

He edged closer to our car and said something. Again, Keith and I could not understand him, his accent being one that we had never heard. We asked him again to repeat what he had just said. Instead of talking, the man smiled and pointed his finger into the night air, and mumbled something. We tried to get him to repeat it once more, but then his eyes grew wide, and he shook his head and walked away.

We could tell he was getting angry at us, and once he left, other people who had been watching started walking toward our car. I told Keith to roll up the window and we took off. It didn't matter which way we went, I just wanted to get out of that neighbourhood as fast as possible.

We found our way back onto the freeway and headed across the Delaware River, into New Jersey.

"Let's go east," Keith said looking at the map, "and watch out for a sign that says Atlantic City' it's the largest city on the coast."

"Yes, sir," I said, "from now on we'll stay on the coast, no matter what. How far is it to Atlantic City?"

"About fifty miles," Keith said. "Do you want me to drive?"

"No, that's okay, I'll make it there."

Soon, we arrived in Pleasantville, a small town on the outskirts of Atlantic City.

It was getting close to supper time, and after the incident in Philadelphia, I was ready to find a place to eat and get some rest. Keith agreed, so we found a diner and went in. We asked the waitress if she knew anything about Atlantic City.

"It's got quite a history," she began, "from being the gambling capital of the world, and also being the entertainment centre for the mob bosses of the 1920s."

"You mean like Al Capone?" I asked.

"Oh yes," she said, "and many more like him; this place was really a party city."

"How about now?" Keith asked.

"Well," she said, "it's all legal now, but the casinos and the partying have never stopped. "It's a real tourist town now. Where are you from?" she asked.

"We're from Miami," I said proudly, "and we have been on a surfing trip for the last few days. Is any surfing done around here?"

"There isn't anywhere that I know of," she answered, "plus it's the beginning of tourist season and it can get pretty crowded at the beach, but hopefully you can find a spot where there aren't too many people. I don't surf myself so I don't really know where that might be, but I have heard stories about a stretch of beach north of here, Long Branch and Asbury Park, that is great for surfing and a lot less crowded."

We thanked her for the information, and after eating, we decided that we had better find a cheap motel to get a shower and clean off some of the industrialized dirt that we had accumulated in Philly and Baltimore. Then we took off to get a closer look at the famous boardwalk of New Jersey.

It was indeed a tourist city as hotels and restaurants lined the beach for as far as the eye could see.

"This reminds me of Miami Beach," Keith said, "but I don't see anybody with surfboards around."

"Yes," I said, "but I can see it being a fun place, with its nice beaches and casinos to gamble your money away."

"Everything that we don't want," Keith added. "Let's go back to our motel, I'm tired."

We spent the evening watching TV, and heard about the continuing trouble with the black people and the civil rights rioting in different cities, Newark, New Jersey being one of them. I also heard a piece of news about the Vietnam war and that the US was winning.

"Isn't Newark just north of here?" I asked.

"Yes, it is," Keith said, "it's right across from Long Island, New York."

I looked at the map, and said, "It would be neat to go to Long Island and see if there is any surfing going on there."

"Yeah," Keith joked, "and maybe we'll get involved in a race riot."

"We won't do anything like that," I said, "but we'll definitely check out the place the waitress told us about."

After a good night's sleep, Keith and I headed for Asbury Park and Long Branch.

As we approached the area, we spotted our first vehicle with boards on top.

"Now this is beginning to look familiar," Keith said.

Asbury Park was first, with Long Branch a few miles north of it. We decided to stop and have a look. There before us, was a beautiful stretch of beach, and the smell of clean saltwater filled the morning air. We spotted a few surfers enjoying the early morning waves, and watched as they caught and rode the waves for a few feet before falling off.

"Looks like beginners," Keith said. "Let's go farther up and have a look."

I agreed, so we took off and made it to Long Branch. We found a motel situated right across from the beach, which had a few vehicles with surfboards on top parked in front.

"Alright," I said joyfully, "this looks like the place we've been searching for."

We parked the car and were soon approached by two guys.

"Hi," they said, "are you new to this area?"

We told them the usual story and they welcomed us to their humble surfing beach. I was happy to see that they weren't impressed with us being from Miami as they asked us to join them for a morning coffee at the burger joint which was right next to the motel.

They told us about Long Branch, and how it evolved from a sleepy town to a college party town, far away from the rich and fancy hotels of Atlantic City.

"We needed a place to unwind after a semester of college," they said, "and so this is it."

"This is exactly what we are looking for," I said, "but how is the surfing? And oh yes, where are all the women?"

They laughed at my question regarding women and they assured me that there were lots of "wahinis" (Hawaiian for female surfers) around and that they would show up soon.

"Now, about the waves," they began, "they aren't too bad. As you can see, there are two-foot waves now, but sometimes we get five- or six-footers coming in, then it gets real interesting."

We talked about the differences of the East Coast versus the West Coast, and we all agreed that going to California would be the real test of our abilities.

"Someday," Keith said, "maybe even next month, we'll make it there, right Allan?"

I told the other two about the newspaper article and the hearse, and wanting to take it to California.

"Now that would be a trip of a lifetime," they said. "Can we come?"

We drank our coffee and soon there were a few more vehicles pulling in that were loaded with surfboards and women. The two guys that were having coffee with us got up and went over to greet them.

Keith and I decided that we were going to get a room, and went straight for the office. Inside, a man smoking a fat cigar greeted us.

"Hello boys," he said, smiling, "what can I do for you?"

"We'd like a room; how much?"

"Ten dollars a night or forty-five for a week," he said. "Can't go much lower than that."

Keith and I looked at each other, then I said, "Okay, a week it is."

After paying the man, he let us know the rules of the motel.

"Although you boys are out to have a good time, I hope you don't do anything stupid, cause if you do, I'll have you thrown out. Is that clear?"

We assured him that we were going to be responsible, but that we weren't sure about how the locals would act.

"They're mostly okay," he said, "but there are a few that might want to take advantage of the situation. I can tolerate a small amount of liquor and pot, as do the police, but please don't let it get out of hand. And one more thing, I don't mind if you have a couple of guests stay overnight, if you know what I mean."

We thanked him and went on up to our room, which included two queen beds, a beer refrigerator, a cooking stove, a bathroom, and a TV. I plopped down on one of the beds, and Keith started changing into his surfing baggies.

"Hey Al," he said, "are you going for a nap or are you going to go surfing?"

"I'm coming," I said, "don't worry about me."

Soon, the beach was alive with about fifty surfers, and the waves increased in size as the day wore on. We surfed for a couple of hours, and then decided to go and get something to eat. I asked Keith how much money he had left and decided that we better start making our own lunches. We found a nearby corner store and bought a loaf of bread, some peanut butter and jam, a six pack of beer, and some popcorn. One guy saw the beer as we brought it up to our room, and he followed us.

He came in and asked if there was going to be a party.

"No," I said bluntly but politely, "now please go."

After lunch, we decided to go back to the beach for some more surfing. It was a beautiful day, and we were truly enjoying ourselves.

There were a couple of girls who were walking on the beach, and they attracted Keith's attention. He surfed in and casually walked up and began talking to them. I watched as he soon had them both laughing. After a few minutes, he came back into the water and paddled over to where I was.

"They agreed to come over to our room tonight," Keith said. "We should get some more beer."

"Sounds good to me," I said. "That didn't take you long' did you get their names?"

"Of course I did," Keith said. "Barbara and Linda."

"One blond and one brunette," I said. "I get the brunette. "What's her name?"

"I think that's Barbara," Keith said. "Who cares?"

It was five o'clock when we decided to go back to our room.

"When did those two girls say they were coming?" I asked.

"They didn't say," Keith answered. "Who knows they might not even show up."

"Well," I said, "I hope they bring the booze, I'm getting low on money."

"Relax," Keith said, "you're always worried about money."

We decided to wait a while for dinner, just in case Barbara and Linda came.

"Maybe they'll bring a pizza or something," I said jokingly.

We watched the six o'clock news, and the two girls had not shown up.

Soon there was a knock on the door. I jumped up in anticipation. I opened the door, and saw Barbara and Linda standing there, each with a case of beer in their hands. Behind them were a bunch of people, who barged in and began opening beer bottles.

"We thought we would give you two a welcome to Long Branch party," Barbara said, as she handed me a beer.

Someone else brought a portable stereo and soon everyone was dancing and listening to music.

I looked at Keith, who yelled out above the noise, "See, I told you they would come!"

I sat on the bed and watched everyone and I thought for sure that the manager would come up and tell us to quiet down.

For the next few hours, we had people coming and going, and the place was getting messier by the minute. Barbara and Linda had since vanished. I went into the bathroom and saw puddles of beer and whatever, and all of our towels were missing. As soon as I saw this, I went out and told everyone, "This party is over, please leave our room."

No one heard me the first time, so I jumped on top of a bed and yelled it again. Then, I jumped off the bed and turned the music down, and everybody looked at me and wondered what was wrong.

"Look," I said, "there's a broken beer bottle in the bathroom, all of the towels are gone, and you are making a mess of our room. Either you take it outside now, or I will have to call the motel manager."

Just then, the manager did show up, and he told everyone that they would have to leave immediately, or he would call the police.

One by one, they walked out. The manager told me that I did the right thing in telling everyone to get out.

"I told you that things could get out of hand real quick, so I'll forget about this time, but please don't let it happen again."

Keith and I told him we were sorry and that we did not plan the party, but he just looked at us and said, "I've heard that one before."

After everyone left, Keith and I sat on our beds, looking at the mess.

"Unbelievable," I said. "Our first night we almost get kicked out."

"Well now we know," Keith said. "Nobody gets in here unless it's a couple of cute girls."

"I'll agree to that one," I said, "but where did Barbara and Linda go?"

"Beats me," Keith said. "I didn't even notice that they left."

"Oh well," I said, "we'll probably never see them again."

"Now what do we do?" Keith asked.

"We could go and look for Barbara and Linda," I said jokingly.

"At least they left us some beer," Keith said. "Want one?"

"Sure," I said, "why not."

We cleaned up the place and then turned on the TV. It was about nine o'clock when I heard a knock on our door. I parted the drapes and took a peek outside.

"It's a girl," I said, "and she doesn't look familiar."

"Make sure she doesn't have the rest of the party people with her," Keith said.

I opened the door and asked her what she wanted.

"I'm by myself, and I don't have anywhere else to go. Can I come in?"

I looked to Keith for his opinion.

"It's up to you, Al."

I thought about it for a moment, and checked to see if she was just trying to get in and start another party, her friends waiting nearby. I couldn't see anyone around so I let her in.

"What's your name?" I asked.

"Oh, it's, uh, Mary."

She made me feel uneasy, but for some unknown reason, I was beginning to like her. Keith could see what was happening so he grabbed his beer and said, "I'll see you later, Al; have a good time."

Mary came in and sat on the bed.

"Do you have anything to eat?" she asked.

"Not really, except for some popcorn and peanut butter."

"Ugh, I hate peanut butter, but how about some popcorn?"

"Uh sure, it's the kind that comes in its own aluminum pan."

I started to make the popcorn, and she got up from the bed and turned on the TV.

"Maybe there's a good movie on," she said. "I like movies."

When the popcorn was ready, I turned around and noticed that her clothes were on the floor. She was in bed, sitting upright, and reading the TV guide. I was surprised, and somewhat amused, so I asked her if she had found any good movies.

"I don't see any good movies," she said, "but please put it on channel 4, 'The Untouchables' is on."

"Oh yes, I know that one," I said. "My parents watch it all the time."

I put the popcorn in front of her and went to sit down on the other bed.

"Hey silly," she said, "aren't you going to join me?"

She pulled the covers back and said, "get in, the show is about to start."

I was now wondering what show she meant, as she didn't have anything on below except her bra and panties.

As I got in she asked me if I always go to bed with my clothes on.

"No, of course not; why?"

"Well then, why are you getting into bed with all of your clothes on?"

I was now a bit embarrassed at the way she was treating the whole situation, but I obliged her and took off my pants and T-shirt. Then she asked me a strange question.

"I have a nickname. Can you guess it?"

"No, what is it?"

"It's 'the Grabber'," she said with a snicker.

I pondered that answer for a second and then she asked me another question.

"Do you wanna know why they call me that?"

"Okay, why do they call you 'the Grabber'?"

"It's because I like to grab guys by the you-know-what."

All of a sudden, she reached for my you-know-what. I blocked her hand from achieving its desired impact, and told her to stop. I jumped out of bed and she did the same. She didn't say anything as she came straight at me, and we both tumbled to the floor. I was now trying to figure out why she was doing this, as I found myself fully engaged in a wrestling match. Was this her strange way of having foreplay? I decided to play along and we proceeded to toss each other around the room. Finally, as we were both panting pretty heavily, I asked her to calm down, and get back into bed.

"No way," she said, "I've only just begun."

Just as she lunged at me again, there was a knock on the door.

Oh my God, I thought, *is it the manager, or what?*

It was as if time had stopped. Both of us sweating and breathing heavily, I asked "who's there?"

"It's me, Keith, let me in."

"Are you alone?" I asked.

"Yes, I am, now open the door."

I unlocked the door and he came in.

He looked at me, and then went straight for his suitcase and grabbed his bottle of gin.

"You won't believe who I ran into tonight," Keith said. "I'll tell you later."

Before I could say anything, Keith was out the door. Mary resumed her attack and lunged at me again.

We wrestled some more, and soon afterward she started getting tired.

"Are we done?" I asked.

"Yes, yes, I'm done," she said, reluctantly. "Let's get back in bed."

We got back into bed, totally exhausted, and began watching TV.

By now I was feeling very horny, so I reached under the covers and touched her thigh.

She slapped my hand and said in a serious tone, "Hey watch it mister. I'm the Grabber, not you."

I was so confused; I didn't know what to think. Just then, there was another knock on the door.

"Go away Keith," I yelled, "we don't want any."

The knocking continued, so I hopped up and opened the door. There before me stood Dennis, the guy Keith and I left behind in Miami. He was not alone, and I recognized Barbara and Linda, standing behind him.

Since I was only clad in my underwear, I quickly ran back to the bed and got in.

Dennis came in, a big smile on his face, and said, "You remember me, don't you?"

"Of course I do," I said, still in shock. "How... When ... What are you doing here?"

"Myself and a couple of other guys are on our way up to Canada for Expo 67 in Montreal. It's just by chance that I ran into Keith down by the beach."

"Wow, I said, I'd offer you a drink, but as you can see ..."

"It's okay," Dennis said, "we'll leave you two alone. I might see you tomorrow if we stay overnight."

I was watching Barbara as she and Linda were talking to one another. Then Barbara stepped inside the room and stared at me. I felt a shiver go down my back as if she was looking right through me. She had a disgusted look on her face as she looked over at the Grabber.

"Come on," Barbara said, "let's get the hell out of here."

The Grabber let out a squeal of delight, as if she had just won a prize, and the three visitors went away.

My mind was now totally focused on Barbara, wishing it was her in my bed and not the Grabber.

I got up to get another beer, and when I turned around to ask Mary if she wanted one, I saw that she was getting up and getting dressed. Without saying a word, Mary, aka the Grabber, left.

After she left, I quickly got dressed. I waited ten minutes and then took a peek to see if she had really gone.

I needed some fresh air after that encounter, so I headed straight for the beach, where a bonfire was the centre of the evening's entertainment.

As I got closer, Keith spotted me coming and yelled out, "Hey lover boy, how's it going?"

I sat down next to Keith, who insisted I tell everyone about my heated encounter.

"So, Al, what exactly did happen after I left?" Keith asked.

Trying to play the innocent one, I replied, "Nothing happened."

The rest of the people wanted to hear more and they insisted that I tell them the truth. I scanned the circle in hopes that I would see Barbara and Linda, but they were nowhere in sight.

I repeated myself, "No, really, there's nothing to tell. We watched some TV and then she left."

They moaned in disappointment at my story, and they started to leave the area.

Finally, after most of them had gone, I told Keith what had really happened.

"You saw Dennis earlier," I said. "Well, he showed up with Barbara and Linda. Even stranger was, once they saw Mary, who called herself the Grabber, they left in a hurry."

Keith looked at me with a quizzical look on his face and asked, "She called herself the what?"

"She called herself the Grabber," I whispered.

Keith's girlfriend started laughing and I knew right away that she knew whom I was talking about.

"Wow," Keith said, "I wasn't sure if you needed any help, but I must say it did look quite interesting. So, come on Allan, tell me what really happened."

I told Keith the whole story, leaving nothing out, and his girl-friend told me that I was lucky that it didn't go any further.

Soon, we were all laughing about the whole incident. Keith's girl-friend, looking at her watch, told him that she had better go home. They kissed and she left. Keith and I headed back to our room.

"I'm tired," I said. "I haven't had an evening like this in a long time."

Keith just looked at me and said, "Just when have you wrestled with a girl that you hardly knew, and who called herself the Grabber?"

We made it back to our room, and decided to clean up in the morning.

We awoke the next morning to hear that it was raining, and decided to head to the diner for coffee. We talked about how our trip was going and what we were going to do after our week was up at the motel.

"So far," I said, "it's been a wild ride, and the surfing has been pretty good."

"I would agree with that," Keith said. "Just think if we had the hearse here, wouldn't that be cool?"

"I'm glad we don't have the hearse," I said. "Sure it's cool but it would probably attract the police as well as the mob bosses that Al Capone use to run with."

Keith laughed at my analogy, and agreed that even without the hearse, we had met some interesting people and even had a surprise visit from Dennis.

"Speaking of Dennis, did you see him after you left me and Mary?" I asked.

"No, I didn't," Keith answered. "Wasn't he with Barbara and Linda?"

"Yes, he was with them when they showed up at our room," I said, "and I got this strange stare from Barbara when she saw that I was with the Grabber."

"Oh well," Keith said, "you probably missed out on a better night with her, than you had with the Grabber."

"Yes," I said, "I think you might be right on that one."

After breakfast, we went back to our room to watch some TV, and get the latest weather report. The ocean was totally flat, not a wave in sight. The weather report told us that the rain was going to end tomorrow, so we decided to drive up north and see what was there. Once we were out of the town of Long Branch, we saw homes that must have cost a million dollars each, spaced evenly along the coast.

"Must be nice to be able to afford a place like that," I said.

"Yes," Keith said, "only the rich and famous could afford a house like that one."

We made it up to Monmouth Beach and the weather was getting worse. There were a few hardy souls trying to catch a wave, but it looked hopeless. We saw a sign that pointed inland to a place called

Red Bank, so we headed there. There were nice houses, meaning we were in an upper-middle class neighbourhood. We drove around some more and I couldn't get my mind of Barbara.

"What are you thinking about?" Keith asked.

"I'm thinking I blew it with those girls that Dennis showed up with, particularly Barbara."

"Yeah," Keith said smiling, "she reminded me of a girl I met in Miami about six months ago at the college. She even gave me her phone number."

"So," I asked, "where does this mysterious girl live?"

"In Connecticut," Keith said.

"You're kidding!" I said. "That's not too far from here."

I took one look at Keith and he looked at me.

Oh no, he isn't, I thought.

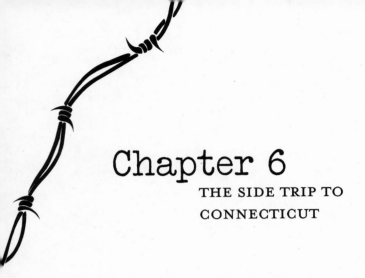

Chapter 6
THE SIDE TRIP TO CONNECTICUT

Keith came up with the idea that since we were very close, we might as well go there, and even get to see some of the Big Apple, New York.

"Alright, what have you got in mind?" I asked.

"I think I still have that phone number in my wallet."

I laughed at what he was suggesting, but I could see that he was seriously thinking of going there.

"I never mentioned it before," he said, "because I didn't know how far we would get. But since we are this close, why not?"

He pulled over and took his wallet out to look for the address.

"Here it is," he said. "She's in Bridgeport, Connecticut. How far away is that?"

I grabbed the map and said, "Hey, it's not that far at all; we just have to go up through Newark, then into New York, and right next door is Connecticut, with Bridgeport being a few more miles east."

"Are you okay with us going there?" Keith asked.

"We still have our room paid for another four days, so why not? Butwhat about our surfboards?" I asked. "Should we go back for them?"

"No," Keith answered. "Who ever heard of going surfing in New York?"

"Alright then," I said, "we're off to see your old girlfriend. But what if she has a boyfriend?"

"We'll worry about that when we get there," Keith said. "I can't wait to see the look on her face."

I sat back to enjoy the ride, thinking, *Oh God, here we go again.*

It was getting close to noon when we arrived at the outskirts of Newark.

"What's that smell?" I asked. "Are we on fire, or what?"

"It smells like gunpowder," Keith replied.

We immediately remembered the news story that told us about the race riots, and it smelled like we were in the middle of a Fourth of July fireworks celebration.

"These race riots are getting ugly," I said. "People are dying for their freedom in a supposedly free country; how weird is that?"

Keith didn't say a word as he was desperately trying to navigate his way through the city.

"Do we want to go to Long Island, or just head straight across the Hudson River and into New York state, and then over to Connecticut?" I asked.

"Let's just head straight for Connecticut," Keith said, as traffic was beginning to get heavier.

"Okay," I said, looking at the map. "We need to find the I-95 freeway leaving Newark, and stay on that all the way to Bridgeport."

"There it is," Keith said. "Good timing."

We followed the signs and were soon into New York, and then into Connecticut.

Finally, we saw a turnoff that would take us into Bridgeport.

Once we got there, we stopped for gas and got something to eat.

Keith took the time to phone his girlfriend. When he came back to the car, he told me that he had talked with her, but that she had told him she was now engaged and would be married soon.

"So now what?" I asked.

"Well," Keith said, "she said she wants to see me one more time, since we took the time to come all this way."

"What about her boyfriend, is that a problem?" I asked.

"She said that he was away on business," Keith said, "and that she doesn't expect him home tonight."

"Uh-oh," I said, "you aren't thinking what I'm thinking, are you?"

"No," Keith said, "but it would be great to see her one more time, just to see what kind of guy she's marrying. She must have a picture of him, right?"

"Yes," I said, "but if we go, you have to promise me that it will just be a short visit; don't even get the idea of spending the night."

"I wouldn't do that to you Al," Keith said, smiling. "Let's go; it's not too far from here."

We made it to the block and found the house.

"Wow," Keith said, "he must be loaded. Look at this place."

"Yes," I said, jokingly, "it must be big enough to house four or five kids."

Keith just looked at me and asked, "Do you want to come with me?"

"No, you go and have your visit with her; I'll just drive around the block a few times and watch for her fiancé."

"Very funny," Keith said. "Give me an hour. That should be good enough."

I looked at my watch and took off. I drove around the neighbourhood a few times and saw that the houses were obviously in the middle to upper class range. After that, I drove back to the gas station, and decided to call my mother to let her know that I was alright, and ask if she could send me some more money. She was delighted that I had called.

"It's been ten days since you left," she said. "When are you coming home?"

"Not for a while," I said. "We are having too much fun. Everything is okay and I'll call you when we decide to come home."

"Alright, son," she said, "I'll send some money right away. Call me when you get it."

"Thanks, Mom," I said. "I'll call you when I get it. Love you; bye."

I looked at my watch and saw that an hour was just about up. I drove back to her house and noticed a car pulling into her driveway. I parked a few houses away and watched.

"Oh my God," I said, "it must be the fiancé."

The man walked straight up the walkway and went in without knocking. I wasn't sure what would happen next. I hoped that everything would be normal, and that I would see Keith coming out soon.

Instead, what I saw made me start laughing. Keith suddenly appeared from the side of the house, stopping for a moment to check and see if I was nearby. I honked the horn, and he saw me and waved. Then he started running across the street to where I was parked. Breathing heavily, he got in and told me to get going as fast as possible.

"Why did you have to leave by the side of the house?" I asked.

Once he caught his breath, Keith started explaining what just happened.

"Everything was cool," he began. "we were having coffee one minute, and joking about the time we spent together in Miami, when all of a sudden, she heard his car come into the driveway. She got so excited and she told me I had to leave by the back door, and that she didn't want me around when he came in."

"I thought she was okay with this reunion," I said.

"Yeah," Keith said, "you and me both."

"Anyway," I added, "you did get to see her. Did you get to see a picture of him?"

"No," Keith said. "I looked for photos, but it's strange that I didn't see any."

"Maybe she took them away so you couldn't see how handsome he was," I said with a laugh.

By now, Keith wasn't listening to anything I said, and we started back to New Jersey.

"I called my mom," I said, "and she is sending me some more money."

Keith was still pondering his short-lived reunion, so I decide not to bother him with small talk.

Even though it was getting late, I felt wide awake and decided to keep on driving. It was still raining, and since there wasn't much traffic to contend with, we made good time. Keith had fallen asleep as I drove through the burrows of New York, and back into New Jersey.

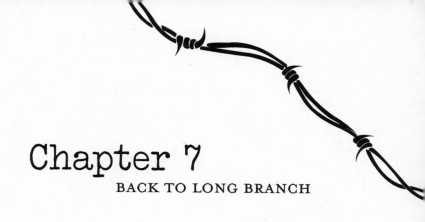

Chapter 7

BACK TO LONG BRANCH

We arrived back at our motel at about one o'clock in the morning. The parking lot looked deserted, except for one other car.

I nudged Keith and said, "Hey man, we're back, let's go."

Once we were in our beds it didn't take long to fall asleep. In the morning, we awoke to the sound of heavy rain.

"It looks terrible out there," I said to Keith, who was still in bed.

"Turn on the TV," Keith said, "and see if there is going to be any improvement today, or if it's going to be like this for the rest of our stay."

I could tell that he was not happy with the way things turned out in Bridgeport, so I offered to go and get some breakfast and bring it back to the room.

Finally, he got up and looked out the window.

"This sucks," he said. "But you know something? I'm going to check out the waves. You never know with weather like this."

I watched him as he left to go outside in his shorts, T-shirt, and sandals. I grabbed my wallet and followed him to the edge of the parking lot and then headed for the diner. I ordered two large omelets and two large coffees to go. Just as the order was ready, Keith came walking in, drenched to the bone. I asked Keith if he wanted to eat here or go back to our room. He pointed to a table and sat down.

I paid for the order and told the waitress that we would take a table and eat in.

Keith sipped his coffee and mumbled something about the waves being pretty big.

"They must be five or six feet," he said, his teeth chattering.

"Well, of course," I said, "there is a storm happening."

Keith looked at me and started laughing.

"What's wrong with you?" I asked.

"Oh nothing," he said. "This hot coffee is really good. Did we really go to see my old girlfriend last night, or was I dreaming?"

"Yes, Keith," I said, "we really did go to Bridgeport to see your old flame."

"Wow," Keith replied, "I don't remember too much, except for the fact that I slept all the way home, right?"

"It's best that you don't remember anything Keith," I said. "Now, how about those waves you were talking about?"

"Huh? Oh yes, I think it would a good idea to try these waves, but this time I think I'll get a wet suit."

"I could not agree with you more." I said.

We finished our omelets and walked back to our room to wait the required one hour before going into the water.

We watched TV and heard the latest news about the war. The usual statistics of how many Vietcong were killed always outnumbered the Americans killed. President Johnson continued to work for peace, but was always telling the public that we were winning the war.

The protests against the war were growing bigger each day, and even Martin Luther King, a crusader for the rights of the black people, came on TV and told young American boys to burn their draft cards.

"I'm sure glad we have our student deferment," I said to Keith. "I don't think I'd make a good soldier."

"Me neither," Keith answered. "Let's hope it's over soon."

"I wonder if any of our friends joined the military and are in the war right now," I said.

"Don't even think about that," Keith said. "It's too depressing."

"How about your cousin Johnny?" I asked. "He seems the type that would go for something like that."

"I don't think he could pass the tests," Keith said jokingly. "But yeah, I'll bet he would drive the enemy crazy."

Finally, our hour of waiting ended and we took off for the surf shop to rent some wet suits.

Because of the weather, we practically had the whole beach to ourselves.

We spent a good amount of time trying to master the larger and more erratic waves that the storm was producing. After a few hours, we were exhausted. We decided to go and get some lunch.

While waiting for our food, Dennis showed up. He made his way over to our table and sat down beside us.

"Hey guys, have you changed your mind about going to Expo 67 in Montreal?"

"No," Keith said, why would we want to go to Canada?"

"It's going to be great!" Dennis declared, as he pulled out a brochure. "See here, it says that there are going to be exhibits from over thirty countries."

"Is Vietnam going to be one of the countries?" I asked sarcastically. "Maybe they can teach us how to grow rice or something."

"Now you're being stupid," Dennis said. "It's going to a learning experience that is better than any college could teach."

"I'm sure you are right about that," I said, "but no thanks. Keith and I are going to stay right here and enjoy our time, surfing big waves."

"Alright," Dennis said, "but you don't know what you're missing. I'll see you back in Miami."

"Okay," we said, "have a good trip."

After Dennis left, we thought about the idea of going to Canada and what it would be like to cross the border.

"I don't know anything about Canada," I said. "Do you?"

"No," Keith said, "there isn't anything taught in high school about it and there certainly isn't anything that I know of in college."

"Yeah," I said, "Canada is always a weird shade of pink when you look at it on the map. It's a big country, but it's all ice and snow, like on that TV show, 'Sergeant Preston of the Yukon;' have you ever seen it?"

"Not really," Keith said. "Hey, let's get back out there, enough about Canada."

We surfed for about an hour until the wind increased and made the waves too choppy and erratic.

"Let's quit for today," Keith said. "I've had enough."

We rode one last wave in, then went up to our room. There was a message from the manager pinned to the door.

"He wants us to come to the office," I said. "I wonder if it's about the money that my mother is sending."

I went to the office and sure enough, the manager told me that he had received a call from the Western Union office in Red Bank about the wired money. Then he asked me if we were planning on staying longer than the week we had paid him for.

"I'm not sure," I said. "We'll let you know soon."

I went back to the room to get my wallet and asked Keith if he wanted to go.

"No," he said, "I'll stay here. You don't need me for that."

As I drove to Red Bank, I started thinking about our plans for the rest of the summer. The weather had changed drastically, and the rain continued to drench the area. We had been away for nearly two weeks now, and we certainly had seen a lot of the east coast. Now it was time to make a decision. Either stay longer, go up to Expo 67 with Dennis, or head back home.

When I arrived back at the motel, Keith was on the phone, talking to his mother. After he was finished, he told me that everything was okay back home. I called my mom to let her know that I had received the money and that we were thinking of heading home.

When Keith heard me say that, he asked, "So now you want to go home?" "Well," I said, looking out the window at the rain, "this weather is making it harder to stick around. It would be different if it were sunny, because we would be out there, instead of in here."

"I agree," Keith said, "but we have paid for a week, so we might as well stay right here. The weather will eventually change."

"I guess you're right," I said. "I promise not to let a little bit of rain get me down."

We spent the rest of the day watching TV and looking to see if the rain had stopped. A few cars with boards would show up, and then leave. We went out for supper, came back to our room, and again turned the TV on. It was boredom at its peak, until we heard a weather forecast saying that the rains were coming to an end in the morning.

"Alright," I said, "we're back to the beach tomorrow."

Sure enough, the weather did turn around, and the morning sun was pouring through our window. We hurried to get dressed and went for coffee and our usual omelet. After eating, we got our boards and waxed them up good. The previous day's storm had taken some of the debris that had been at the high tide mark, such as logs, seaweed, and miscellaneous garbage, and turned the beach into a messy and dangerous situation.

"Be careful," I said to Keith, "you don't want to hit anything."

We spent a good three hours having fun while dodging the floating debris, and seeing who could stay on their board the longest.

When we agreed to stop, we made a beeline for the freshwater showers, and washed the sea weed and other crap off. The parking lot was now totally full of surfers and tourists. It was only yesterday that

I was ready to go home, and now the wait for good weather made it all seem worthwhile.

The next couple of days were spent enjoying the good weather, and as our first week in Long Branch was coming to an end, we were faced with the decision of whether to go or stay for another week.

Keith and I talked it over, and decided it was time to move on and head back south.

On our last night, we were having dinner at the local burger joint, when a couple of well-known local surfers showed up. We told them that we might be heading out in the morning, and that this was the best beach that we had encountered on our trip. They shook our hands and told us that we were welcome to come back any time. They left and went out into the parking lot, where I could see that they were talking to another group of surfers. I also noticed that they kept looking back in our direction, and I could sense that something was being planned.

"You don't think that they are planning some kind of farewell party?" I asked Keith.

"Who cares," Keith answered. "They can have all the parties they want, as long as I'm invited."

"Yeah," I said, "it will probably be down at the beach with a bonfire and all of the friends we've made; I sure hope that Barbara comes to it."

"Quit dreaming about Barbara," Keith said. "She's probably long gone by now."

After dinner, we went and told the manager that we would be leaving in the morning.

He just looked at us and laughed, "Well, I'm sure you've had a ton of fun. Take care driving back down to Florida."

We thanked him and went back to our room where we took turns looking at the map, trying to decide where we should go. There wasn't anywhere that looked inviting, and so we decided that we should go home.

I called my mother and told her that news, and Keith did the same.

After we called, we could see that a large crowd of people was forming in the parking lot. I watched as they started to come up to our room.

"Oh no," I said, "I knew it."

"What?" Keith asked. "Is someone coming?"

"Yes, there is," I said. "At least twenty people, I would say."

They were carrying cases of beer and as they made their way to our door, I asked Keith if we should let them in.

"Might as well," he said. "It is our last night here."

I took another glimpse outside, in the hopes that I would see Barbara, but she wasn't with them.

I opened the door and they came in. I recognized most of them, and some I had never seen before. They proceeded to fill our room, and soon the music was turned up, and the beer was flowing freely. Everyone told us that they were going to miss us, and some of them wanted our addresses so they could visit us in Miami. I gave a few of them my phone number, and Keith did the same.

As the party wore on, I heard the sound of glass breaking in the bathroom. I walked in and saw a guy standing in the bathtub with all of his clothes on. He stood there looking at a broken beer bottle on the floor. I told him to stay there while I cleaned it up. He just smiled at me, and then he turned the shower on.

"Keith, I yelled, get in here!"

Keith came in and shut the water off, while I picked up the pieces of glass.

We helped him out of the tub, and gave him some towels to dry off. A couple of his friends came in and apologized for his behaviour, and took him outside.

While this was happening, there were others who were now dancing on the beds, jumping from one to another.

I looked at Keith and said, "Oh well, we're leaving tomorrow; the manager can't do anything to us, right?"

"I guess not," Keith said. "Let's just hope that nothing else happens."

Chapter 8

THE FRATERNITY HOUSE

It was nearly midnight, and the farewell party being thrown for us was still going strong. They not only filled our room, but there was another dozen or so directly outside on the balcony. Keith was having fun, dancing with a couple of girls, so I decide to join him.

Just then, I noticed the office porch light come on. Stepping outside, the manager stood there, looking at everyone. I grabbed Keith's arm and pointed toward the office.

"He's coming up here," I said. "I hope he understands that it is not our fault."

The manager made his way up the stairs, pushing his way through the crowd. I went to meet him before he saw the mess inside our room.

"Hi," I said. "I guess we're a little bit noisy tonight. They decided to throw us a going away party."

He barged right past me and took one look inside the room. He then turned around and screamed, "Everyone, get out, now!"

I shut the music off, and tried to calm him down.

He was now red in the face, and threatened to call the police.

"I want you two, and everyone else, out of here tonight, do you hear me?"

He then stomped out and went back into his office.

Everybody was stunned to hear the manager say this.

"He's never been like this before," one person said.

"Yeah," said another, "maybe he's just mad at something else and won't bother us again; turn on the music."

Someone did turn on the music, but I went and shut it off.

"Listen everyone," I said, "Keith and I appreciate the party, but you have to admit, things here have gotten out of hand. There are broken beer bottles in the bathroom, all of the towels are gone, and someone has broken a lamp. So please, we thank you for the party, but you'll all have to leave."

After they left, Keith and I sat down and looked at the mess.

"What are we going to do?" I asked.

"Good question, Al," Keith said. "One I don't have an answer for."

Just then, there was a knock on our door.

"Uh-oh," I said, "I hope that's not the police."

I opened the door and saw one guy standing there.

"What do you want?" I asked.

"I think I can help you two out," he said. "I heard that you were kicked out by the manager."

"Come on in," I said. "How can you help us?"

"Well," he began, "it's obvious you need a place to stay tonight, so I'd like to help by offering you a room at my fraternity house."

I was speechless at first, and then Keith jumped up and said, "We'll take it. where is it?"

"It's about a twenty-minute drive from here," he said. "And my name is Dave."

I looked at Keith and said, "Why not? It is better than staying here and maybe getting arrested."

"You got that right," Keith said. "Let's get our things together."

"I'll wait for you down in the parking lot," Dave said. "I'm parked right next to your VW."

Keith and I hurried to get our things together, then rushed down to the car.

We strapped our boards on and followed Dave to the fraternity house. Since it was almost 2:00 a.m., we were thankful that this stranger had taken it upon himself to help us out.

"I wonder why he's doing this?" Keith asked.

"Who knows," I said, "maybe he's been surfing next us the whole time and we just never met."

Dave unlocked the front door to the building and we walked down a long hallway.

"Being summer break, this place is empty right now except for one odd traveler and his two buddies," he said. "Here's one room, and there's another one next to it, and if you're hungry, the kitchen is just down the hall."

"Why are you doing this?" Keith asked.

"I just want to help out two guys who need a place to stay, that's all." Dave answered.

"Well," I said, "thanks a lot for everything. Will we see you in the morning?"

"No," Dave said, smiling. "I'm staying at my girlfriend's place tonight. If you decide to stay another day or two, that's okay, just clean up before you go."

"No problem," Keith said. "Good night."

Keith and I looked at the two rooms and decided that they were both the same.

"Well," I said, yawning, "I'll see you in the morning."

I slept until 10:00 a.m. I went to Keith's room and knocked on his door.

"Come in," he said.

As I went in, I could hear someone arguing down at the end of the hall.

"What's all the commotion about?" Keith asked.

"It must be those characters that Dave was talking about," I said. "So, what do we do now?"

"About what?" Keith mumbled.

"I mean, do we stay here or do we go home?"

"I thought we already decided to go home," Keith said, as he was getting up.

"Let's go to the kitchen and see about making some coffee," I said, "then we'll decide."

We walked down the hallway and saw a guy coming out of a room.

"That guy looks familiar," I said to Keith.

"Oh my God," Keith said, "it's Dennis."

Just then, Dennis turned around and spotted us.

"Hey," he said, with a surprised look on his face, "what are you two doing here?"

The three of us went to the kitchen, and I saw Dennis's two friends in their room.

We explained to Dennis what had happened at the motel, and then it was Dennis's turn to explain.

"We are still going to Canada for Expo 67," he said. "It's only because one of them is waiting for his parents to send him some money that we are still here."

"Well," I said, "Keith and I are heading back to Florida. We've seen enough around here."

"Okay," Dennis said, "remember, if you change your mind ..."

"We won't," I said. "See you later."

Keith and I drank our coffee and left. We decided to drive back to the motel and tell the manager that we felt bad about what had happened. When we arrived, the cleaning crew was already busy in our room, so we went straight for the office.

The manager saw us and he immediately held up his hands and said, "Why, boys, why?"

We explained to him that it wasn't our idea of having the whole community show up in our room, and that we couldn't control them once they were in the room. He accepted our apology and told us that we would be welcomed the next time, whenever that was going to be.

Keith and I left his office and went back to the car.

"Well," Keith said, "this is it. Back to good old Florida, the hearse, and our jobs."

"Yes," I replied, "I'm going to remember this place forever, even if I didn't get to meet the girl of my dreams."

"You mean Barbara?" Keith asked.

"Yes, I do," I answered. "Perhaps in another time."

Before leaving the parking lot, we saw Dave running over to our car.

"I wonder what he wants?" Keith said.

"Hey guys," Dave said, "you'd better get out of here fast."

"Why, what's up?" I asked.

"I just got a call this morning from some of the frat brothers, and they told me that some items were stolen from the house. Do you have any idea who took them?"

"No, we don't," I said. "What kind of things are you talking about?"

"There were some fireworks and clothes taken," Dave said. "I didn't think it was you two. Do you suppose that it was that Dennis guy and his two friends?"

"I would suspect it was the other two guys," I said. "We know Dennis and I don't think it was him."

"Well," Dave added, "you had better get going before the frat brothers show up. They're looking to beat somebody up."

Just then, someone came over and told Dave that the frat brothers were on their way to the motel. Keith and I heard this, thanked them both, and took off. We left the parking lot and saw Dennis, who saw us and stuck out his thumb. We stopped and told him to get in.

Allan Glass

"Did you hear what happened?" he asked.

"Yes, we did," I said. "Now get in before we all get mobbed."

Dennis got in and said, "It's probably those two idiots that I hooked up with; I'm almost positive of that."

"You're probably right, I said. "What are your plans now?"

"I'm still going to Montreal," Dennis said, "so could you drop me off at the freeway entrance?"

"Yeah, sure," I said, "anything to help you on your way."

We drove Dennis to the on-ramp of the freeway and said goodbye.

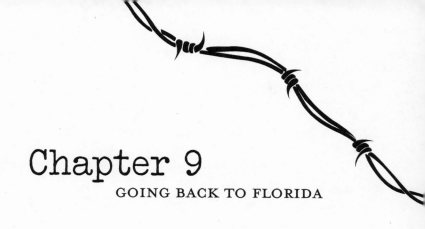

Chapter 9
GOING BACK TO FLORIDA

We took off and got onto the freeway heading south. Neither of us spoke a word. After twenty miles, I broke the silence and asked, "Do you think we are doing the right thing?"

Keith just laughed and said, "Al, look, we have only been gone a couple of weeks, and in that time we've been through nine states. I'd say we have done a lot of traveling, wouldn't you?"

"Yes," I said, "but it seems like it was just yesterday that we left."

"Well, where would you like to go now?" Keith asked.

"I don't have a clue," I said. "I guess we'll go home. At least we'll have the hearse to play with, although I'm not sure of what we can do with it."

"We'll have a blast with it," Keith said. "Just think of all the women that will be attracted to it when we take it to the beach."

"That's true," I replied. "It will be a whole different world driving that huge black thing."

I started thinking about the hearse, and how my mother was getting used to the fact that she had a hearse sitting in front of the house. Then I remembered the VW, and how we came to acquire it.

"Keith," I said, "what do you think we should do with the VW?"

"What do you mean?" Keith asked.

"Well," I said, "I've thought about this ever since we took it, and now that we don't need it anymore, I think we should simply give it back. I mean, do you really want a stolen car sitting around your place?"

Keith was silent, and I could tell that he was thinking very seriously about what I had just said.

"Let's worry about that when we get home," he said. "For now, we can keep it at Johnny's."

I sat back and thought that it was at least a start to changing Keith's mind about giving it back.

The trip home was a quick one, as we made only one overnight stop in Myrtle Beach. I called my mother and let her know we would be home the next day.

When we arrived, Keith dropped me off at my place. I saw both my car and the hearse, proudly sitting where I had left them.

"I'll call you tonight," Keith said.

"Okay," I replied, "but I'll probably spend tonight with my mom."

"No problem," Keith said. "We'll do something tomorrow; bye."

My mother was there to greet me with a hug, and she asked me if I was hungry.

We had lunch and I spent the next half hour telling her all about the trip, well, at least part of it.

Then she asked me about the hearse. "What do you plan on doing with that thing?"

I tried to explain to her that it was a one of a kind vehicle, an antique, and that it might have some historical value to it, as well as being the coolest surfing vehicle
in Miami. She just sat there, looking at me like this was the craziest idea that I had ever come up with.

"It might be cool to you," she said, "but the neighbours have told me that it looks creepy and evil."

"Oh Mom," I said. "That's your religious side coming out, isn't it?"

She tried to convince me that her Catholic upbringing had nothing to do with this, but I didn't believe her for a second.

"Alright, Mom," I said, trying to be nice, "how about I move the hearse up alongside the house, so you can't really see it from the road?"

"Well," she said, "I guess that would be better."

I phoned Keith that night and asked him about keeping the hearse at his house.

"There's no room here," Keith said, "and we don't want to keep it at Johnny's. Remember, he's got the VW."

"Okay," I said, "I'll put it beside my house for now. See you tomorrow, or are you going to work?"

"No, I'm not going to work," Keith said. "I haven't called my boss yet; I'll do that tomorrow. What about your job?"

"I'll probably go there tomorrow," I said, "and see if they need me."

The next day I drove to the supermarket. The manager saw me and smiled.

"You're back," he said. "It's been more than two weeks; can you come in tomorrow?"

"Uh, yeah," I said, "I wasn't sure if you would still need me."

"Oh yes," he said, "I need you. We've got other people here waiting to take their vacations, so can I expect you to be here at 9:00 a.m.?"

"Alright," I said, "see you tomorrow."

I left feeling pretty good about being wanted. I was into my third year of working at this store, and it was the kind of work that I enjoyed doing. Even with my long hair, an attribute that other jobs would not accept, my manager would just joke about it from time to time, saying, "You don't want to look like a girl, now do you?"

I went over to Keith's and told him that I was returning to work. He told me there wasn't much work at the gas station and that he was going to try and look for work elsewhere. Meanwhile, the question of what to do with the VW came up.

"Johnny doesn't want it at his place," Keith said, "so I guess we should return it to that Cuban guy."

"I'm glad you feel that way," I said. "When do you want to do it?"

"The sooner the better," Keith said. "I drove past his house and saw that he has a different vehicle, and it's not another bug."

"How about tomorrow night, around midnight?" I suggested.

"Sounds good," Keith said. "Come over around nine and we'll wait at Johnny's."

I told my mother that I was going to a party, but instead, I picked Keith up and the two of us went to Johnny's.

When the clock struck midnight, Keith drove the VW to the exact spot we took it from, and walked over to where I was waiting.

As soon as Keith got in, I took off in a different direction.

"I sure wish we could see the look on his face when he wakes up and sees a bright yellow VW in front of his house," I said. "How long do you think it will take him to realize that it's his?"

"I don't care about that," Keith said, "but I'm sure when he saw that his car was gone, he called the cops, then probably the insurance company. I wonder if it was the insurance company that got him the new car."

I drove back to Keith's and dropped him off, and then I went straight home.

As I lay in my bed, I knew that returning the car was the right thing to do. It also put an end to the worries that had bothered me in the short time that we had the car.

For the next couple of weeks, my life seemed to return to normal, with Keith and I doing the things that we loved the most, surfing and going to parties with my hearse. As the month of June and my twentieth birthday passed, I was ready to spend the rest of summer having as much fun as possible. In September, it would be time to go back to college and prepare for my career as a professional deep sea diver.

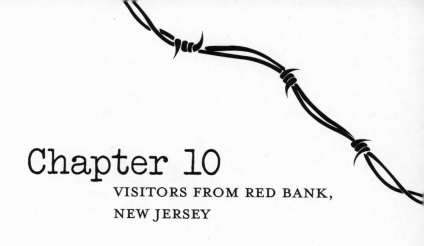

Chapter 10

VISITORS FROM RED BANK, NEW JERSEY

Just as things got back to normal, I received a call from Dennis, the guy whom Keith and I had left in New Jersey, and who was going to Montreal for Expo 67.

He explained to me that he had spent one week in Montreal, then decided to come back to Miami, but that wasn't why he had called.

"The reason I'm calling you is to ask if you remember the time that you were in the motel room with that girl, the Grabber, and I showed up with two other girls?"

"How could I forget that night?" I asked. "What's up?"

"Well," Dennis continued, "I just got off the phone with them and they are here in Miami, right now!"

"Really?" I said. "You mean Barbara and Linda? Those two?"

"Yes, they drove down in Barbara's car, and are staying in a motel. They want us to show them around while they are here, so can you come and pick me up? They're expecting us."

"Yes!" I said. "I'll come and pick you up in about half an hour."

I quickly showered and told my mother that I wouldn't be home for supper.

After picking Dennis up, he told me that he was attracted to Linda, and that I would have to settle for Barbara. I told him that was okay with me.

When we arrived at the motel, I saw Barbara standing on the balcony, her long auburn hair blowing in the breeze.

I sat in my car and stared up at her, thinking, *she's so beautiful.*

"Come on," Dennis said, "let's go."

Anxiously, Dennis and I walked up to their floor and greeted them both.

"Hi," I said, "I'm Allan."

"I know," Barbara said with a smile, "I'll bet you're surprised to see us."

The four of us went into their room and Barbara offered me a beer.

I looked over at Dennis and Linda. They were making out on Linda's bed, so I asked Barbara to go out onto the balcony.

"Yes," Barbara said, "let's go out."

"So," I asked, "what brings you two to Miami?"

"We've been planning to come down for some time now, so here we are."

"I thought you would plan to come down in the wintertime, not the summer. Isn't it too hot here?"

"Well, it's because we wanted to drive down, and you can't really do that with a brand-new Plymouth Barracuda in the winter, now can you?"

I looked out into the parking lot and saw the shiny new 'Cuda.

"Is that it over there?"

"Yes, it is," she said. "And I see that you have a very nice car yourself; what is it?"

"It's a 1965 Malibu Super Sport."

"Very nice indeed. I can't wait to go for a drive in it."

"Oh yes, we'll definitely go for a ride in it. So," I said, "how long did it take for you to drive down?"

"Only two days," Barbara said. "Linda and I took turns driving."

Barbara and I continued our small talk, and then she surprised me by asking me why I was with the Grabber.

"When I first saw you at the beach," she said, "I was attracted to you. Then, when I saw you in bed with her, I couldn't believe my eyes. How did you end up with her?"

I told her the shortened version and convinced her that nothing happened.

"That sounds like her style," Barbara said. "I knew her from high school, and she was always the big tease. Eventually, she got her nickname from one of the guys she dated."

We finished our beer and Barbara asked me if I wanted another one.

"No thanks," I said. "Would you like to go for a ride?"

She got up, opened the door to her room, and took a peek inside.

"Let's go for that ride," she said, laughing. "They're under the covers."

After I got a closer look at her car, we took off in mine. The hot summer sun made me wish I had a convertible. Barbara liked the interior of the car, saying that she knew someone in New Jersey that had one just like it.

As we left Hialeah, I drove straight for the causeway that linked Miami Beach to the mainland.

"It's sure beautiful here," Barbara said, as we made our way into the area that only the rich and famous lived.

As we drove past the most famous Miami Beach hotels, I could tell that she was in her own little world, dreaming of what it would be like to live here.

I also dreamed of being rich and driving around town with the most beautiful girl in the world sitting next to me.

All of a sudden, I heard my stomach growl, which made us both laugh.

"Are you getting hungry?" she asked.

"Well yes," I said, looking at my watch. "It is one o'clock."

"Let's look for a place to eat," she said. "Have you been to any of these places?"

"Are you kidding?" I said. "Do you do realize where we are?"

"Oh," she said, feeling a bit embarrassed, "we can head back to the motel, if that's what you would rather do."

"The thing is," I said, "I probably only have about five dollars on me right now, and I don't think that it would buy very much around here."

She just giggled and said, "Alright, then, let's find a restaurant that doesn't look too expensive, and I'll buy, if that's alright with you."

I bit my tongue and agreed with her, saying, "I'll just keep on driving, the farther we get from these expensive hotels, the cheaper it will be. Just let me know when you want to stop."

Just then, I spotted my favourite, a Burger King, but I kept silent.

Suddenly she saw it too, and said, "Hey, there's a Burger King, do you want to go there?"

"Sure," I said, "I didn't know they had one of these here."

"Why not?" she asked. "Rich people like Burger King too."

During lunch, I told her about living with my mother, working at the local supermarket, and going to the junior college so I could get my degree to get a job as a professional diver.

"Sounds exotic," she said. "You never know which area of the world you'll be going to next."

I then asked her about her life, and she told me that she was working as a secretary at her father's business in Red Bank.

"It's not very glamorous," she said. "They make different parts for the auto industry, and it's not the kind of job that I want to stay at forever."

I wanted to ask her about her plans for marriage and having children and wanted to ask her to marry me, but instead I asked her,

"What's a single, beautiful girl like you want to do for the rest of your life?"

"Whoa," she said, with a surprised look on her face. "I haven't even thought about that. Right now, I just want to travel around to different parts of the US and see where it takes me."

"Alright," I said, "fair enough. At least you women don't have to worry about that stupid war in Vietnam."

"That's true," Barbara said. "I've never thought about it. At least you can avoid it by staying in school, right?"

"Yes, that's right, and I plan on doing just that, because I have no intentions of fighting a war that I know nothing about."

"I knew a couple of guys that joined up when the war started," Barbara said, "and I haven't heard anything from them since. It makes me wonder what happened to them."

With that remark, we finished eating in silence and then headed back for the motel.

When we arrived at the motel, we decided to knock first.

"Come on in," Linda yelled. "Dennis left a few minutes ago. He's weird."

She looked at me, expecting me to defend him, but I just told her that I didn't know him that well, that Keith and I had just met him before we went on our trip.

"I don't like him or dislike him," I said, "but he just doesn't fit in with me and Keith."

The three of us sat and talked awhile, then they asked me what my plans were for dinner. I told them that although I was still living at home with my mother, I was free to go anywhere I wanted.

"The motel has a barbecue out back," Linda said. "Let's get some steaks, potato salad, and some wine, and eat here."

"We'll get them at the store where I work," I said. "Besides, I have to go in and check out my schedule for the coming week."

The three of us took off in Barbara's Barracuda, and I was impressed by the car's power.

"Hey Barbara, do you know what size engine is in this?"

"Of course I do. It's a 426 cu inch Hemi, with approx. 370 horsepower."

"Well it has mine beat by about 100 cu inches and 20 horsepower."

"That's still a big engine," she said. "Probably from the Corvette model, right?"

"You are correct. How did you know?"

"Remember, I work for Daddy, who makes parts for cars, so that kind of information is used every day."

"Oh yes," I said, feeling very humbled. "I forgot."

We arrived at the store and went in. I saw the manager and went over to talk to him, while the girls grabbed a shopping cart and took off.

"Hi," I said. "They're some people I met while I was in New Jersey, and they have come down for a visit."

"They look very nice," the manager said. "Don't forget now, you are scheduled to come in to work tomorrow morning."

"Don't worry, I'll be here."

I caught up with the two of them as they were throwing things into the cart. Everything from snack foods to expensive cuts of meat, they were on a shopping spree, and money didn't seem to matter.

"Where's the beer and wine?" they asked.

"The beer is under the meat counter," I said, "and the wine section is over next to the produce."

After getting the beer, we headed over to the produce department. I spotted the produce manager, and decided to play a little game. I knew that he was a real ladies' man, and that he always tried to flirt with the women who came to his department. I crept up slowly, close enough to hear them, but staying out of sight. As Barbara and Linda approached him, his eyes grew wide, and I could tell that he was getting ready to cast his spell on them.

"Hello ladies," he began, "may I help you?"

Barbara turned around to see if I was nearby. When she saw that I wasn't, she sensed that something was going on, so she playfully accepted the produce manager's come-on. When she started asking him questions about the different kinds of produce, I almost burst out laughing as I could tell that she was stringing him along, and acting like she was really interested in him. Linda didn't clue in to what was happening as she looked over the selection of wine.

"Hey Barb, what kind of wine do you want with your steak?" she asked.

"Oh," Barb answered, "any kind will do."

I decided to get in on the fun, so I walked up to where they were.

"Hi, Jim," I said, "how's it going?"

"Everything's fine, Al," Jim said, as he went back to giving Barbara all of his attention and expertise in picking the ripest melons.

I acted like I was an expert in produce and began giving Barbara my tips for picking the same melon.

Jim finally got a little ticked off and asked me what I thought I was doing, since he was the expert.

"Who's the manager of this department, me or you?" he asked.

"Why you, Jim, of course," I said. "I'm just here helping these two ladies do some shopping."

Jim looked stunned, but he smiled and asked, "They're with you?"

"Yes, they are," I said, gloating. "Did you girls find what you are looking for?"

"Not really," Barbara said as she winked at me. "We didn't find anything here that I like. Come on, let's go."

Meanwhile, Linda was busy putting bottles of red and white wine into the cart.

"There," she said. "That should do us for a couple of days."

I looked at Jim, whose mouth was still agape, and said, "Thanks, Jim. I'm working tomorrow, so I'll see you then."

Jim just shook his head in awe of my two beauties and went back to playing with his melons.

The checkout lines were full, so I asked the manager if I could open a till just for them.

"Sure, he said, go ahead with number seven; it's all set to go."

After shopping, we went back to the motel. Linda mentioned to Barbara that they should check out the barbecue and make sure that it was clean and ready to be used. The three of us went and the manager told us that it was all set to go.

That evening, Linda, Barbara, and I shared one of the best barbecue steak dinners I have ever had, and the red wine that Linda had picked out for the occasion was perfect. Afterward, we relaxed and spent the rest of the evening talking and listening to music, and of course drinking more wine. When the clock struck eleven, I remembered that I had to go to work the next morning, and that I didn't have any work clothes with me. When I told them that I would have to leave, Barbara came close and put her arms around me.

"Can't you get them in the morning?" she cooed. "I don't want to be alone tonight."

I looked at Linda for help, but she was busy getting ready for bed herself.

"Alright," I said, "but I'll have to get up around eight, in order to go home, get changed, and get to work by nine."

"No problem," Barbara said, "I have an alarm clock right here."

She set the clock for seven thirty and placed it on the nightstand beside the bed.

"There," she said, smiling. "Are you happy now?"

"No," I said, "not yet." And I hopped into bed and turned out the lights.

The next thing I remembered was the alarm clock going off. I looked at Barbara, who was sound asleep, as was Linda. I gave her a kiss and slowly got out of bed.

I scribbled a note and left it on the table telling them to come to the store, and left.

That day, I couldn't stop talking to all of my co-workers about my new girlfriend, especially to Jim, who still could not accept the fact that Barbara was with me. The girls did not show up so I decided to go home after work and get another change of clothes.

My mother asked me what I was up to, and when I told her the truth, she seemed worried that I was never going to see her again.

"I'm all alone here, Allan," she said. "It's not fair."

"It's okay, Mom," I said. "They are just here for a little while, to have some fun, and then they'll go back home to New Jersey. Then I'll be back here with you, and start school in September."

I left feeling a little bit guilty, but the thought of being with Barbara made me forget all about that.

When I arrived at the motel, I saw Barbara and Linda carrying their belongings downstairs. My mind was racing with the idea that they had changed their minds and were moving out and going back to Jersey.

I ran up to them and asked them what they were doing.

"We're moving to a ground level room," they said. "It's bigger and has a better TV and refrigerator."

"Don't just stand there," Linda said. "Grab something so we can get this finished faster."

I kept the part about my thinking they were leaving to myself, and started helping them. When we finished, Barbara came up to me and gave me a kiss.

"Did you remember to bring your work clothes with you this time?" she asked.

"Yes, I did," I said. "They're in the car; I'll go and get them."

We went into their new place and I immediately smelled something wonderful coming from the kitchen. "What are you cooking?" I asked.

"We're having turkey tonight," Linda said. "The manager let us start it this morning, right after we asked for a bigger place."

"Oh, I get it," I said. "You were just waiting for me to finish work, so I could help you move all of your other stuff."

"Well yeah," Barbara said, jokingly, "you've got to earn your dinner, right Linda?"

"That's right," Linda said. "But now it's time for a chilled glass of white wine."

"That sounds good," I said wiping the sweat off my brow.

While the turkey was cooking, I asked Linda if she thought Dennis would come back.

"I hope not," she said.

Then they told me that a friend of theirs from New Jersey was flying down to Miami tomorrow, and that he would be staying here with them.

"You'll really like him," Barbara said. "His name is Bruce. He's a friend we went to school with, but he doesn't quite fit in with the college crowd. You'll see what we mean when he gets here; he is quite the character."

They described him as being six feet tall and weighing a hundred pounds.

"He sounds pretty weird," I said, "but with Linda's cooking he'll double his weight in no time."

Finally, Linda looked at the time and proudly announced, "Dinner is ready."

While we were eating, Linda and Barbara mentioned Bruce's name again.

"We're hoping that he brings some of the good stuff. When I asked them what they meant by "good stuff," they would just giggle and tell me that I would have to wait.

The next day, the girls showed up just before quitting time, and Bruce was with them. He was definitely a tall, skinny kid, with a smile that never quit. We shook hands and left the store.

"We'll see you two back at the motel," Barbara said, as she got into my car.

"Do you have to go home for anything, or can we go straight to the motel?" she asked me.

"To the motel it is. Did Bruce bring the good stuff?"

"Yes, he did. Can you figure out what it is?"

"I would say it's marijuana, am I right?"

"How did you know?" she asked. "Have you ever smoked pot?"

"A few times. Keith's friends had some once, but it's not something I go looking for."

That evening, we had another wonderful dinner, and Bruce declared that it was time for a joint.

I noticed that it had a reddish-brown colour to it so I asked him about it.

"It's called Panama Red," he said. "From Panama of course."

"This is quite different than the traditional green Mexican pot, and even the Acapulco gold that I have tried," I said. "Is it expensive?"

"Oh yes," Bruce said. "It's twice the price of regular Mexican."

We smoked a joint, had a beer, and sat watching TV.

"This stuff also has a peculiar taste to it," I said. "Completely different from anything else I've smoked."

We began discussing the future and the idea came up of Barbara and Linda moving out of the motel and finding a small house to rent.

"I don't feel comfortable in this motel," Barbara said. "It would be nice to have a little more room and of course some more privacy."

"That sounds like a good idea," I said. "Have you got any ideas as to where you would look for such a place?"

Linda jumped up and grabbed the newspaper.

"There are a couple of places near here that sound alright," she said. "We'll check them out tomorrow."

"I've already told the motel manager that we were thinking of moving out," Barbara added, "so we don't have to worry about that."

I mentioned my hearse to them, and asked if I could keep it at their new place, so my mother would not have to put up with it.

"You've got a what?" Bruce asked.

"Oh yes," I said, "I forgot to tell you that I own a 1941 Cadillac hearse."

"That sounds really cool," Bruce said. "I can't wait to see it."

The next day, I went to work for a half day, and when I drove to the motel, the manager said that they had moved out, and he handed me a piece of paper with the new address.

I thanked him and took off. It was a modest neighbourhood, with small houses and big yards. Barbara's 'Cuda stood out prominently on the street so I had no problem finding their new home.

It was a Mexican-style adobe house, made out of red clay.

I heard music playing from inside as I neared the front door. I knocked and Barbara answered.

"Hey silly," she said, holding a beer, "you don't have to knock, just come in."

I gave her a hug and looked around.

"This is a really cute place," I said. "Nice find."

I was given a beer by Linda and Bruce offered me a joint.

"No thanks," I said. "I still have to go back to my place and see my mom."

"Are you going to bring your hearse back here?" he asked.

"I could," I said, "but I would need someone to drive me there."

"I'll take you," Barbara said, "and also meet your mom."

"Sounds like a plan," I said.

We drove back to my mother's house, and walked up to the door.

My mother was watching us the whole time, so when I opened the door, my mother started freaking out on Barbara.

"So," she began, "you are the one that is stealing my son away from me!"

"Excuse me," Barbara said, "but I'm not stealing your son. Besides, he's old enough to make up his own mind."

I went to my room and got the keys for the hearse, and hoped that they would eventually see eye to eye. While my mother kept arguing with Barbara, I told her that I was taking the hearse away, so she wouldn't have to look at it any more.

"You should put that woman in that hearse," my mother said. "That's where she belongs."

Barbara had heard enough and walked out.

"It's alright, Mother," I said. "Please don't be so mad at her. It's me that wants to do this."

She had a look of shock on her face when I said that, and she went into her teary-eyed story of how I was her only son and ...

"Don't worry, Mom," I said, "I love you, and I'll see you later."

I jumped into the hearse and took off.

We arrived back at the house, and half the neighbourhood came out, staring at the strange vehicle arriving. Bruce came out with his mouth wide open.

"Wow, this is really beautiful; where did you find it?"

"At a used car lot," I said, "For $400. The salesman even told me that it was used to carry Al Capone."

"No kidding!" Bruce said. "What do you plan on doing with it?"

"Well, I bought it when Keith and I were planning our trip, but that fell through because it uses a lot of gas. Before we left though, we used it a couple of times for surfing, and taking people for rides, which seems to be the only thing that it is good for."

"I'd like to go for a ride in it," Bruce said, "just to see the look on people's faces when we drive by."

"Yes," I said, "it does have that effect on people."

That night, the four of us decided that we should go for a ride in the hearse.

We all squeezed into the front and took off. Linda said something about getting some outdoor plants to fix up the front yard, which at present, resembled a desert.

"That's a good idea," I said, "but where are we going to get that sort of thing?"

Just then, Barbara spotted a nursery, and yelled, "Look, there's a place over there!"

I drove by it and sure enough, it was an outdoor garden centre.

I parked across the street and we went over to investigate. Barbara and I went to one side and Linda and Bruce went to the other side.

Within a few minutes, I heard Bruce yell out, "Come on, I've got one!"

Barbara and I looked over and saw him running across the street to where the hearse was parked. He was carrying a palm tree, and Linda was right behind him carrying another type of tree.

Barbara shrieked when she saw this, "Oh damn, what are they doing? Those crazy idiots!"

"Come on," I said, "let's go before somebody sees us."

We ran across the street and began helping Linda and Bruce put the trees into the back of the hearse.

Then Barbara, Linda, and I got into the front seat, while Bruce stayed in the back.

I started up the motor and took off. No sooner were we a block away, than a police car came up from behind and turned his red and blues on.

"Oh great," I said, "here we go again. Stay calm everybody; I'll handle this."

I asked Linda to get the registration out of the glove box as the policeman came to my window.

"Good evening," he said politely, "what do we have here?"

He took his flashlight and proceeded to look at my papers, and then he handed them back.

"Please step out of the vehicle," he demanded. "Is there anyone in the back?"

"Uh, yes, officer," I said, "there is one person."

"Please open the back then," he said. "I'd like to take a look, if you don't mind."

"Oh, no," I said, "he's just making sure the plants don't fall over."

The cop looked at me strangely as I opened the doors, and there was Bruce, peering out between the potted trees.

"Alright you," the officer said, "come on out."

Bruce was stoned on pot so he almost fell as he made his way out of the hearse.

"Have you been drinking?" the cop asked.

"Yes, I have, sir, but it was only a couple of beers."

"Do you all have ID?" he asked.

I was the only one who had brought my ID, so I explained to him that these were my friends and that I was just taking them for a short ride in my antique hearse.

Barbara told him that she had rented a house not too far from here and that we were on our way home now.

"Good to hear that," the cop said. Then he looked at me and said, "I did notice the 'tag applied for' sign. I suppose you have applied for such a tag?"

"Oh yes, sir," I said, "I've only had it for a few days now, and they told me it would take at least two weeks before I get it."

"Just make sure you don't take it on the main highways," he said. "I'll let you go this time. It is a beauty though, so take care and have a good night."

"Thank you," I said. "You have a good night too, officer."

The four of us got in and took off. We couldn't stop laughing about what we had just gone through.

"That was great!" Bruce said. "He thought I was drunk. I guess he couldn't smell the pot that I had just smoked back there."

"He was probably more concerned with the hearse," I said. "It's not the first time this has happened."

On the way home, I proceeded to tell them about the other times I got stopped, which brought on even more laughter.

Once we arrived back at the house, we carried the trees to an appropriate spot beside the house.

"There," Barbara said. "That adds some green to this place, but I think we'll need some more to make it complete."

"Well," I said, yawning, "definitely not tonight."

As the days and weeks passed, Bruce and Linda decided to fly back to New Jersey. I had moved in with Barbara, telling my mother that we were going to live together for the summer, and I continued to work at the supermarket.

September arrived, and I was ready to start working toward my new career. I had purchased my new textbooks and spent a few nights looking over them with Barbara.

"Did you take chemistry in high school?" I asked.

"No," she said. "I, like you, barely passed biology, and when I did try it out, it was a disaster."

"What did you do then?"

"Well, they let me take business courses, like you did."

"So, I guess I can't come to you for help when it comes time for a test," I said.

"Don't worry," she said, "you'll do just fine."

Her confidence in me helped me to at least think I had a chance, but that all changed the first day of school.

I found my chemistry room, and went inside. Most of the students were busy looking at their new text books.

I sat down beside one guy and he introduced himself.

"This course is going to be a breeze," he declared. "I got straight A's in high school."

"You did?" I said. "You're lucky. I never even took high school chemistry."

"Then why are you in here?" he asked.

I explained everything to him, and he assured me that he would help me out if I needed it.

"Thank you," I said. "I think I'm going to need it."

The teacher came in, and after he introduced himself, he told us that we were going to be given a test that covered high school chemistry.

"It's just a way for me to evaluate everyone's level, and to see if the grades that you got in high school are what they should be."

He passed out a two-sheet exam paper, and told us to begin.

I looked at all of the questions, and threw my pencil down. I didn't have a clue as to what I was looking at. Signs, symbols, equations; it was as if I was reading a foreign language.

I was determined to go over it again, and I found one question near the beginning, that I knew I could answer. It was converting Fahrenheit to Celsius.

I had remembered the formula so it was a simple math question, and I completed it in no time. Then, I stared at the rest, trying to make some sense of it.

After ten minutes I stood up, to the amazement of the rest of the class, and walked up to the teacher. I placed my test papers in front of him, and whispered in his ear, "I have no idea what I am looking at, except for question two."

He was sympathetic to my cause, and told me to come back after class for a talk. I accepted his help and told him I'd be back.

When I spoke with the teacher, I told him that I wanted to become a diver, not a chemist. He just laughed and said, "Even divers must have some knowledge of chemistry. It just might help to save your life."

I had to agree with him, so I told him I would continue on and try to do my best.

When I went home, I told Barbara that I didn't feel good about my chances to succeed.

She convinced me to keep trying, and that I just might be able to do it.

The first month of school was spent rehashing high school chemistry, and I was able to understand some of it, but not all of it.

By the end of the second month, I knew I was losing ground, and everyone else had test scores to prove it.

November arrived, and instead of going to school, I found myself either staying home with Barbara, or taking my hearse to the beach with Keith. My friendship with Keith was waning somewhat, as he had moved in with his girlfriend, and the two of us were into a whole new chapter in our lives.

In December, Barbara's parents were asking her about returning home for Christmas. Barbara mentioned that since I had never experienced a Christmas up north, that I should go and spend it with her and her parents. We talked it over and I decided that it would be a chance for me to leave Miami again, and rethink my future. After I said yes, I phoned my mother to let her know of my plans.

"What about school?" she asked. "Are you thinking of quitting?"

"No, Mom," I said. "It's the holiday break for everyone, so I'll be back at school in mid-January. I promise I'll see you before we go. I love you."

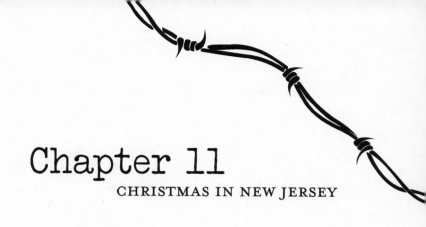

Chapter 11

CHRISTMAS IN NEW JERSEY

A week before Christmas, I went and saw my mother, and gave her Barbara's parents' phone number.

"I'll call you when we get there," I said. "Sue will always be here to help you if you need it."

"Take care," she said, "and have a good time without me." It was her favourite saying to make me feel guilty about leaving her.

Barbara and I took off for New Jersey. We took turns driving, because we wanted to get there as quickly as possible. As we headed north, the signs of winter were soon everywhere. When we arrive in Jacksonville, Florida, we began to notice the change in temperature. Following the coastline, it reminded me of the trip that Keith and I took.

It wasn't until we reached North Carolina that we decided to stop for dinner.

A chilly evening indeed, and the waitress told us there was snow in the forecast. We ate quickly and filled the gas tank. A light snowfall greeted us as we drove around Washington, D. C. We agreed to keep driving all night as traffic was light and we could make good time.

"This doesn't feel like Christmas in Miami," I said.

"You've never seen snow or had a snowball fight?" Barbara asked.

"No," I said, "the closest I've been to snow is what I've seen on Christmas cards and TV. A few times there would be a bit of frost in the morning, but no snow."

"What did you do for heat?" Barbara asked.

"We have a kerosene heater, the portable kind where you put kerosene into the base, and then you light a big round wick, kind of like a big candle. I would have to go to the corner gas station with our metal kerosene can and get the guy to fill it up. It was truly the sign that a severe winter blast was here. How do you guys up north heat your homes?"

"We have an oil furnace in the basement that heats the whole house," Barbara said, "plus a large wood-burning fireplace in the living room."

"Just like in the Christmas cards," I said. "Sound real cozy."

After we passed Baltimore and Philadelphia, we headed straight for Trenton, New Jersey. From there, we drove due east for Barbara's home town of Red Bank.

Barbara was getting anxious as we got close to her home.

"Remember," she said, "I've been telling my parents that you are just a friend, not my lover, so you'll have to stay in my brother's room."

We arrived just before noon, the snow was continuing to fall, and there were a few inches on the ground.

Heading up the driveway, I could tell that this was a middle-upper class neighbourhood; it looked similar to the one Keith and I drove around.

"Watch out when you get out," she said, laughing, "it might be slippery."

She was right. I got out of the car, and put both my feet on the ground. Just as I was going to say that there was nothing to it, I went down.

Barbara came running around and helped me up.

"I told you it might be slippery. Are you alright?"

"Yes, I'm fine," I said, as I gave her a hug and a kiss.

I looked up at the large snowflakes falling and watched as they settled down on her hair. It made me feel like we were actors in a romantic movie.

"What are you thinking about?" Barbara asked.

"Oh nothing" I said. "Now get me out of this beautiful but horrid weather."

As we turned to walk up to the front door, the door opened. Barbara's mother, father, and younger brother were standing in the doorway, smiling.

"Welcome home, Barbara," they said. "Get in here, it's freezing."

Barbara gave her parents a big hug and then introduced me to them.

"This is my mom, Grace, my dad, Richard, and my little brother, Mike."

"Let's go into the kitchen," Richard said. "Grace has just made some hot chocolate, and some of those little sandwiches that you like, Barbara."

He looked at me and said, "Unless you want something stronger."

"No, thank you," I said, "hot chocolate sounds really good at this time."

Barbara mentioned that this was my first time up north in the wintertime, and joked that I was still shivering from being out in the cold for a whole five minutes.

"Here you are," Grace said, placing the hot chocolate in front of me.

"Umm, that is good stuff," I said, as I drank the whole thing in one gulp.

They all laughed, and Grace offered to refill my cup.

"Yes, please," I said, "I'm starting to thaw out now."

I figured a little humour was a good way to break the ice.

"So, is this the man you and Linda met back in June?" Richard asked.

"No, Daddy," she said, "that was Dennis, a friend of Allan's, and it was Linda who met Dennis and got his phone number and address before he went on his way up to Canada for the Expo 67 event. When Linda and I went down to Miami, it was Dennis that we phoned in Miami. Got that so far?" she asked.

"Yes," Richard said, "go on."

"Well, Dennis phoned Allan and told him about Linda and me, and the rest is history."

Changing the subject abruptly, Barbara said, "Did you know you can go swimming in the ocean down there, even in November? That's something we can't do here."

"Not true, sis," Mike said. "Yesterday I saw a few surfers. They were wearing wet suits of course, but they're still crazy. Sorry Allan, I didn't mean you."

"No offense taken," I said, "but I have been known to go surfing in Miami, just before a hurricane gets too close."

"Oh my," Grace said, "that sounds dangerous."

"I know," I said, "but it's the only time we get big waves, and we don't go too far out. Still, there's always a few that get swept out to sea and have to be rescued by the Coast Guard."

"Yes," Richard said, laughing, "we get to see those idiots on the six o'clock news."

"Speaking of the time," Barbara said, "I'd like to have a shower, and then go visit a few friends. You won't mind entertaining Allan, would you Mike?"

"No problem," Mike said.

As everyone got up from the table, I sensed that Barbara was using this chance to prove to her parents that I was just a visitor, who had shown their daughter a good time while she was down in Miami, and nothing else.

After Barbara left, Mike took me up to his room.

"As you can see by my collection of books, I'm interested in US history and political science."

"So, do you want to be a politician?" I asked.

"I haven't made up my mind yet," he said, "but yeah, that would be cool."

Mike was turning eighteen soon, and was into his final year of high school.

We talked about the choices that a high school graduate faced, and that going to college was truly the only choice. I told him about my first career choice of becoming an accountant.

"My father says a good accountant is very important to a successful business," Mike said, "so why did you decide to change?"

"I was bored to death of crunching numbers, while what I really wanted was a career that had something to do with the ocean. My sister's husband was working in underwater communications, and he told me that if I got a two-year marine biology degree, I could get a job with him. It sounded so good at the time that I decided to switch majors."

"I can see how you would be tempted to do that." Mike said.

"The only thing wrong with that," I said, "is that I couldn't understand chemistry, since I never took it in high school."

"That's too bad," Mike said. "Now what do you plan on doing?"

"I just might have to go back to what I know best, and that's being an accountant. It sure beats getting drafted into the army."

"I know a couple of guys who signed up last year," Mike said, "and I haven't heard from them since."

"I also knew a couple of guys who signed up just after we graduated in '65, the year the war began."

"I'm a history junkie, remember?" Mike said. "And I've been studying communism. Since Vietnam shares a border with China, I can see why they might be interested in keeping the Americans out of there. The US is claiming that it was a Chinese boat that attacked one of our ships in the Gulf of Tonkin, and that's what started this whole thing."

"Who knows why these things happen," I said, "but I do know that I will definitely stay in school."

"Yeah," Mike said, "me too."

Our conversation then turned to Barbara.

"You like my sister," Mike said. "I can tell."

"What do you mean by that?" I asked, trying to avoid the truth. "We're just friends."

"Well, Allan, I don't know you very well, but I do know my sister, and I can always tell when she is up to her old tricks."

"What do you mean by her old tricks?" I asked.

Mike realized that he had said more than he should have.

"Oh, nothing," he said, "just forget what I said."

I decided to give him the benefit of the doubt, and began to read some of his history books.

Barbara came home around six o'clock.

"Hi everybody," she said, "am I late for dinner?"

I wanted to run downstairs and give her a welcome home kiss, but I couldn't.

"No," Grace said, but dinner's almost ready, so go and wash up."

Mike came back upstairs and told me to use the washroom there, while his father and Barbara went to the main bathroom.

It was during dinner that Richard asked Barbara if she was ready to go to work with him in the morning.

"Don't you ever take a holiday, Daddy? She asked.

"Not when I'm wrapping up a big order for GM," he said proudly. "It means bonuses for everyone, including yourself."

"Oh, that sounds wonderful Daddy; now I can go shopping."

"You mean you didn't get anything while you were down in Miami?" Grace asked jokingly.

"It's hard to get you guys anything that you don't already have," Barbara said, "so I'll need your lists tomorrow after work."

Everyone laughed, except me, because I thought she was being serious.

"You see, Allan," Grace explained, "Barbara was always the one that would start buying things right after the last Christmas, keeping them at a friend's house."

"You'll also have to give me some ideas for yourself, Allan," Barbara said, "since I haven't got you a present."

"You know," I said, "I feel really bad because I haven't bought any presents."

"Don't worry about that," Barbara said, "I'll take you shopping as soon as Daddy will give me some time off."

"Alright," Richard said, "you can go shopping with Allan the day after tomorrow, but I do need you to come in with me and help with some paperwork."

The next morning, I awoke to find Mike still asleep, and so I made my way downstairs. I found Grace in the kitchen, and she told me that Barbara and her father had already left.

I looked outside and as the snow was still falling, I told Grace that it made for a picturesque scene that was right out of a Norman Rockwell painting.

"Yes, it is very pretty at this time of the year," Grace said, "but then I guess you're not really used to it."

I had to be careful of what I said to her, because it was hard to hide the truth about me and her daughter.

"No," I said, "I still can't believe I'm here, but I'm glad I came."

"Barbara brings someone different each year," Grace said, "but this is the first time we've had someone from Florida. We're glad to have you, and we hope you enjoy your first white Christmas."

She hinted about my telling her of my upbringing, without being too forward, so I proceeded to tell her everything.

"So, if your mom is from Indiana, and your dad is from Massachusetts," Grace said, "then they've definitely seen a lot of white Christmases while they were growing up. Where did you say is your dad now?"

"He's in Japan," I said. "Last year, during the summer, I went with my mother and sister to visit him for two weeks, and we even experienced a mild earthquake."

"Wow," she said, laughing, "I'd like to go somewhere like that, but they can keep their earthquakes."

Just then, Mike came downstairs and demanded coffee.

"You know where it is," Grace said politely. "Allan, do you want me to make you any breakfast or can you wait till I get back from the store?"

"I'll wait," I said, "unless Mike wants to make my breakfast."

"I don't do breakfast," Mike said, still half asleep. "Mother, go ahead and do your shopping; we'll be fine."

Mike and I continued our conversations about the US government's history of being involved in different wars. It didn't take long for me to realize that Mike was against the war in Vietnam.

When Grace returned from shopping, Mike left to drop off some Christmas presents for his friends.

The snow was still falling, and I decided to go out for a walk.

Barbara returned at 2:00 p.m. and she told her mother that she was ready to take me to the mall and do some shopping.

"Daddy will be home soon," Barbara said. "We shouldn't be too long."

We sped out of the driveway and I asked her if anything was wrong.

"Oh, nothing," she quickly replied.

When we arrived at the mall, she leaned over and gave me a kiss.

"What was that for?" I asked.

"It's been a few days now, and I'm beginning to miss our ..." she stopped short of finishing her thoughts, and she jumped out of the car.

"Come on," she said, "let's get this over with before the mall gets too crowded."

She held my hand as she led me around to her favourite stores.

We went into a very upscale clothing store, and without hesitating, she picked something out for her parents. She told the salesperson to gift wrap them, and paid with cash.

"How about Mike?" I asked.

"His gift from you will be your choice," she said. "Do you have any ideas?"

"Well," I said, "he does like books on history and politics, so if there is a book store nearby ..."

"Over there," she said, pointing.

We went in and she asked the salesman about the genre that I had mentioned.

"Right over here," he said. "We have a fine selection of presidents' memoirs as well as famous historical events; so, if you need any more help, just call."

I took my time going over the selections, and finally decided on a book by John F. Kennedy, called *A Nation of Immigrants*. It wasn't published until after his assassination, and the foreword was by his brother, Robert.

Barbara looked at it and frowned.

"What?" I said. "He was my favourite president, and I am kind of drawn to the idea that America is a nation of immigrants, except of course the Indians."

"Okay," Barbara said, "but remember, my dad is a Republican."

I stayed with my choice and Barbara paid for it.

We ran around the mall like children, looking at all of the decorations and doing some more window shopping.

"I don't think I could afford most of this stuff," I said, "unless I won the lottery."

"Don't even think about that," she said. "Come on, we'd better get home."

The next two nights were spent singing Christmas carols around the tree, with Richard and Grace each taking turns playing the piano. Meanwhile, Barbara and I were finding it impossible to keep up our charade of just being friends.

Christmas arrived, and we all had fun opening our presents.

I received a book on surfing from Mike, and we all had a good laugh when he opened my gift, and saw that it was also a book.

Richard took one look at it and said, "JFK, he was a Democrat that I didn't care nor vote for."

"Now, dear," Grace cut in, "let's not get into a debate on politics, especially on Christmas Day."

Richard and Grace gave me a sweater, and last but not least, Barbara gave me a T-shirt that had a surfing scene from Hawaii on it. When she opened my gift to her, a gold charm bracelet, she let out a gasp that was sure to alert her parents as to our relationship.

Her mother asked to see it, and said, "This is really nice, Allan. Did you get it in Florida?"

"Yes," I said, "but it's really not that expensive."

"Well, I like it," Barbara said, as she put it around her wrist. "It's the thought that counts, right?"

I felt like telling everyone the truth, that I loved her, and that we had been sleeping together now for six months, but of course I didn't.

We spent the rest of the day drinking eggnog with rum, and singing along to a Christmas album that Barbara had bought earlier. We then topped it all off by having a wonderful Christmas dinner.

As the evening was coming to an end, Mike went to bed, as did his mother. Richard, Barbara, and I stayed up watching the eleven o'clock news.

Afterward, Richard said, "I'm going to bed. Good night."

"Good night, Daddy," Barbara said. "We're going to stay up a little bit longer."

"Alright," Richard said, "see you in the morning."

After Richard closed the bedroom door, Barbara slid over next to me and started kissing me.

"Hey," I said, "I'd like to, but what if your dad comes out and sees us?"

"I don't know how much longer I can take this," she said, as she kept up her amorous actions.

Just then, her father did come out, and he headed straight for the bathroom.

I pushed Barbara away, and said, "See, I told you he was going to do that."

Richard came out of the bathroom and mumbled something about us calling it a night.

"Yes, Daddy, we're turning off the TV now. Good night."

With that said, I hurried up to Mike's room and thought about what would have happened if her father had caught us.

The next morning, Grace made a huge omelet for everyone.

"After last night's dinner," Barbara said, "I'm not that hungry."

Everyone else dug in and took some.

"So, Allan," Richard said, "are you staying for New Year's?"

His question made me think that he had noticed me and Barbara last night, so I looked at Barbara for the answer.

"Yes, Daddy," she said, "he doesn't have to be back at school until mid-January."

"Well," Richard said, "I hope you aren't planning any more trips. I need you to come in to work tomorrow. There's been a change to that big order from GM."

Barbara didn't answer him, and I could feel a bit of tension brewing between the two of them.

That evening, Barbara and I were alone, watching TV. Richard and Grace had gone out to visit friends, and Mike had done the same.

"I wish we could tell them the truth," I said, "or just go back to Florida. We will after New Year's, of course?"

"You heard my dad," she said, "he needs me for at least tomorrow, then we'll talk about going back, okay?"

I agreed to let it stand and I made it known that I was getting impatient about a few things.

"I've got a plan," she said, "so when my parents come home, just follow my lead."

At about eleven o'clock, her parents came in.

"I'm tired," Richard said, as he took off his winter coat. He came into the living room and saw Barbara and me. "If you're coming to work tomorrow, you should be calling it a night."

"Yes, Daddy," Barbara answered.

I started to get up but she grabbed my arm and put her finger to her lips.

Richard and Grace went into their room and closed the door.

"Time to put my plan to work," Barbara whispered. "Just wait."

A few minutes later Richard came out. He looked at us and then his watch.

"Alright you two," he said, "time to go to your rooms."

Richard went into the bathroom for a few minutes and then came out.

"Good night," he said to the two of us. "See you in the morning Barbara."

After Richard went into his room, we waited about five minutes and then Barbara motioned me to follow her. She led me into the bathroom, which was twice the size of most bathrooms, and proceeded to take some large towels from the cabinet. She started spreading them on the floor, and then she started to undress.

I looked at her in total disbelief, and then I proceeded to do the same. She locked the door, turned out the lights and we started to make love. I didn't know whether to fear for my life, or start laughing, as the whole thing had to be done in relative silence. After only five minutes, I thought I heard a noise, and then, there was a knock on the door.

"Barbara, are you in there?"

It was her father's voice, and everything that Barbara and I were doing came to a screeching halt.

We got up slowly, and Barbara turned on the light. While I was getting dressed, she again put her finger up to her lips.

"Yes, Daddy," she said, "it's me."

"What's going on, Barbara?" he demanded. "Is Allan in there with you?"

"Yes, Daddy," she said, "he's got a splinter in his finger and I'm trying to get it out."

I rolled my eyes at her feeble attempt to convince him that we weren't doing anything wrong as she found a Band-Aid in the medicine cabinet and wrapped it around my finger.

"I see," Richard said. "Well, come on then, you better hurry up and get to bed."

"Alright, Daddy," she said, "I will."

We listened intently as we heard him walking back to his bedroom, or at least I was hoping that he was.

"When you leave," Barbara whispered, "go straight up to Mike's room, even if he's still up."

I remembered the two hunting rifles that were hung above the fireplace, and thought that I was going to be looking down the barrel of a shotgun. I gathered my courage and opened the door. He wasn't there. I tiptoed to the stairs and hurried up to Mike's room.

Mike was awake, and he asked me what was happening.

"My father will forget about it," Mike said. "Barbara has always talked her way out of these situations."

I asked him what he meant about "these situations."

"Oh, nothing," he said, "don't worry about it."

For some reason, I didn't believe him.

When I awoke the next morning, everyone except Mike and me were gone. After breakfast, Mike repeated himself and told me not to worry about it, and left to visit friends.

Just then, the phone rang. It was Barbara.

"My father gave me the silent treatment on our way to work," she said. "We'll be home around 3:00. See you then."

I hung up and tried to think of what might happen, and then realized that I might be worrying for nothing.

I was listening to music when Mike and Grace returned. Neither one of them would talk about it, and the silence made me feel uneasy.

Barbara and her father came home at 3:00. Barbara came over to where I was sitting, and told me to come outside with her.

"My father bought a bus ticket," she began with a tear in her eye, "and he told me to give it to you."

"So, where's the ticket?" I asked.

"I tore it up and threw it at him," she said, "and then I told him that I had feelings for you."

"What did he say then?" I asked.

"He told me that I should have been truthful about the whole thing from the start," she said, "and that I have done this before."

"You've done what before?" I asked.

"I've had other boyfriends," she said, sobbing, "and I always try to keep my parents from knowing."

I wasn't shocked to hear that she had other boyfriends, but I couldn't understand the part about her not telling her parents.

"So, what happens now?" I asked.

"He expects me to replace the bus ticket I tore up, and that you have to leave our house immediately. I've thought about it and have decided to get you a motel room so you don't have to leave."

"Does this mean that we can stay there together?" I asked.

"No, not really," she said. "I mean that if my father suspects anything, he could cause trouble for you, and I don't want that."

"Wow," I said, "I was hoping that this whole thing would pass, and that we would eventually get a place together."

"We should go now and put your things into my car," she said. "I'll tell my dad that you will be taking the bus home."

We loaded up her car and left quietly. I felt bad about not being able to say thank you to Grace, but Barbara assured me that she would take care of that.

We stopped at a store and she bought me a few groceries. When we arrived at the motel, she told me to wait in the car. She went to the office to pay for the room. It was a fairly nice motel, and I asked her if it was expensive.

"Don't worry about that," she said, as we took my belongings up to the room.

"I'll call you tomorrow," she said, "and remember, don't phone me at my parents' house."

"Don't worry about that," I said. "I'll wait for you to call or come over."

We hugged and kissed, but as she left I had a feeling that something wasn't right.

That night, she phoned me and told me that she wasn't going to be able to see me on New Year's Eve.

"Why not?" I asked. "Are you going somewhere else that's more important?"

"No, don't be silly," she said. "It's just that my parents expect me to be here with them and their friends."

"Well, okay then, I guess, but it's sure going to be hard to bring in the new year without you. You'll let me know if anything changes, won't you?"

"Yes, I will," she said. "Now remember, don't phone or even think of showing up here. I love you; bye."

After hanging up I decide to go for a walk. Her parents' home was a good half-hour walk from the motel, so I headed in the opposite direction.

When I got back to the motel, I got a phone call from Mike.

"Hi Al," he said, "I'm calling you because I thought you'd like to know that I overheard my sister on the phone, and she was making plans to go somewhere on New Year's Eve."

"She told me that she was going to spend it with your parents," I said.

"Well," Mike said, "because I got to know you and all that, I'm willing to lend you my car so that you can see where she is going."

I was stunned to hear him say this.

"How are you going to do that?" I asked.

"Before she leaves, I'll tell my parents that I'm going over to a friend's house. You meet me around the corner and I'll give you my car, and hopefully you can follow her after she leaves."

Mike then gave me an address and a phone number, and told me to bring the car there when I was finished with my investigation.

It sounded crazy to me at first, but then I thought about it and said, "Okay, I'll do it."

New Year's Eve arrived, and I did as Mike said. I was so nervous that I couldn't eat, and I took off just after 7:00 p.m. I arrived near Barbara's house and waited. Mike showed up at about 8:00 p.m., and I thanked him for doing this.

"She's getting all prettied up," he said, "but I still don't know where she is going."

I got in, drove around the block, and parked within viewing distance of her house.

At 9:00, Barbara started up her Barracuda and backed out of the driveway. I started Mike's car and began following her.

I could tell that she was heading straight for the ocean, but instead of going towards Long Branch, she headed north for Sandy Hook, a small town at the end of a narrow stretch of land. I began seeing expensive-looking houses that were right on the beach, a quarter of a mile apart.

There weren't many vehicles on this stretch of road, so I stayed well back. I saw her brake lights come on, so I slowed down and watched her pull into a driveway.

I stopped and watched her get out and walk up to the front door. I drove up closer and waited, hoping to see her come out after a few minutes, but she didn't.

My pulse was racing as I was feeling both betrayed and angry.

I drove into the driveway and got out. As I approached the front door, I could see her talking to a man. They noticed me and came to see who it was. When Barbara saw me, she looked embarrassed, and then she saw her brother's car.

Barbara quickly told the man who I was.

He smiled and said, "Come on in."

"I'm so sorry you had to find out this way," she said, "please sit down and I'll explain everything."

I started to do as she commanded, but then thought better of it.

I asked her if this was her boyfriend. She said that he was a good friend, and that he was the one who had paid for her and Linda's trip to Miami. She wanted to tell me more but I had heard enough.

"I don't want to hear any more excuses," I said. "You have been leading me on the whole time we've been together. I really loved you Barbara, but it's over now."

I left the two of them standing there, and got into Mike's car.

Barbara came out and shouted, "I'll call you tomorrow, Allan."

I drove away, feeling both angry and foolish for believing that she loved only me. While driving to the address that Mike had given me, I tried to rationalize everything that had just happened.

I arrived at Mike's friend's house, and knocked. Mike opened the door, and he could tell just by looking at me, that I had just been dealt a dose of reality by his sister.

He turned and told his friend that he was leaving, and the two of us walked back to his car.

"I followed her to a man's house in Sandy Hook," I said. "Do you know anything about him?"

"All I know is that she's had a few mysterious boyfriends in the past," Mike said, "and that they've never come to meet my parents."

"It is strange," I said, "to think you know someone, and then it all goes away in seconds."

"Did you get to talk to him?" Mike asked.

"Oh yes," I said, "I confronted the two of them, right inside his house, and she admitted to me that it was him that paid for her and Linda's trip to Miami."

"So that's it, Mike said. "I thought there was something going on just before she left."

Mike drove me back to my motel room and I thanked him for his help.

"You can tell her it was my idea to borrow your car and follow her," I said.

"I can handle my sister," Mike said. "Besides lying to my parents, she lied to me too."

I spent the night watching TV, with the hope of Barbara calling and apologizing.

The next day, around noon, I got a call from her.

"Allan," she began, "please don't hang up. I've got some important news for you from your mother."

"What is it?" I asked.

"She called last night and talked to my mother. The US Army has sent you a draft notice and they want you to come in on the fifteenth of January."

I was stunned and speechless. I just lost the woman I loved, and now I was getting drafted into the army.

"My mother must be doing this to get me to come back home," I said. "It's a good way to get me to leave you and be with her, but I don't believe her."

"Well," Barbara said, "you should call her right away and find out if it's the truth or not."

"Yes, I will," I said, hanging up.

I sat on the bed and felt my whole world crumbling around me. I thought for sure that my mother was lying, so I decided to call her.

"Hello, Mother, this is Allan. What's this about the army wanting to draft me?"

"It's true," she said. "I got the letter yesterday. They want you to come into their office on the seventh."

"Can you please forward me the letter? There must be some mistake."

"It says on the front of the envelope that it can't be forwarded. I called them and asked them to explain how a college student could be drafted, and they told me that you haven't been going to school for the last three months. Is that true?"

"Yes, Mom, it's true," I said. "I've been so wrapped up with Barbara that I didn't think it would matter, but even that has blown up in my face."

"What do you mean?" she asked. "What has she done to my boy?"

"It's a long story," I said. "I'll have to call you back and let you know what I plan on doing. Bye, Mom, I love you."

I called Barbara back and she answered right away.

"Is it true?" she asked. "Did the Army really send you a draft notice?"

"Yes," I said, "my mother wasn't joking. Anyway, it doesn't concern you anymore, so I'll handle this. Goodbye."

"Wait!" Barbara screamed. "I don't want our relationship to end this way. Please let me help you with this; I'm coming over."

I hung up and wondered how she was going to deal with my newest misfortune.

Barbara arrived within minutes, and when she walked in, she could tell that I was feeling pretty sad.

I looked at her and said, "I can't believe what is happening to me. First, it was you going to see what's-his-name, and second, my mother, or should I say the Army, literally drops this bomb on me. I feel like ..."

Barbara interrupted me and said, "It's all my fault. I never stopped liking you, but I'm afraid of saying the words 'I love you,' and I don't know why."

"Well," I said, "I can't tell you what love is. The closest I've ever been in love, was, I guess, my high school girlfriend, and that too ended pretty bad."

"Enough about love," Barbara said. "What about this army thing? Did you find out when you have to be there?"

"Yes, I did, on the seventh."

"Of this month!" Barbara exclaimed.

"Yes," I said, "this month. That's only a few days away."

"Wow," she said, "that doesn't give us much time."

"What do you mean by that?" I asked.

"Well, I've been thinking about it, and I have decided to stay with you while you go through this whole ordeal."

I gave her a quizzical look, and asked what she had in mind.

"We'll drive back down to Florida together, get a motel room, and I will stay with you until ..."

"That's very good of you to suggest this," I said "but what happens when I am drafted into the army for real? Do we write each other while I'm in training or what?"

"Whoa," Barbara said, "you haven't been drafted yet, so let's take it step by step."

The two of us embraced for a while, and we started to cry.

I looked at her and said, "Barbara, whatever happens, I will always remember the good times that we had, even the time you saw me in bed with the Grabber."

This made the two of us start laughing, and we sat back down on the bed.

"I am so glad that you have come back to me," I said, "even if it is under these circumstances."

"So," Barbara said, "are you ready to leave this ugly weather and head back to sunny, warm Florida?"

"Yes," I said. "I only wish that it were for a different reason."

"Me too, she said. "Think positive, and who knows, they might even reject you."

"That would be great," I said. "Maybe I should flunk all their tests on purpose."

The mood of the room changed quickly. A minute ago, we were feeling bad about everything, and now, we were feeling upbeat. I felt that the magic of being together with her was definitely back.

"Oh, wait a minute," I said. "What about your parents? What are they going to say when you tell them you're leaving again, with me?"

"Don't worry about that," she said. "I'll think of something."

"Yes," I said, "you always do."

We agreed to leave the next day, but before she left, I hugged her tightly and told her that I loved her.

"I love you too," she said. "I'll call you and let you know when I am ready to go."

I called my mother and told her that I would be taking a bus home and that I would see her soon.

The next day, Barbara phoned and told me she was on her way over. The snow had stopped falling, and the sun was shining brightly. As we left the motel, I began thinking of what was going to happen to me, and wondered whether or not I could convince the US government that I was ready to go to school, thus keeping my deferment from military service.

Although it was a beautiful start to 1968, it was also the end of having fun, fun, fun.

PART II:

Guns,
Guns,
Guns

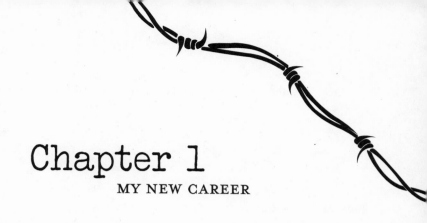

Chapter 1

MY NEW CAREER

The trip back to Miami was a sombre one, unlike when we went to New Jersey a week before Christmas.

Arriving in Miami the next day, Barbara and I went directly to the motel that she and Linda had stayed at. She went in and paid for the room and then she asked me if I wanted to go straight to my mother's house, or wait until the next day.

"I had better get this over with. Remember, I'm hoping that she wasn't telling me the truth about the Army."

Barbara drove me to my house and I told her to wait in the car.

The door was locked, so I knocked loudly.

"Who is it?" my mother asked.

"It's me, Mom, your son. Open the door."

She opened it a bit and looked at me. Then she hugged me and told me that she was happy to see me.

"So, where is this letter?" I asked. "The one that the Army supposedly sent."

"You still don't believe me," she said. "It's in your room, on top of your dresser."

I went in, and there it was. A large brown envelope, addressed to me, with the US government's logo in the upper left corner.

My worst fears were beginning to come true, and I took the letter out and read it.

I went back out to the living room, and my mother was watching TV, like nothing else mattered.

I sat down and looked at her, holding the envelope up.

"This is wrong," I said. "I'm a student and they just can't change my status. I'll go and talk to them tomorrow."

She sat there, silently watching her program, and I could tell that she was in one of her "see, I told you so" moods.

I got up and started to leave.

"Where are you going?" she asked. "Did that girl Barbara come back with you?"

"Yes, Mother, she did and I'll be staying with her. Goodbye."

I got into Barbara's car and showed her the envelope.

"It's true," I said. "They want me to come in for an evaluation in a few days."

"What about your student deferment?" Barbara asked. "Aren't you going to try to get it back?"

"Yes indeed," I said, "it's the only thing that I can do."

We spent the night watching TV and trying to come up with a solution to my problem. One newscast told us that the war was escalating, and another showed President Lyndon Johnson telling the American public that the US forces were making significant progress, and that the enemy would be defeated soon.

Also on the news were two large anti-war protests, one at the Pentagon, and one at the Lincoln Memorial. Then there were the race riots still happening, and it seemed that the American government was getting attacked from both sides of the political spectrum.

"The US is fighting two wars," I said to Barbara. "One at home and the other in Vietnam."

"It's crazy," Barbara said. "I know my brother is also watching to see what is going to happen."

I turned off the TV and changed the subject.

"Enough about the war," I said. "Can I ask you a question about the man you went to see on New Year's Eve in Sandy Hook?"

"What about him?"

"How did you two meet?"

"I met him while I was working at my father's business. He was the owner of another car parts business that wanted to do a partnership deal with my father. He simply came in where I was working, and we started talking."

"So, he took one look at you and swept you off your feet, right?"

"Well, sort of. He had a wedding ring on, and when I asked him about it, he told me that they were separated. When my father noticed this, he reminded me that although he was a very wealthy man, he was still married. I was curious at first, but after a couple of dates, we decided to become friends instead of lovers."

"So, he was just a guy whom you admired, has money to burn, and who paid for your trip with Linda down to Miami, am I right?"

"Yes," Barbara said, yawning, "that's about it. Now let's get some sleep."

Barbara fell asleep quickly, but I was wide awake and thinking that if she could have any rich man she wanted, why was she with me. I gave up trying to find the answer and fell into a deep sleep. I dreamt that my mother was yelling at us from outside the motel. I must have started laughing, because it woke Barbara up. I assured her that it was nothing, and we soon fell back to sleep. We stayed in bed until 10:00 a.m., and then made our way to the nearest diner for breakfast.

"So, what do you plan on doing first?" she asked.

"I guess I'll go to the college, and see if I can re-enroll or something and hopefully get my student status back."

"Okay, then," Barbara said, "let's go."

Barbara drove me to the college and we went directly to the office. I spoke with the secretary, who told me that the records office was just down the hall. We went there and met with the person in charge. He took down my name and the list of my courses and then he went to his filing cabinet. He pulled my file and began looking at it.

It says here that your last known attendance was October 15, is that correct, Mr. Glass?"

"Something like that," I said, "I'm not really sure."

"Well," he said, opening an envelope that was attached, "there is a notice here that pertains to the US military. It says that because your attendance has not been satisfactory, your student deferment has ended and that you are immediately eligible for the draft."

My heart started to pound as I searched for an excuse as to why I had stopped going to school, but I could not come up with a viable one.

"Isn't there someone that I can talk to and re-enroll and get my student status back?" I asked.

"You can try and talk to the dean, and the board of education," he said, "but you're not the first one to experience this change of status. The college, of course, isn't the one that is making the rules; it's the US military."

I thanked him for his honesty and we walked out of his office.

"Boy," Barbara said, "it sounds as though there isn't any hope of changing the minds of the military. They can draft those who do not go to school, or in your case, forget to go for a few months."

I looked at her and snapped, "I didn't forget, Barbara, and it's partly your fault that I'm in this mess."

"Why is it my fault?" she asked. "I didn't do anything but have a good time with you. You could have still gone to school."

She was right. I was in this mess because I was too oblivious to the consequences, and now I was faced with being inducted into the US Army in just a couple of days.

We drove back to the motel room and I called Keith.

"Hi, Keith," I said, "how's everything going?"

"I'm okay. What have you been up to lately?"

"Oh, I'm just getting ready to join the army and go to war. What have you been doing?"

"You're what?" Keith shrieked.

"You heard me," I said. "My student deferment isn't valid anymore, because they say that I haven't been going to school. My mother got the letter from the military while I was up in New Jersey with Barbara for Christmas. The school says that they can't do anything about it, so it looks like my only hope is to ask the army for a chance at re-enrolling."

"That is terrible news, my friend," Keith said. "I haven't been going to school either, but I was lucky to meet a girl whose father is a psychiatrist, and he agreed to write me a letter saying that I was mentally unfit for service. It cost me $400, but it was well worth it."

"Can you get him to do the same for me?" I asked.

"No," Keith said, "he won't do it anymore. He has been writing these letters for his friends, and has been questioned by the military."

"I'm going to the draft office tomorrow," I said. "I'll call you afterward and let you know what happened."

I then called my mother and told her everything.

"I hope you can change their mind, Allan," she said. "You should be in college, not going over there to fight this war."

"I know, Mom, and it's my fault," I said. "I'll call you tomorrow after I see them."

The next day, Barbara gave me a ride to the draft office.

As I approached the office, I saw posters of Uncle Sam pointing his finger and saying, "We want you."

I entered and got in line behind two other guys who were waiting to talk to the man behind the desk.

One by one, the two others talked briefly, and then left with a bunch of papers and took their seat a large table. I stood there next, and the man asked for my name.

"I don't see your name here, young man. Are you sure your report date is today?"

"My date to report isn't today, but a couple of days from now," I said.

"Well then," he said, smiling, "you come back then and we'll see that you are taken care of, alright?"

"Well," I said, "I'm here to see if I can change your mind about me getting drafted."

He started laughing, and said, "That's the first time I've heard that one! You're kidding, right?"

"No sir," I said. "There's been a mistake about me not going to school, and I'd like to talk to someone about it."

"Oh, I see," he said, with a surprised look on his face. He picked up the phone and made a call.

"We've got another one," he said. "Okay, I'll send him in."

"Go right in," he said, pointing to a door. "And good luck."

As I left, I could hear him chuckling to himself.

I knocked and went in.

Sitting at his desk, in full military uniform, was an Army officer who looked to be old enough to have served in World War II.

He looked at me and told me to sit down.

"I'm Colonel Smith," he said. "What can I do for you?"

"Well, sir," I began, "I've been going to college for the last year and a half, and decided to take some time off to go to New Jersey with my girlfriend for Christmas, and now I'm being drafted into the military. Can you help me?"

He just stared at me and started laughing.

"That's the first time I've heard that one," he said, "but I'm sorry, there isn't anything I can do. You know that when you join, you can choose from a wide variety of careers, and it's all paid for by the US government."

"Yes, sir, I know that, but a career in the Army wasn't what I was looking for. I just want to become a professional diver, and work with my brother-in-law."

"Then you should join the Marines, or the Navy," he said smiling. "They sure could use you over there."

"Over where?" I asked.

"In Vietnam, of course," he said. "And you even get to blow things up too."

I just sat there thinking, *This guy is totally into this war, and he doesn't give a crap about what I want.*

"Okay," I said, "so what you are telling me, is that I can't re-enroll in college and go back to what I was doing before."

"Yes, son," he said, "that is exactly what I'm saying. You have to stay in school to keep your status as a student. I'm sorry, but you're in our system now, and we need you to help win this war."

I knew this was the end of my attempt to change everything, so I thanked him and walked out.

The recruitment officer that I had talked to earlier saw me come out and said, "See you in a couple of days."

I left feeling overwhelmed with emotion, and as I got into her car, Barbara took one look at me and said, "You didn't change their mind, did you?"

"Not even close," I said. "Once you're into their system, there's no going back."

We drove back to the motel and I called my mother to tell her what had happened.

"Is there anything I can do?" she asked.

"No, Mom, it's out of our hands now. They told me I have to go into the draft office in a couple of days and begin my paperwork for becoming a soldier."

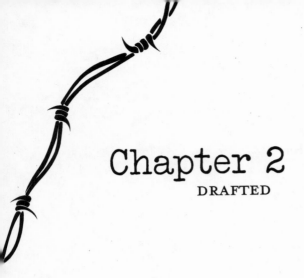

Chapter 2
DRAFTED

Barbara gave me a ride to the draft board office, and I told her to go back to the motel and await my phone call.

"I don't know how long this is going to take," I said.

I walked in and was met by an MP, a military policeman, standing at the doorway. He pointed and told me to go stand in line. There were a dozen or so young men in front of me, some of them looking like they had just turned eighteen. One by one they would answer a few questions, and then take their paperwork over to a large table. After receiving mine, I proceeded to the table. It was a general questionnaire concerning basic medical and school records, and I quickly filled it out and was told to get in another line. Two more MPs were standing in a corner, smoking and joking around. I handed my questionnaire to the officer, and was given some more papers and told to go into another room. Once inside, I realized that this was the beginning of my military career: obeying orders, and doing as I was told.

I saw a team of doctors looking everyone over. They weighed us, then looked into our ears, nose, and throats, and asked us if we were allergic to anything. They hastily wrote everything down, handed the papers back to us, and then told us to go into the next room. I felt like I was in a herd of cattle, soon to be led to the slaughterhouse.

Just then, one guy came out of a room screaming, "I won't do it," and ran toward the front door. The MP grabbed him and took him to another room.

"If anyone else has the same bright idea as him," he said sternly, "then I suggest you tell me now!"

No one dared to challenge his authority, and we silently went back to our examinations.

When it was all over, the officer in charge took my papers and told me that I would be contacted in a day or two, and that I shouldn't make plans to go anywhere.

I phoned Barbara to come and get me.

"How was it?" she asked.

"This is the worst day of my life," I said. "It's like being a robot and controlled by someone." After I said this, I started laughing nervously, and Barbara asked me why.

"If they think that I'm going over there to kill people, then they are totally mistaken. I'd rather go to jail than go to Vietnam."

"How long does the training take, did they tell you?" Barbara asked.

"No, of course not," I said. "Why?"

"Well," Barbara said, "the war might end before you are finished with it."

"Yes," I said, "that would definitely be a miracle ending to this nightmare."

Barbara could see that I was depressed and suggested that we go to a nice restaurant for lunch.

"Sure," I said, "anything you want."

While we were eating, Barbara tried to cheer me up by bringing up all of the good times we had. I stopped eating and realized that I had not been listening to her.

"I'm sorry," I said, "I know what you are trying to do. It's why I love you and want to be ..."

Barbara cut in and said, "It's alright Allan, I understand how you must feel. I just wish there was something I could do to help."

"Hey," I said, "just think of the training I'll get. I'll learn how to kill people and blow things up. What could be more fun than that?"

I slammed my fork down on the table and everyone around us stared.

Barbara grabbed my hand and asked me if I was ready to leave.

"Yes," I said, "let's go."

We drove back to the motel and turned on the TV. More protests against the war continued to dominate that news. President Johnson kept telling the public that we were negotiating with the North Vietnamese, and that they would probably surrender soon. But the reality of the war, which started in 1965, was totally different. As the bombing of Vietnam kept escalating, Johnson's popularity was dropping. The number of race riots also increased, and America's cities were being torn apart.

I looked at Barbara and told her to turn the TV off.

"I haven't heard one valid reason for this war," I said, "and it's beginning to look like there is no immediate end in sight."

After a couple of days, the Army phoned my home and my mother called me.

"They want you to come into their office tomorrow to sign some more papers," she said.

"Alright, Mom, I'll go there."

The next day, Barbara and I went to the draft office and I was handed a couple of official-looking documents. One was a medical clearance document and the other was for the actual oath of allegiance into the army.

I looked them over and wanted to tear them up. Instead, I swore out loud that I would never go to war and kill anyone.

The desk sergeant heard me and smiled as I signed and gave them to him.

"Thank you very much," he said. "You will soon be receiving a letter with detailed instructions on where you are to report to for the beginning of your training."

I left the office feeling like I had betrayed myself.

"What's wrong?" Barbara asked as I got into her car.

"I just signed my death warrant," I said, "and it makes me sick to my stomach."

We drove back to the motel room and I called my mother to tell her what I had just done.

"I don't know who I am anymore," I said to her. "I feel like a different person."

"Well, son," she said, "you will serve your country and do what is right. I'll tell your father when he calls."

"I know only this, Mom," I said, "I don't think I will ever go over there; it's just not right."

"You know, son, your father has always told you to do what you think is right, and not follow others. The two of us will support whatever decision you make."

"Thanks Mom," I said, "that makes me feel better."

I looked at Barbara who was listening to every word, and I told her that I had made up my mind.

"I'll go through their stupid training," I said, "and hope that the war will end by the time I finish."

"Did they tell you when and where you have to go?" Barbara asked.

"I'll know soon," I said. "They will send a letter."

Barbara and I spent the next few days partying with Keith and his girlfriend, and letting everyone know that I was against the war.

Then I heard some disturbing news. I met with the parents of a former classmate, and they told me that their son, who had enlisted in 1966, had been killed recently. They had been for the war, but were now speaking out against it, saying the army never fully explained how or why it happened.

The next day, my mother called and told me that the letter had arrived, and that I was going to Fort Jackson, South Carolina, for my training.

I looked it up on a map, and saw that it was in the middle of the state, directly across from Myrtle Beach.

I joked with Barbara, saying that I should take my surfboard and show the other soldiers how to do it.

"I can drive you there if you would like," she said.

"No," I said, "the military sent a plane ticket, and said that they would meet me at the airport. You might as well call your parents and tell them you are coming home."

We picked up the letter with the ticket, and I said my farewells to everyone.

The next day, Barbara gave me a ride to the airport, and as I gave her one last hug, I told her I would write to her every day.

"You do that," she said.

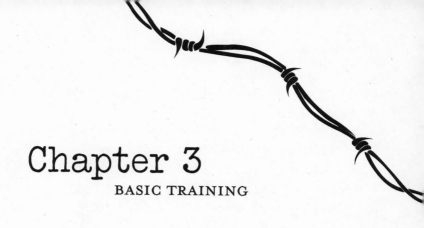

Chapter 3
BASIC TRAINING

It was a cool, crisp start to January when I arrived in South Carolina. I was one of thirty men who were directed to get on a military bus that would take us to Fort Jackson. When we arrived, we were told to pick up a large duffel bag and run up a hill toward a large building. Some of us made it with little or no difficulty, while some lagged far behind. I saw this as an intimidation tactic, to prove to us that some of the men needed to work a little harder if they wanted to become soldiers in America's army.

A few more buses came, and everyone went through the same routine. We dropped our duffel bags and went inside a large auditorium with a stage at the front. At least two hundred men sat there, some whispering and some laughing and joking, then three heavily decorated officers came out on stage.

"Good day gentlemen, I'm Lieutenant Scott. Today is the beginning of your basic training, during which you will spend eight weeks getting both your body and your mind in shape. Some of you, I hope, will go on to become career soldiers, and some of you will spend your time here and then serve the rest of your two years helping to keep America safe. Whichever category you fall into, I trust that your stay here will give you all of the tools necessary to become a better man. I now hand the microphone over to our base commander, Major Leroy Stevens."

A round of applause was given, as the major took the microphone.

"Greetings, my fellow Americans. You are here today because your country needs you. As you know, we have been fighting in Vietnam now for two years, a battle to keep the Chinese communists from taking over the entire Southeast Asian continent. This battle has been an ongoing one, as history has shown. The French have tried, but they have not been successful in stopping them. Now, it is up to us to give back control of Vietnam's country to the Vietnamese people. Thank you."

Major Scott handed the microphone over to Captain Wilson.

"Welcome to Fort Jackson," he began. "We will begin our training tomorrow morning, at 0800 hours military time, which to you means 8:00 a.m. After that you will rise at 0700 hours for the remainder of your first week. Then, for the rest of your basic training, you will be rise at 0530 hours, and be in the mess hall by 0600 hours. Anyone who is unable to meet this requirement will be subject to KP duty, or, as I like to put it, working in the 'grease pit.' You will now be taken to the cafeteria for lunch, and then be taken to the theatre to watch a movie. Thank you for wanting to serve your country, as you are now part of the finest group of fighting men that I have ever known."

The three walked off the stage and we were instructed to file out of the auditorium and follow a sergeant to the cafeteria.

While eating, I quickly found out that some of these guys had just turned eighteen, the minimum age for joining the military. I, on the other hand, had just passed the midway mark to my twenty-first birthday. I also found out that they had different reasons for being here.

Some told me that they were pressured by their parents, either for financial reasons, or pure patriotism. The one thing I knew was that my time spent in training would be two months of hoping the war would end.

After lunch, we headed over to the theatre. An officer came out on stage and began to describe the film that we were about to see. Once he finished, we all sat back as the film began.

It started with a dozen or so American GIs sitting around a camp, smoking cigarettes, and playing cards. The sun was shining, and the palm trees in the background were swaying gently in the breeze. I looked around and I could see that everyone was enjoying this scene, when all of a sudden, a loud thunderous explosion filled the room. Everyone jumped. The scene that we had just watched had vanished, and now the only thing visible was a cloud of smoke. As the smoke cleared, we watched with our mouths open. All that was left of the once happy, card-playing GIs was a mass of bloody corpses. Everyone had been blown up and killed. We continued to watch, hearing only the yelling and screaming of their fellow soldiers running over to see what had happened.

The film stopped, and the officer came back out on stage.

"What you have just seen," he said, "is actual footage of this war, and a reminder that this is not a game."

He walked off and the film started up again. We were shown scenes that vividly depicted the viciousness of the enemy, the Viet Cong, and the cruel and unusual methods that they were using to kill and even torture American soldiers.

I could tell from the reaction of the crowd that we were being brainwashed into hating the Viet Cong and wanting to kill them. There wasn't one scene that showed American GIs killing them. After the film ended, I heard remarks like, "I can't wait to kill those ..." and "send me over there now ..."

I now understood that the Army was going to train these men, both physically and mentally, to become skilled killers, and never ask why.

During my two months of training, we would be faced with the same routine every day. Get up early, have breakfast, and stand in formation for roll call. We would then spend most of the day running or marching around the grounds. We were also fed a constant diet of films, usually three or four a week, which would inform us about the latest tactics being used by the enemy.

As we got to know each other, small groups started forming. The majority of us came from the southeastern states: Florida, Georgia, and North and South Carolina. We would trade stories of how and where we grew up, which eventually would lead into why we were here. Most of the men were drafted, who on becoming eligible at the age of eighteen, had nothing else to do. Or like myself, had stopped going to school. The few who had joined before they received their draft notice usually did so because of pressure from their parents.

Basic training accomplished two things. First, it got us used to working together as a group, and second, it taught us to obey orders.

I accepted these rules as being an essential part of any team, and it made me think about World War II, and how cooperation from the countries involved were so important in the defeating of Germany.

The only thing I could not accept was the reason for this war, or invasion of another country as I liked to call it. Every time I asked this question, they simply answered that it was "stopping the spread of communism."

I wrote to Barbara a few times, and told her that there had been a few guys who questioned the war and that they wanted out. Some of them wanted out on religious grounds, so they were given the chance to talk to the base chaplain. After that, they were brought in front of the base commander, who would give them two choices. The first was that they would receive a dishonourable discharge and spend two years in a state prison in Leavenworth, Kansas. The second was they could agree to finish their training and continue on with their required two years of service. Most of them usually chose the latter, with only a couple of guys taking the first alternative. I never received anything back from Barbara, so I stopped writing to her.

I decided to swallow the bitter pill of my basic training and try to make the most of it. I especially had fun with the drill sergeants, some of whom were only a year or two older than I was.

It was the end of February when our basic training ended. We were given a small graduation ceremony, with some receiving promotions to private first class, which included a small pay raise, while the rest of us remained as privates. Most of us were also given orders to report back to Fort Jackson on March 10, to begin AIT, which stood for Advanced Individual Training.

I said farewell to the friends I had made, and got on a plane for Miami.

Chapter 4
GOING HOME

When I got off the plane, I was greeted by the warm Florida sunshine. I had just gone through two months of basic training in South Carolina, which meant getting up early and dealing with below freezing temperatures. I phoned my mother and told her I was at the airport, and she came and picked me up.

"You look so different," she said. "It must be that short haircut."

"I had long hair before I left, and as it turned out, I had the longest hair of anybody there," I said. "All of the barbers were pointing at me and saying, 'I want him.'"

"I must admit that I like the way you look now," she said. "I wasn't too happy with your long hair."

We arrived home, and I called Keith.

"Come on over," Keith said, "and tell us all about it."

I went over to Keith's house and was met by his mother, as well as Johnny, Keith's cousin. Johnny was teasing Keith about him being "too crazy" to be accepted into the army. On the other hand, Johnny wanted me to tell him all about my two months of training, and asked if I got to shoot any guns.

"We did carry old World War II rifles around," I said, "but the purpose of our training was more physical and mental rather than learning how to shoot a gun. That will happen when I go back for AIT, Advanced Individual Training, on March 10."

"I wish I could go," Johnny said, "I'd love to kill some gooks!"

"Johnny!" Keith's mother shrieked, "Don't talk like that."

I had lunch with them and then Keith and I went back to my house. I couldn't wait to start up the hearse and relive the good times we had before I left.

"Let's go to the beach," Keith said. "I haven't been there since you left."

"There's hardly any gas left in the tank," I said. "Maybe tomorrow."

We sat in the hearse, talking about what I had just been through, and I restated my vow of not wanting to go to war. Keith agreed and then he told me a story about a friend of ours who had been recently killed in Vietnam.

"Wow," I said, "this war is beginning to hit close to home. You don't really think of the consequences until someone you know dies, then you ask the question 'why are we there?'"

After Keith left I went inside to talk to my mother. I told her about my friend who was killed, and she started to cry. I tried to console her but I knew that it wouldn't help, so I went outside.

During dinner, we talked about my training, and I explained how it was being used to brainwash everyone. She just nodded in agreement and then told me that my father would be in Japan for at least another six months.

"Well," I said, "I'll be real close to him if I go to Vietnam."

"Oh son," she cried, "I hope this thing is over before you have to go."

"I do too," I said, "but don't worry, I'm not there yet; who knows, maybe I'll get sent to Hawaii, or some place in Europe, that would be good."

"Yes, it would," she said, "then your father could go and visit you."

"That's true," I said, "it would be really great to see him."

We finished dinner and went into the living room to watch some TV.

"They are showing more of the war on TV," she said, "but I don't like watching it."

The newscast started off with a report about a protest by approximately five hundred New York University students, who were upset at the Dow Chemical Company for bringing recruiters to their campus. Dow Chemical is the principal manufacturer of napalm, the toxic chemical burning agent used by the US Military to defoliate the jungles of Vietnam.

This was followed with a report by renowned newsman Walter Cronkite, who talked about his recent trip to Vietnam, and the aftermath of the Tet Offensive.

"On January 31," Cronkite began, "approximately 70,000 North Vietnamese troops took part in an all-out attack, starting in South Vietnam's second-largest city, Da Nang. They continued their assault in other cities and villages, and even penetrated the centre of Saigon. The North Vietnamese hoped to stir an uprising among the people of South Vietnam, but they were wrong. The people did not revolt, and the Viet Cong suffered tremendous losses. Instead, they won a different kind of victory, as the attack was an embarrassment to the US. We were supposed to be winning the war, and after the Tet Offensive, the people who had been for the war started blaming President Johnson for mishandling it."

After this report, the station showed TV's first on air war execution. American photographer Eddie Adams photographed South Vietnam's General Nguyen Ngoc Loan, a security official, as he shot a Viet Cong prisoner in the head. The photograph is another rallying point for anti-war protestors, who use it to question the morality of the American allies, the south Vietnamese.

My mother and I sat there watching the shooting, and were completely shocked by what we saw.

"I can't watch this anymore," she said, getting up. "I'm going to bed."

I continued watching as the news turned its attention on Richard Nixon, a Republican from California. He had announced his presidential candidacy in February, and told the American public that if elected in November, he would bring an end to the war, "one way or another."

I wondered what he meant by that, as there was no explanation of how he would end the war. I turned off the TV and went to bed.

The next day, I called Keith and the two of us went for a drive to the beach.

When we arrived, we sat in Keith's car and started talking about the good times we had.

"Do you realize that it wasn't long ago that we were having a great time traveling up the coast? I sure wish we could do that again," I said. "After I found out the truth about Barbara, everything started to come apart."

"If you would have just kept on going to school," Keith said, "you wouldn't be in this predicament."

"Yes, I know that now," I said.

"Hey," Keith said, "we could always go across the border to Mexico, and hide out there."

"Oh yes," I said, laughing, "that would be one way of getting out of going to Vietnam, but we also might end up in a Mexican jail, and never get out. No, I think I'll stick it out and hope that it ends before the rest of my training is up."

"I hope that it ends too," Keith said, "so we can get back to the more important things in life like watching these girls surf."

"I couldn't agree with you more," I said.

I mentioned to Keith that the Army was letting us have our own cars at the base while we were in AIT, and that I would be driving my car back to South Carolina.

"Why don't you take the hearse?" Keith asked. "That would be so symbolic."

"I don't think that they would look at it that way," I said, "but thanks for the idea."

We spent the next hour having lunch and afterward, Keith and I went home. He dropped me off at my house and when I went in, I found my mother writing a letter.

"Who are you writing to?" I asked.

"The US Army, she said. I'm asking them to let you stay here with me, because I need you here, not over there fighting that ridiculous war."

"I don't think that will work, Mom," I said, "but please go ahead and try, if it will make you feel better."

She slammed the pen down and tore up the letter, and started to cry.

"I just don't know what else to do," she said. "I need you here with me."

"I know, Mom," I said, "I know."

I told my mother not to worry, and that I would be back home in a couple of months. She took a picture of me in my uniform, and then I got ready to make the drive back to Fort Jackson, South Carolina.

Chapter 5
AIT

The drive back to South Carolina by myself gave me time to think about what I was going to do if the war did not end soon. If I refused to go, the Army would surely send me to jail for two years. If I went, I wondered how I would react to the situation of having to kill or be killed. I replayed in my mind parts of the films I had watched in basic training, and each time I shuddered with the thought of taking another person's life. I came to the conclusion that I was not going to a war that I did not understand or agree with.

I arrived at Fort Jackson on March 9, and went straight to the company's headquarters that were listed on my papers. The sergeant at the desk welcomed me back, and he gave me the name of my training officer, as well as directions to my new barracks building.

"Once you get situated," he said, looking at his watch, "you can go over to the mess hall and get some dinner."

I thanked him and left.

My new home wasn't any different than the one I had in basic training, although it did make me feel like I was no longer on the bottom of the ladder. I was greeted by another sergeant, who told me to pick any bed, and that he would be back later to fill everyone in on tomorrow's activities. Within an hour, the sergeant came back and told us that we would be awakened at 0600 hours.

"After breakfast," he said, "you'll take some more tests in order to evaluate your MO, or Modus Operandi, which is Latin for your job title with the Army.

I spent the night getting to know the guys who were bunking next to me and we tried to imagine what kind of jobs we would be doing.

After breakfast, I was one of twenty who were directed over to a building, while the others headed into another one. We were greeted by a large black man, who introduced himself as Warrant Officer Williams.

"The reason you are here is because each of you has had some college experience, and therefore qualify to take the Army's visual flight test."

He then handed us each, a ten-page booklet and told us we had an hour to complete it.

"There will be no grade given," he explained, "but the top three scores will qualify for helicopter pilot training school, but only if you want it."

I opened my booklet and saw some diagrams that resembled the dashboard of an airplane. From my days of flying with my father, and seeing the cockpit of a few airplanes, I soon figured out what I was looking at. I finished the test in half the time and handed it in. Warrant Officer Williams took it and smiled and told me to wait until the others had finished. Everyone finished before the hour was up, and then he asked us if we had any questions. I asked about the length of time for becoming a pilot as well as where these schools were.

"Eighteen months," he said, "in Alabama and Texas."

"How soon will we know who will be picked to take this course?" I asked.

"The top three scores will receive some more paperwork to be signed, with three more on standby, just in case the first three do not want it," he said. "That will be all for now, you can join up with the others and take some more tests."

The Army basically wanted to know how our minds worked, and how we would solve everyday problems. A psychological testing of sorts, that included some math and science skills that we learned in school.

After our testing, we were taken back to the mess hall for lunch. I found out from talking to the nineteen others that took the pilot test that there were about five of them who were also thinking of going. I told them that I loved flying, and that my dad worked for Pan Am. They asked me if he was a pilot, and I told them he works in the tower as a flight dispatch person. Because of this, I felt that taking the course and getting my pilot license would be a smart thing to do. Not only would I be safe from going to Vietnam for eighteen months, I would be a licensed pilot, something I knew would make my father very proud.

Meanwhile, the six of us waited anxiously for word of who had been accepted, and who was on standby. Finally, the Warrant Officer who had given us the test called out our names during the morning formation. He took us aside and handed me and two others a set of papers. He informed us that we had the highest scores, and that we could either sign them or hand them back unsigned. I immediately asked for his pen and signed, as did the other two.

"That's what I thought you would do," he said with a smile. "I'll file these and start your applications, and then you will receive some more papers to sign within a week."

He told the other three that they were the backups, and if any one of us decided to back out, they would be first in line. We thanked him and went back to our company's barracks.

I sat on my bunk and realized that my situation had totally changed. I now had eighteen months of going to school to become a helicopter pilot, as well as a nice pay raise of a Warrant Officer, which was equivalent to being a First Lieutenant.

I called my mother and told her the good news. She was ecstatic, to say the least, and she told me she would immediately tell my father.

The three of us spent the next few days patiently waiting for the rest of our paperwork, while the others went about their daily routines of getting placed into the different areas of AIT. Most were placed as foot soldiers, or "grunts," who were taught how to use the M16 rifle, grenade launchers, and M60 machine guns. One of the guys who had a bunk next to mine told me about his MO. He was part of a four-man crew that got to ride around in a jeep, which had a 120 mm recoilless rifle mounted on the jeep.

"What are you going to shoot with that thing?" I asked.

"They said it's for shooting tanks," he said, smiling. "I didn't know they had tanks in Vietnam."

"I didn't either," I said, "but at least you get to ride around in a jeep, instead of having to walk or run everywhere."

Finally, our wait was up, and we were told to report to the Warrant Officer's office. The three of us eagerly ran over, knocked on his door, and went in.

"I'm afraid I have some bad news for one of you," he said, "and it concerns you, Allan. It seems as though they have forgotten to send your paperwork."

He checked the names on the papers he had before him, and handed them to the other two.

"There must have been a mistake," he said to me, "but I'll find out what happened."

"You'll make sure I get mine later, right?" I asked.

"Oh yes," he replied, "I'll look into right away. For now, though, you will have to wait."

I watched as the other two eagerly signed their copies and handed them back to the officer. He then gave us some pamphlets that described the two cities that were giving the training, and told us to have a look at them.

"That's all for now boys," he said, "and Allan, I'll let you know as soon as I get yours."

"Alright," I said nervously, "I definitely want to be a heli pilot."

The three of us walked out, and the two joked about me not getting my papers.

"Don't worry, Allan," they said, "you'll get yours soon."

"I sure hope so," I said, feeling very uneasy about what had just happened.

After a few days, I went over to see the Warrant Officer. He told me that he was doing everything possible to locate my paperwork.

"Why can't they just make out new ones?" I asked.

"It's out of my hands," he said apologetically. "The Army has their own way of dealing with things like this."

I sadly walked out of his office, and began to think of what the Army would do with me. After a couple of days, while we were having lunch, I found out from the Warrant Officer that it was too late to fit me into their schedule. In front of the whole company, I started yelling at the Officer.

"This can't be true! I want to become a helicopter pilot, not some fucking foot soldier!"

The Officer was surprised by my outburst, as he apologized and walked away. I sat back down, and stared at my half-eaten lunch. The other two who had signed up were next to me ,and they agreed that since it was the Army's fault for losing my paperwork, that they should give me another chance. I felt so bad that I couldn't finish my lunch. I got up and went to see the Warrant Officer, to try to see if doing anything else could change the situation. The Warrant Officer explained that he had called everyone he could think of, but it didn't do any good.

I walked out of his office and went straight over to my car. I grabbed one of my 8-track tapes and began listening to music. I sat there, feeling like I had just gotten punched in the stomach. My emotional roller-coaster ride consisted of hate, disgust, fear, and finally despair. I thought of leaving the base immediately and running away, but of course I didn't. As I settled down somewhat, I told myself that I should continue on with my AIT, and hope that my application for pilot training would be revived.

It was Friday when we were told that everyone was being given a two-day weekend pass. Since I was not accepted for the pilot training, I was told that I was being placed on the four-man jeep crew, and would start my new MO training on Monday. I called my mother and told her about the Army losing my paperwork.

"That's awful," she said. "I'll call your father and give him the news."

Monday arrived and I went with the others to where they kept the military vehicles. I was a week behind in my training, but the crew assured me that up until now they had just been in the classroom.

"We've been shown how to camouflage a jeep," Derrick said.

"We've also been shown how to destroy a tank with just one shot," Mike added.

"It's really cool to see the 'bullet' flying through the air a half mile away." Joe said.

"It sounds as though this training has got you guys all excited," I said.

"Not only that," Derrick said, "but we get to ride in the jeep when everyone else is running."

"I can see how that's attractive," I said, as we approached the yard. A sergeant was there waiting for us and he told us that we should drive over to the learning centre and check in with our instructor. We found our jeep and got in.

"I'll drive," Derrick said, "it's only ten minutes from here."

When we arrived, the instructor welcomed me and the five of us went in.

"Because Allan has not been shown the films regarding the safety issues related to the 120, we will spend an hour going over the major points."

He started the film and proceeded to show what would happen if you stood in the wrong place when the gun was fired. A dummy, placed ten feet behind the jeep, was blown to shreds as the back blast completely destroyed it.

"Okay," I said, "I get the picture."

A few more films showed me the basic steps on how to fire the weapon, the range that it covered, as well as techniques used in camouflaging the jeep. The instructor then told everyone that today we were going to a firing range to practice the shooting of the 60 mm tracer round, before moving on to the 120.

As we drove to the range, we chuckled at the sight of the other soldiers, who were running back and forth.

Once we arrived, we were shown the firing mechanism used to shoot the tracer round. It was mounted on a turret and faced an arcade-like backdrop, which resembled a jungle. The instructor walked over to a small shed and told us to watch what was going to happen. The backdrop began moving, and from the left-hand side a small metal replica of a tank appeared. It slowly moved across the backdrop, and then it stopped. The instructor told us that in a real case scenario, we would first place the enemy tank into our sights, read the distance, and then fire the round.

"In short," he said, "once you see the tracer round is going to hit your target, you let the big round go."

"Yeah," Derrick said, "then you get the hell out of there."

"Why do you have to leave?" I asked.

"Because if you don't, they have the technology to fire a round at you," the instructor answered.

"But, I thought we were camouflaged?" I asked.

"We are," Derrick said, "but they have heat seeking gadgets that automatically turns their gun on us and fires, even before our round hits them."

"Wow," I said, "so much for being the first to shoot."

Our training with the 120 mm recoilless rifle was in fact more interesting than I had thought. After our first week, I had forgotten all about my future as a helicopter pilot, and settled in for two more months of learning how to destroy tanks in Vietnam.

The four crews being trained became close friends, as we had to rely on each other to work as a team. At the end of our training, we were surprised to find out that only two of the four crews would be given the official title of Anti-Tank Warfare Unit.

When I asked our instructor what the other crews were going to do, he just threw up his hands and said, "That's not my job, but I'm sure they'll find something else for you to do."

We were also told that the names of the final two crews would be listed on the bulletin board on graduation day. Graduation day for me meant that I had one month of leave, and then it would be off to either another country, or jail.

Finally, graduation day arrived, and we ran to the bulletin board to see whose names were on the list. I scanned the board and did not see mine. The ones whose names were there jumped for joy, as they ran away to the mess hall. I didn't care if my name was or wasn't there, but I did wonder what kind of MO the Army had given me. I stopped my sergeant in the hall and asked him about it.

"You'll find out shortly," he said. "When you graduate, you will be given your completion of training diploma as well as your new MO and reporting date."

I thanked him and he wished me all the best for the future, then I walked back to get ready for the ceremony.

We began the ceremony with each of our companies flying their respective flags and marching to a grandstand filled with dignitaries and the families of the soldiers who were graduating.

After a few short speeches, they began calling out our names. I heard mine and went to collect my papers. Once I returned to my place, I looked at them. The words "Republic of South Vietnam" jumped right off the page and hit me like a ton of bricks. As I kept reading, I saw that they had changed my MO to that of Infantry. I couldn't believe it. I had been hoping for a different destination. I showed it to the guy next to me who had also just received his papers, and he too was being sent to Vietnam. The other important items were the date and place of where I was reporting to next. It was June 10, at the Oakland, California Army Base.

After the ceremony, I said goodbye to my friends. I then called my mother, and told her I was coming home.

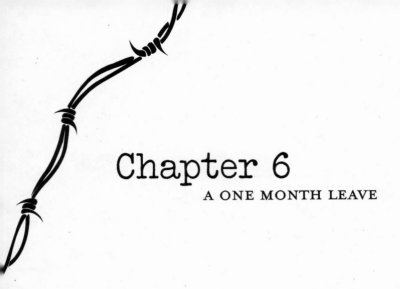

Chapter 6

A ONE MONTH LEAVE

It was the beginning of May, 1968, when I arrived back home in Miami. The first thing I noticed was that the hearse wasn't where it was supposed to be. I went in, thinking that Keith might have taken it, and asked my mother her about its whereabouts.

"Oh, son," she said, with tears coming down, "I hope you won't hate me for what I have done."

"What's that?" I asked.

"I had to sell it," she said. "The neighbours weren't happy with it sitting there all this time. It has been almost a year that you've had it, and since you are going off to war ..."

"Stop!" I shouted. "You had no right to do this. You could have told Keith to move it or something. When did you sell it, and to whom?"

"It was to the driver of the garbage truck," she said. "He gave me twenty dollars for it."

I went outside, as I was beginning to lose my temper with her. After I settled down, I knew I had to find out who had bought it and get it back. I drove over to Keith's and told him what had happened.

"I knew that she was thinking of doing it," Keith said, "but I didn't think she would actually go through with it."

"You've got to help me get it back," I said.

"How do we find out who bought it?" Keith asked.

"My mother told me it had something to do with the trash men," I said. "That's all she would say. First I get ordered to Vietnam, and then I lose my hearse."

"You're going where?" Keith asked.

"The Army has given me one month of leave," I said, "and then I'm off to Vietnam."

"You're not really going, are you?" Keith asked.

"Not on your life, brother," I said. "I'll go to jail first."

"You'd better not tell that to Donny," Keith said. "He's going to become a cop."

"That's a surprise," I said. "He never told us about that."

"He just started last week," Keith said, "and I can already see the changes in him."

Keith and I talked about where the hearse could be, and came to the conclusion that if they had signed all of the necessary papers, and my mother had acted as the seller, then it was a done deal.

"So, what happens at the end of your month's leave?" Keith asked.

"I'm supposed to report to the Oakland Army Base in California," I said.

I went back home and told my mother that I was sorry I yelled at her. She assured me that it was the neighbours that pressured her into getting rid of it. I felt that it was her way of saying, "you're going off to war and I don't need a hearse to remind me of it."

I didn't bother her any more about it. I asked her about my father and if she had spoken with him lately.

"Yes," she said, "I called him this morning and told him you were through with your training and that you would be going there soon."

She started sobbing again, and I tried to console her by telling her that I wasn't sure if I should go.

She stopped crying and sat up.

"What do you mean by 'you aren't sure'?"

"I'm not sure," I said, "because nobody could give me a good enough reason to convince me that we should be there."

"I thought it was because of the Chinese communists," she said, "and that they want to take over the world; that's what they are telling us on TV."

"That's the only reason I've heard," I said. "It's not like World War II, when Hitler wanted to take over Europe, but it does sound a lot like Korea, where one group of politicians wanted to take over the whole country and another group opposed them. I was told during my training that the French armies were there first, but that they weren't good enough to win the war, and so they left. Now, the only thing that our government has said is that some US boats were supposedly shot at while they were patrolling in the Gulf of Tonkin in August of 1964, and that we are retaliating for that attack. We are also being told that the North Vietnamese want to take control of all of Vietnam and eventually all of Indochina. It's called the domino theory. So, I concluded, if I'm going to be sent over there to kill those people, I need a better reason than that."

"It sounds as though you have made up your mind about not going," she said. "Have you considered the consequences of going to jail?"

"Yes, I have," I said, "and I'm ready to stand up for what I believe is the right decision."

"Well then," she said, "I'm sure your father and I will support whatever decision you make, because we love you."

"Thank you, Mom," I said. "I needed to hear that."

With that taken care of, I went to the window and looked out to where the hearse once stood and thought about how things might have been different, if I had only stayed in school.

The United States first involved itself in Vietnam in 1950, when President Harry Truman began to underwrite the costs of France's war against the Viet Minh, with approximately $15 million in military aid, and over $3 billion over a 4 year period. Later, throughout the fifties and early sixties, the U.S. Stepped up its political, economic, and military commitments in Indochina. This took place under Presidents Dwight Eisenhower and John F. Kennedy. In opposition to the increased American presence, many prominent senators had begun to criticize the administration's decisions.

http://library.thinkquest.org/27942/war.htm
"Radical Times: The Antiwar Movement of the 1960's"

I spent the month of May having as much fun with Keith as possible, going to the beach every day. I also wrestled with the thought of either going to war or going to jail. With one week left of my leave time, my mother got a call from my father.

"Your father has friends in Belmont, California," she said, "which is about sixty miles south of San Francisco, and they are willing to let you stay with them. They'll even take you to San Francisco and show you around, then they'll take you to the base in Oakland."

"I don't know, Mom," I said, "but I'll think about it."

"Okay," she said, "but I need your answer by tomorrow."

That night, I agonized over the plan, and tried to think of what would happen if I went there. I'd always hoped of going to California with Keith, but this was totally different. I wasn't getting any new ideas from my family to help in my decision making, so I decided to go to California. The next day, I told my mother that I had decided to go to California, so she called the people in Belmont and my flight was booked for the next day.

My last night with my mother, June 5, was spent watching TV, and the news couldn't have been worse.

We heard the news anchor say, "On the evening of the California Primary, June 4, Robert Kennedy was assassinated just after midnight, as he left the stage at the Ambassador Hotel in San Francisco. He is currently in the hospital and undergoing life-saving surgery. He had been addressing a large crowd of supporters, after his victories in California and South Dakota, when he was shot."

"My God!" Mom screamed, "What is going on with our country?"

"This happened in San Francisco, I said. "Isn't that were I'm going tomorrow?"

"Yes," Mom said, "are you sure you still want to go there?"

I thought about what we had just heard, and said, "Yes, Mom, I'm still going to go."

The next day, June 6, I put on my army uniform and packed my duffel bag with the rest of my army clothes. My mother grabbed her camera and took a couple of pictures, saying I looked handsome in my uniform. Then we drove to the airport and I boarded a direct flight for San Francisco.

Chapter 7

GOING TO BELMONT, CALIFORNIA

I arrived at San Francisco Airport at 4:00 p.m., picked up my duffel bag, and went looking for my father's friends. As I walked around, I noticed that a lot of people were looking very sad. I heard Robert Kennedy's name mentioned in one conversation. He had died in the early morning hours, succumbing to an assassin's bullet the night before. He was forty-two.

I finally spotted two people holding a sign with my name on it. They introduced themselves as Jim and Martha, and the three of us left for Belmont. Jim told me that he had worked with my father while they were in Japan, and Martha added that she was a teacher at one of the local high schools.

"The two of us have some time off," Martha said, "so when your father asked us to show you around we couldn't say no."

"I appreciate this," I said. "I've never been to the West Coast."

"Well then," Jim said, "tomorrow we will take you back to the big city, and have dinner at one of the many fine restaurants."

I sat back and enjoyed the ride to Belmont, which took us along the San Francisco Bay. I kept looking out at the bay, and looked for any signs of surfing.

"Is there any surfing here in the Bay?" I asked.

"No," Jim said, laughing, "that's more of an L.A. thing."

"Oh yes," I said, feeling a bit foolish, "I forgot."

Once we arrived at their apartment, Martha started to prepare dinner, while Jim told me all about him working with my dad. During dinner, the two of us talked about the politics of the war.

"We don't believe in it," Jim said. "It has gone on for far too long, and there doesn't seem to be any end in sight. President Johnson has told us he isn't going to seek reelection, and Robert Kennedy, brother of President John F. Kennedy, was recently assassinated. The US is definitely going through a troubled time because of this war, and even the leader of the civil rights movement, Martin Luther King, who was assassinated a couple of months ago, has brought on more rioting in many large US cities."

I was glad to hear that they no longer believed in the war. After dinner, Martha suggested that we look at the brochures that she had taken while they were waiting for me at the airport.

They were from the many restaurants in San Francisco, and she asked me to pick out a few. After looking at them, I decided on a seafood restaurant at Fisherman's Wharf, one Italian and one Spanish. Martha looked at my choices and told me she had not been to any of them.

"We'll go to a different one each night," she said.

"Alright," I said, I really do appreciate everything you are doing for me, thank you so much."

Each night was like going to a different country for dinner. After dinner, we would go for a cable car ride, and visit different parts of the city. One was the Presidio Military base, which overlooked the entrance to the San Francisco Bay near the Golden Gate Bridge.

"One of its uses in World War II," Jim said, "was to keep the Japanese Navy from entering the Bay. It's now a place where soldiers returning from Vietnam come to unwind and serve out their remaining few weeks of service."

The next few nights were spent having a good time. Each restaurant had its share of people in military uniforms, and I wondered how many of them were faced with the same fate as I was. I also knew that the time for making the biggest decision of my life was close at hand.

The media reports kept telling us that there were daily protests, some with students burning their draft cards. The opposition to the war here on the West Coast was increasing, and with a presidential election coming up, people were beginning to voice their opinions.

The day before I was supposed to report to Oakland, Jim and Martha told me they were inviting a few friends over for dinner. One of them was an Army Captain who had been to Vietnam and who was also planning on going back.

"You can ask him about the war," Martha said.

"Yes," I said, "I'll do that."

While Martha prepared dinner for their guests, as well as my "last supper," Jim and I were watching TV. It was June 9, and they were showing the funeral service for Robert Kennedy, which was being held at St. Patrick's Cathedral in New York. Senator Edward Kennedy, the youngest brother of John and Robert, delivered the eulogy.

The guests and the captain arrived, and we were all introduced to each other.

"Hello, Private," he said, "I'm Captain Matt Cooke; I understand you're heading off to Vietnam tomorrow."

"Yes, sir," I said, saluting him, "tomorrow I'm going to war."

"Oh," he said, throwing up his hands, "it's not as bad as you might think it is."

I just looked at him and decided to keep my true thoughts to myself.

We went into the living room while Martha and another woman went into the kitchen.

"Dinner's ready," Martha said, "Mary and I will set the table."

While we were eating, the conversation got around to the war. The captain kept talking about how the war was going to be over soon, and how America's army was vastly superior to that of the North Vietnamese. He then looked at me and asked about my training.

"I was trained as an anti-tank crew member using the 120 mm recoiless rifle."

"I've never fired one," Matt said, "but I have heard of them."

"When I got my orders for Vietnam," I continued, "the Army changed my MO to the infantry, something that I didn't even train for."

"Let me tell you," Matt said, smiling, "once you get over there, they might even make you a cook."

Everyone except me laughed at Matt's remark. I just glared at him, and my heart started to beat faster.

"It was even worse," I said, "when they lost my paperwork for going to helicopter pilot school at the beginning of AIT."

"So, it sounds as if you're not happy with the way things turned out," Matt said.

"That's an understatement," I said. "The Army doesn't seem to care what happens to the guys that receive special training, and then change it to suit their needs."

"Well," Matt said, "I wouldn't be here today if it wasn't for the Army taking care of me. One thing you must remember is that although you are a member of a team, you are responsible for your own actions, good or bad. For example, I was leading a team into a village that we thought was on our side when they started shooting at us. I ordered my men to kill everyone, because we could not tell the good guys from the bad."

"That is why we shouldn't be there," I said loudly. "We can't even tell who the enemy is."

The captain and everyone else could see that I was becoming agitated, so Martha changed the subject quickly, and asked if everyone would like some more wine.

I declined and got up from the table and went into the living room. Jim followed me out and asked if I was alright.

"I'm okay," I said, "but I wish that captain would leave."

"He's going to be staying overnight with us," Jim said, "so try and keep calm."

Jim went back into the dining room while I started to think of what I was going to do next. I didn't want to wait until the morning and cause a scene by telling Jim and Martha that I wasn't going to Oakland. Even though I had begun to trust Jim and Martha, and had thought of telling them the truth, everything changed with the captain being here. If I refused to go, he would surely call the Military Police and have them escort me to Oakland, or jail. I finally came up with the idea of leaving the apartment in the middle of the night, and thus eliminating any connection of my escape to Jim and Martha.

Jim came out and asked me if I was going to finish my dinner, but I told him I had lost my appetite and wanted to stay in the living room. The other guests, sensing there was something going on, decided to leave after they finished their dinner. After the guests had left, the captain and Jim came out to the living room.

"That's your sofa," Jim said, pointing, "and Allan, the other one is yours."

The captain ignored me as he started up a conversation with Jim about baseball, while I pondered my next move.

Then, Jim turned to me and asked, "What time do you have to be at the base in Oakland?"

"Noon," I said, "or whenever I get there."

"You had better be there on time," the captain said. "You don't want to be classified as being AWOL on your first day now, do you?"

"No, I don't want that," I said.

I thought that I should at least make them think that I was ready to go, and not raise their suspicions that I would be changing my mind.

It was time to call it a night, and the captain and I prepared our sofas with the blankets that Martha had given us. The sofas were facing each other, and after the lights were turned out, I was thankful that the watch I was wearing had a luminous dial, so I could easily read the time. Jim had told me that they would wake me at 7:00 a.m., and that we would leave by 8:00.

I watched the captain as he tossed and turned on his sofa, hoping that he would soon fall asleep. Meanwhile, I was wide awake, but tired, and it was time to make the biggest decision of my life. I knew I didn't want to wait until Jim and Martha woke me, so I decided to leave the apartment sometime in the middle of the night.

Suddenly, I woke up sweating. I realized that I had indeed fallen asleep. I quickly looked at my watch, it was 1:00 a.m. Now I really felt tired, as well as nervous and anxious, and yet I was determined to stick to my plan. One more hour of sleep, I told myself, just one more. Again, I awoke and glanced at the time, 2:00 a.m. The captain was snoring, which made me smile, and I thought, *just one more hour.* This time, I awoke to see that my hour had gone an extra fifteen minutes, it was 3:15 a.m.

I thought to myself, *Now is the time to go.* I slowly got up and walked past the captain, went through the kitchen, and back out again. I stood beside my duffel bag, with the clothes I was going to wear on top, and proceeded to get dressed. The captain made a groaning noise, and I froze. He had turned his body so that he now faced directly toward me. *Oh well,* I thought, *if he is watching me, so be it.* I had made my decision to leave, and was ready to accept the consequences of getting caught. I made my way to the door, and opened it. The cool, foggy air hit me hard as I stepped outside and closed the door behind me.

PART III:

Run,

Run,

Run

Chapter 1
LEAVING BELMONT

As I walked away, I glanced back to see if anyone was following. I looked down at my name tag on my jacket, and decided to tear it off. *I don't need this anymore*, I thought, and tossed it into the bushes. I had no idea in which direction I was headed, but I knew that I wanted to go to San Francisco, and hoped I would meet up with some people who could help me.

As I made my way onto the main street in Belmont, I saw a police car coming. I hid behind a bush until it passed me, and then I continued on. After an hour of walking, I could see some bright lights farther up the road, which told me I was getting close to some businesses. At 5:00 a.m., I came to a gas station, and saw the attendant putting out the displays.

When he saw me coming, he stopped what he was doing and said, "Good morning. You're out for an early morning walk."

"Yes," I said, "would it be possible to use your washroom?"

"Well," he said, eyeing me up and down, "okay; I'll go and get the key."

I thanked him and went in to wash up. When I was done, he asked me if I as in the military.

"No, I'm not," I said, "these are just some clothes a friend gave me. Is there a bus that goes into San Francisco from here?"

"Why yes," he said, looking at his watch, "but you're headed in the wrong direction. It should be coming any minute now. In fact, here it comes now."

I thanked him and ran across the street. I got on the bus and asked the driver, "How much to go into the city?"

"Two dollars and fifty cents," he said, "but if you're in the Army, it's free."

"Thanks," I said, "but I'm not in the Army."

The bus was empty, so I went to the back and sat down. I looked at my watch. It was 6:00 a.m., and I realized that by now, someone in the apartment might have gotten up and noticed that I was gone. My emotions were running high as I tried imagining who I would eventually meet in San Francisco.

As we headed into the city, everyone who got on wearing a suit and tie made me feel more paranoid. *The sooner I get off this bus*, I thought, *the better I'll feel*. Finally, we arrived at the bus station at 7:00 a.m. I knew now that it was up to my instincts to find someone that would understand my situation and could help me.

I left the station and started walking uphill. Just ahead of me, I spotted two young men; both were wearing backpacks. As I got closer, I started feeling more comfortable about talking to them.

I ran up beside them, and asked, "Excuse me, but are you from around here?"

Startled, they both turned to look at me.

"Hello, and yes, I'm from here and my friend is from Santa Rosa."

"Look," I said, "I just got off the bus, and I'm running away from the Army. Can you help me out?"

They stopped and looked at one another. Then they looked back at me, and introduced themselves.

"I'm Greg, and this is Mike, and you are welcome to join us. We're heading to Golden Gate Park right now."

I knew right away that these two were just the type of people I was looking for, and we made our way up the hill.

"So," Greg said, "you say you are running away from the Army?"

"Yes, that's right. I'm still legally in the Army, and have been ordered to report to Oakland at noon today, then it's off to Vietnam."

"Did you just leave from a military base nearby?" Greg asked.

"No, I'm originally from Florida, and I was staying with some friends of my father, in Belmont."

"Do your friends know you are doing this?" Mike asked.

"No, they don't. I just left their place early this morning, before they got up. I'm sure by now they are calling the authorities."

"Wow," Greg exclaimed, "you're cool with us."

We arrived at the park and Greg took out a blanket for us to sit on. Mike, looking at his watch, asked me if I was hungry.

"Yes," I said, "but I'm more tired than hungry."

Looking into his wallet, Mike said, "I'm going to go and get us some fish and chips and three coffees."

After Mike left, Greg told me that he was eighteen years old, and Mike was only sixteen.

"We've been traveling for a month now, down to LA and Mexico."

"You're eighteen," I said. "So that means you are eligible for the draft, right?"

"Yes," Greg said, "but I plan on going to college."

"I went to college for a year and a half, but I made the mistake of not keeping up my grades and lost my student deferment."

"Wow," Greg said, "I'll make sure I don't do that."

Mike came back with the food and coffee, and before we ate, Greg reached into his backpack and took out a bag of marijuana. He looked at me and asked if I had ever tried it.

"Yes, I have and I like it," I said. "It's better than cigarettes."

"I agree with that," Greg said, as he took out a joint and lit it up.

There were a lot of hippies and straight people walking by, and I asked them if they were worried that someone would call the cops.

"Not here," Mike said. "Just about everyone's either a pot smoker or they don't care."

Once the joint was finished, we dug into the fish and chips. After eating, the three of us fell asleep under the warm California sun.

When I awoke, I looked at my watch, and saw that it was almost noon.

Soon, I'll be officially AWOL from the Army, I thought. Greg and Mike also awoke and I told them about my new status with the military.

Mike and Greg told me that it would be a good idea to get some different clothes, because my khaki pants and dress shoes were a dead giveaway as to my connection with the military, not to mention my short haircut.

They took me to a secondhand store that was nearby, and I got changed.

"You can keep the jacket," Mike said, "everybody is wearing them."

We went back to the park, and thanks to my new wardrobe, I now felt like a new man.

"What do you plan on doing now?" Greg asked.

"I haven't thought about that," I said. "It was hard enough to make the decision to get to this point."

"Well," Greg said, "you are welcome to come home with me; my parents will let you stay at our house."

"Mine would too," Mike said, "they don't believe in the war."

"Where is Santa Rosa?" I asked Mike.

"It's about sixty miles north of here," Mike said.

After giving it some thought, I came to a conclusion.

"If I stay here with Greg," I said, "it will be easier for the Army to find me, so, I have decided to go with Mike to his parents' home in Santa Rosa."

Greg accepted my decision and told me if I ever needed any help, he would be available.

"It will take us a couple of hours to get home, so we should get going," Mike said.

I shook Greg's hand and thanked him for everything, and Mike and I took off.

We made our way out of the park and headed for the Golden Gate Bridge.

Traffic was heavy as Mike and I went to a spot near the entrance of the bridge.

"We won't get hassled by the police here," Mike said, as he stuck out his thumb.

One by one, the cars went whizzing by, and I thought it was going to be a long time before someone would stop for us.

About twenty minutes went by when the traffic slowed to just a few cars. Then we spotted a car coming to a stop right in the middle lane. It was a convertible with two guys in it and they were waving at us.

"Come on!" Mike yelled, "They're waiting for us."

We dodged a few cars as we ran out to their car, which was an older model Buick.

"Get in, quick," the passenger said.

Mike and I got in and we sped away.

The passenger was a young black man who introduced himself as Vince.

"That's Richard," he said, pointing to the driver, who was a bit older and white.

As we drove onto the bridge, Vince asked us where we were going.

"Santa Rosa," Mike said.

Vince just smiled and repeated our destination to Richard.

Once we got to the other side, Richard pulled off the road, and stopped.

"We are going to Reno for the day," Richard said, "but you're welcome to come with us. After that we'll bring you to Santa Rosa."

I looked at Mike, who was trying to decide what to do.

"Sure, why not?" Mike said. "I've never been there before, and I'm in no hurry to get home."

The three of them looked at me for my answer.

I quickly explained my military situation, and then told them that I would definitely stay with Mike, and go with them to Reno.

As we drove through Sausalito, Vince showed us a bag of marijuana and asked if we wanted some.

Mike and I both nodded, and soon the four of us were quite stoned, and on our way to Reno, Nevada.

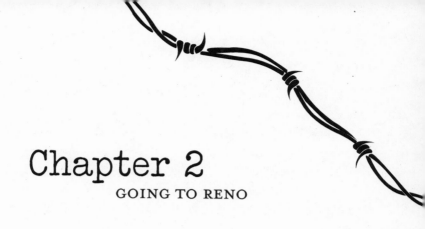

Chapter 2
GOING TO RENO

We made it to Reno just before 5:00 p.m. Richard told us that he was going to spend about an hour or so gambling at one of the smaller casinos, and asked us if we wanted to come along.

"I'm not old enough," Mike said.

"I don't gamble," I said, "and besides, I don't have any money."

After Richard left, Vince told us he never gambled.

"I'm going to see a friend nearby," Vince said.

Mike and I decided to walk around one of the most famous cities in America.

"'The Biggest Little City in the World,'" Mike said, "that's what they call Reno."

"With all of these neon lights and giant hotels," I said, "I have to agree that this is definitely a spot for tourists who like to have a good time, while throwing their money away."

After an hour, Mike and I went back to the car, and saw that Vince was back.

It was 6:30 when Richard showed up. He got in and started up the car.

"Did you win a lot of money?" Vince asked.

"No," Richard said, "they took it all this time."

Vince just smiled as he turned to Mike and me.

"Good thing we got these credit cards," he said, holding up a stack that had to be two inches thick.

I immediately thought, *Who are these guys and what are they doing with all of those credit cards?*

"I'm hungry," Richard said, "let's go and get something to eat."

He drove to the closest restaurant and parked the car. I noticed that the restaurant was very fancy, with expensive cars surrounding our old Buick.

The four of us walked in and were greeted by a man who asked us if we had reservations. Richard told him we didn't, and asked if it would be a problem to find us a table.

"No," he said, smiling, "not at all. Come this way."

We were seated at a table and given menus, and then asked if we wanted anything to drink. Richard and Vince both said they wanted a beer and I ordered one for myself as well. The waiter looked at Mike, who was expecting to be questioned about his age; but he wasn't, so he too asked for a beer.

"Will that be on one bill, or individual ones?" the waiter asked.

"Put it all on one bill," Richard said.

While the waiter went to get our beers, Richard told us that we could choose anything we wanted, even the most expensive steak on the menu. The waiter came back with the beer and asked if we were ready to order. Richard, Mike, and I ordered the steak, while Vince surprised everyone with an order of spaghetti. We tried to convince him to change, but he insisted on having the spaghetti.

"If I want spaghetti," Vince said mockingly, "then I want spaghetti!"

The waiter laughed, and told Vince that they had the best spaghetti in town and that he would not be disappointed.

We kept on kidding Vince about his choice of dinner, but when we saw it, we were amazed at the sight of the large meatballs, sitting atop a mound of noodles and sauce, as well as an assortment of grated cheese that came with it. The smell, which was also very enticing, had us wanting a taste of it, to which Vincent vowed that we would have to order our own if we wanted some.

The steak dinners were excellent, and it took almost an hour to finish our meal. The waiter brought us the bill, and Richard took the stack of credit cards out of his pocket and selected one.

Richard placed the card on the tray and the waiter told him he would bring back the receipt.

I started to think of everything that could go wrong with this whole scenario, and my paranoia was starting to build. I began to pray that those cards were legitimate and that the restaurant would accept them.

Soon, the waiter came back, smiling, and handed the card and the receipt back to Richard.

"I hope you gentlemen enjoyed your meal," he said, "and that you will visit us again soon."

I felt relieved as we all stated our enjoyment of the meal, and left.

The night air was beginning to cool as we piled into the Buick. I put on my jacket, and Richard mentioned something about putting the top up once we got out of the city. We left the parking lot and started down the street. We got into the left-hand lane to make a turn, and I saw Richard glance into his rear view mirror.

"Uh-oh," he said, "the cops are behind us."

Chapter 3
BUSTED

I froze, and started to sink lower into my seat.

As we made the turn, I could see that the police car had turned on its flashing red and blue lights. Richard let out a groan and pulled over.

"Stay calm," Richard said, "it's probably just a taillight or something."

The cop came up to Richard and asked for his driver's license and registration.

Vince got the registration from the glove box and handed it to Richard. To my surprise, Richard claimed that he didn't have a license. Hearing this, the cop went around to Vince and asked him for some ID. Vince told him he didn't have any. The cop then looked at me and asked me for my ID. I handed him my Florida driver's license, and after that he looked at me and asked me if I had a draft card. I told him that I had lost it, and that I hadn't had time to get another one. Then he surprised me with his next question, and asked me if I was in the military.

"No, sir," I said, "I'm not."

He then looked at Mike and asked him for some ID. He looked at it and asked Mike if he was indeed only sixteen years old. Mike confirmed his age and then the cop asked everyone to get out of the car. By this time, three more police cars had shown up, and we were completely surrounded.

"I'm taking everyone in," the cop said, citing different reasons for each of us.

I started feeling sick to my stomach, as it seemed my whole plan of leaving the Army was ending far too soon.

As the four of us were getting handcuffed, I mentioned to the cops that our jackets were still in the car. He went and retrieved them, and as he was making his way around the rear of the car, he shined his flashlight into the well of the car, where the convertible top folded down. He stopped and reached into the well, and pulled the bag of pot out.

Holding it up for everyone to see, he asked, "Who owns this?"

I just stood there in silence, trying to figure out how it got there, while the others just shrugged their shoulders in denial.

Soon, a paddy wagon arrived and the cop in charge told Richard, Vince, and I to get in. I asked him about Mike, and he told me that he was being taken to a juvenile detention place, where he could call his parents.

Once inside the wagon, I asked Richard and Vince about the pot and how it ended up in the well.

"I had it in my pocket," Richard said, "and when we were told to get out, and I was walking around the back of the car, I simply tossed it in."

Vince reminded Richard that because of his previous record of spending two years in the Washington State prison for cocaine possession, he wasn't going to admit ownership of the pot.

"Don't worry," Richard said, "I'm going to tell them that it was mine. How about you, Allan, are you going to tell them about your status with the Army?"

"I guess so," I said. "Since I've only been gone for ten hours, maybe they'll just send me to back to the military."

We arrived at the city jail where we were placed in a temporary "cage." One by one, we were called to a room to be booked on individual charges. Richard was booked for the possession of marijuana, Vince for having no ID, and me for possibly being AWOL from the Army.

After being led back into the cage, the sergeant in charge of booking came to us and said that we were all being charged with possession of marijuana, and that we were now being taken to the larger county jail. We were shocked to hear this, and I asked him about what would happen with my military status.

"First, you'll have to face this pot charge," he said, "and then the military will come and get you."

"Oh great," Vince said, "now I'm probably going to end up back in the Washington State prison."

"I know a lawyer in San Francisco," Richard said. "I'll call him tomorrow and see if he is available."

The ride to the county jail didn't take long. Since it was late, they had to turn the lights back on and announce to the twenty other guys in there that they had some new arrivals.

Once inside the cell, we were given five minutes to find an empty bunk bed, then the lights would be turned off. I quickly found a bed and sat down, having only a few minutes to look around my new home. The guard announced that the lights were being turned off, and I lay down on my bed.

That night was one of the worst nights of my life, knowing that I was sleeping next to people who might have been convicted of unspeakable crimes. At 6:00 a.m., we were awoken first by the turning on of the lights, and second, by the sounds of the breakfast carts being wheeled down the hallway by the trustees who were in charge of feeding us.

I watched as everyone got into a line to receive their tray of food. Richard, Vince, and I were last in line, since we were the new guys. As the line went through, I watched as there seemed to be a hierarchy of prisoners, with the leaders getting their food first, and seating themselves at the first table. We ended up at the last table, and stared down at some kind of slop on our trays.

"What is this?" I asked one of the guys who was there before us.

"It's porridge," he said, smiling, "if you don't want it, give it to me."

I thought about it for a minute, and saw two pieces of toast sitting next to it.

"Here," I said, "you can have the porridge, but I'll keep the toast."

After he gulped down his bowl of porridge, he gladly took mine and had it eaten before I finished my toast. He was an older man, probably in his fifties, and I felt sorry for him.

"What are you in here for?" I asked.

He just mumbled something and started in on his toast.

I looked at Richard and Vince to see if they had eaten theirs. Richard had given his portion to Vince, who was busy gulping it down.

"So, Richard, are you going to call your lawyer friend today?" I asked.

"Definitely," Richard said. "The sooner we get out of here the better."

"I couldn't agree with you more," I said. "This place really freaks me out."

After breakfast, the three of us began talking about our arrest.

"You know," I said, since they found the pot in the well of the car, and not on us personally, I don't see how they can convict us. That would be the first thing I would tell your friend."

We kept on tossing around ideas, when one of the guards came and called out Richard's name.

"It's time for you to make your phone call," the guard told Richard. The other prisoners, hearing this, demanded that they also be given a phone call, something that the guard was used to hearing.

Soon, Richard came back and told us that his lawyer wasn't available, and that he had told the guard that we wanted a state appointed lawyer.

"I wonder how long that will take," I said.

"They told me a couple of days," Richard said.

While we waited to find out who was going to represent us, we quickly got to know how things were being run inside the cell, and just who was pulling the strings. Tommy, a six-foot-four-inch former heavyweight boxer, was in for assault with a deadly weapon, and Ray, a mean looking 260-pound, five-foot-two-inch man, was in for armed robbery. Even though they were kings in this place, they eventually told me that they were someday going to the penitentiary, or the "big house," as they called it.

After a few days, we were told that our state appointed lawyer was here to talk to us. We were led into a room and told to sit and wait. When he entered, what I saw made me start laughing to myself, because he was dressed in a white suit and was wearing a white cowboy hat, and weighed over two hundred pounds.

"Hello," he said, sitting down, "my name is Robert." He opened a folder and asked us our names. Then he placed our individual sheets in front of us.

"Please read these and tell me if you agree or disagree with the statements made concerning the charges stated below."

I read mine and handed it back to him.

"There is one part that I don't agree with," I said. "The part about our knowledge of the marijuana being in the car, and also there is no mention of where they actually found the pot."

"I see," Robert said. "So, where did they find the pot?"

"They found it at the bottom of the well compartment, where the convertible top folds down."

"Oh yes, I understand," Robert said, as looked at Richard and Vince for their say.

"I agree with Allan," Richard said, "they didn't find the pot on us."

"So, Richard, why did you agree to say that the pot was yours?"

Richard went on to explain Vince's situation, and that I was just a hitchhiker who got caught up in this whole mess by accident.

"All you have to do," I humbly suggested to Robert, "is tell the judge that the pot could have been place in there by anyone while we were in the restaurant."

"I will take your story back to the prosecutor's office, and see what he has to say about this," Robert said.

As Robert got up from his seat, I pleaded with him that my story was the truth, and that the charges should be dropped.

"I'll see what I can do," he said. "I'll keep you informed as to what they are planning to do. Goodbye for now."

After he left, we were escorted back to our cell.

"I get the feeling that he isn't going to do anything soon," I said. "He's probably getting paid by the day."

"You've got that right," Richard said.

Another week went by, and there was no communication from Robert.

"We need to get a 'real' lawyer on our side," I told Richard. "This is ridiculous."

I thought of phoning my mother; it had been ten days since I left Jim and Martha's. I asked the guard for a phone call and was told I could have one tomorrow. I called my mother and told her the whole story. She told me that Jim and Martha had called her the day I left, and that they had been looking for me ever since. When I told her that the Reno Police department knew of my status in the military and my reporting to Oakland, she told me that no one had called her to tell her what was going on. When I asked about her getting me a lawyer, she just told me that she would ask my father.

The days went by, and I didn't hear anything more from my mother about getting a lawyer. Meanwhile, Richard received a call from another friend, who told him that a lawyer from nearby Lake Tahoe would be arriving in a few days to take our case.

Robert finally showed up and told us that we would be going in front of a judge for our preliminary trial in one week.

"What happens at a preliminary trial?" I asked.

"It's where you go before a judge," Robert said, "and the prosecutor gets to ask you questions concerning the charges. The important thing to remember is that all of this questioning happens while you are not under oath. Then the judge takes all that into consideration makes a recommendation for either going to a trial or dismissing the case altogether."

"That sounds good to me," I said, "but it sure is taking a long time to get to this point."

"Yes," Robert said. "The courts here are certainly backed up with a lot of cases."

The lawyer from Lake Tahoe finally arrived, and after talking with the three of us, he decided to wait until after the preliminary trial to see if his services were needed.

There were more delays and our preliminary trial kept getting pushed back. Weeks soon turned into months, and the strain of being penned up like animals was starting to get to me. Every night was filled with anxious moments, with inmates fighting with one another, and threats of death being constantly uttered.

Finally, nearly three months after our arrest, we were brought before the judge and prosecutor.

The preliminary trial started with a short speech by the judge, who briefly explained the rules, and said that we would have the opportunity after questioning to speak freely if we wanted to. After hearing the charges read by the prosecutor, I realized that our state appointed lawyer, Robert, had not been successful in getting anything changed.

The judge then asked the three of us if anyone wanted to go onto the witness stand to answer questions from the prosecutor.

I raised my hand, and told the judge I wanted to take the stand.

"Remember," the judge said, "you're not under oath."

The prosecutor grabbed a piece of paper from his table and approached the witness stand.

"Mr. Glass, have you ever smoked marijuana?"

I was stunned to hear his opening question, and at first I wanted to yell out, "Yes, I have." I took a deep breath, and stared at my lawyer. *He should be objecting to this type of question*, I thought to myself, but instead, he just sat there and said nothing. Then, I looked over at the judge and waited to hear him say something.

Finally, when the judge saw that I wasn't going to answer, he told the prosecutor to ask another question, and quickly scolded him, saying that he wasn't legally entitled to ask a person if they had broken the law.

The prosecutor just smiled, fully knowing that he couldn't ask such a question, but had tried to get me to answer it anyway.

He then asked me questions that led up to my being in the vehicle, and whether I had any knowledge of there being marijuana in the car.

I told him the truth about my hitchhiking with Mike, but that we knew nothing about the marijuana.

Once the prosecutor was finished, he asked Richard and Vince if they had anything to say. They declined and the whole thing was over in less than half an hour. The judge thanked everyone, and told us that he would be giving his verdict in a few days.

We were notified a few days later that the judge was ready to see us again. When we got into the courtroom, I spotted a chalkboard, which had a crude diagram of a car, complete with an X marking the spot where they found the pot.

First, the prosecutor got up and made his case to the judge, followed by our lawyer. Our lawyer used the chalkboard diagram to show the judge where the marijuana had been found.

Upon hearing this, the judge asked the prosecutor if this was indeed true, to which he said, "Yes, your honour, it's true."

"Well then," the judge said, raising his gavel, "case dismissed."

It was so anticlimactic that the three of us sat there completely stunned. For three agonizing months, I had been telling our lawyer this fact, and it ended up being the reason for finding us not guilty.

The judge told Richard and Vince they were free to go, and he reminded me of my military hold. We left the courtroom and were taken back to our cells.

I congratulated Richard and Vince on getting released, and they assured me that if I ever needed a place to hide from the Army, they would help me.

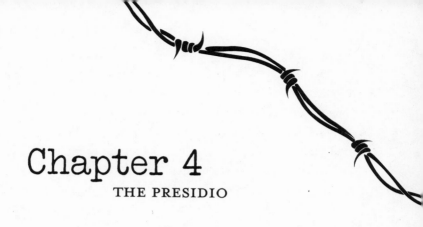

Chapter 4
THE PRESIDIO

My last days at the Reno County jail were spent wondering what the Army was going to do with me. I also witnessed a big change in attitude concerning Tommy and Ray; they found out that they were getting transferred to the State Penitentiary.

An inmate told me, "Once you are in the 'Pen,' it don't matter how big you are." These two big men, who were kings inside our cell, now found themselves being demoted to jacks in the deck of prison life.

On September 10, my name was called and I was told the military was here to take me. I was greeted by two MPs, who led me out to their van. I asked them where we were headed and they told me San Francisco, with a stop in Sacramento. When we arrived in Sacramento, I saw that they were going to a coffee shop.

"Hey," I shouted, "I've got to go to the bathroom."

I was escorted to the washroom by one of the MPs, while the other went into the coffee shop.

As we walked toward the washroom, I thought of making a run for it, but decided to wait for a better chance, as the time spent in jail had taken a lot out of me, both physically and mentally.

After the other MP came out of the coffee shop, they told me that they were going to the city jail for another pickup. Soon, I was being introduced to Mark, an eighteen-year-old from Sacramento. Mark told me that he had been drafted a couple of months ago, and had gone AWOL midway through his basic training.

"I refused to go any further," Mark said, "because I don't believe in this war."

"What about going to college?" I asked.

"My parents can't afford to send me to college."

I told him my story and the two of us instantly became friends.

"So, where are we going?" Mark asked.

"San Francisco," I said. "Have you ever heard of a place called the Presidio?"

"No, I haven't. What's the Presidio?" Mark asked.

"It's an Army base that was originally built to prevent the Japanese from entering the Bay, during WW II," I said. "Now, I assume that they are using it for the guys who are returning from Vietnam, to serve out their remaining time, as well as for keeping fuck-ups like us there."

"Do you think we will be put in jail?" Mark asked.

"I don't know," I said. "Our situations are quite different."

"I've never been in jail," Mark said.

"Well," I said, "it can't be worse than the county jail that I just came from."

A few hours later, we were driving through the front gates of the Presidio. A long, winding road, with large trees on either side, made this part of the Army base look like a park. As we passed a large building that was surrounded by a twelve-foot-high chain-link fence, a cold shiver ran down my back. On top of the fence was barbed wire, and I knew that I was now looking at the stockade, and possibly my new home.

We finally stopped in front of some smaller buildings, were led into one of them, and told to sit and wait.

"This is where you will be processed," the MP said, as he took up his position at the door.

Just then, a washroom door opened and a rotund staff sergeant came out. He acknowledged the MP at the door, and the two of them started talking.

"How's it going Gus?" the MP asked.

"Great," Gus replied, "only one more month to go."

"How many years does that make?" the MP asked.

"Eighteen, then it's retirement for me," Gus said. "It was way back in 1950, I was only eighteen, when I joined."

Gus looked at Mark and asked, "How old are you, son?"

"I'm eighteen. sir," Mark said.

Gus and the MP laughed at Mark for calling Gus "sir."

"Sit down, boy," Gus said, "you don't have to call me 'sir.'"

After the MP gave Gus our paperwork, it was our turn to answer some questions from Gus. After processing, we were led to another building, where we were put into another room which already had ten guys sitting on a couple of benches. I began talking to them and asked what was happening. One guy stood up, and introduced himself as Ron.

"I came here last night," Ron said. "So far, we haven't been told anything and we haven't had any breakfast."

It was now getting close to one o'clock, and I too was getting hungry. I went back to the door and tried to open it, but it was locked. I started banging on the door, and demanding that we get fed.

I could hear someone yelling back at me, as the door opened. It was Gus, along with two other MPs.

"What do you want?" Gus asked.

"I'm hungry," I said, looking at my watch, "and how come these guys haven't been given any breakfast?"

Gus smiled and said, "Look, son, you have just arrived here and already you are making demands. Don't worry, you'll soon be taken care of."

He slammed the door in my face and left. Ron and the other guys seemed to enjoy my little skirmish with Gus, and they congratulated me for saying something.

"They can't do this to us," Ron said, "we're still American citizens and should be treated accordingly."

The guys clapped and yelled out anti-war slogans like "power to the people" and "right on."

Another hour dragged on and then Gus came in and told everyone that we were going over to the mess hall for lunch.

"I want to remind all of you," Gus said, "that you are still in the Army, and I expect you to act accordingly. After lunch, each of you will go before the base commander for an interview."

We were escorted by two MPs, and as we entered the mess hall, the smell of real food made me feel a little bit better.

Ron and I sat together, and we started telling each other the story of how we ended up here in the Presidio. Ron was from Fresno, and like me, was attending college, but had been gradually getting into other things, like protesting the war, and his grades dropped below the required average.

"That's what happened to me," I said, "only I wasn't protesting. I was just madly in love with the wrong girl."

The MPs stood their guard, watching us, and soon afterward, we were informed that we would be going for our interviews. We were taken to another building and told to wait in a room that had benches situated around the perimeter.

"Sit down on these benches and face the wall," one MP snarled, "and don't talk."

I looked at Ron, and the two of us started laughing.

The MP heard us, so he came over and asked, "What's so funny?"

He asked Ron if it was him who was laughing.

"No, sir," Ron said.

"How about you?" he asked me.

"No, sir, I said, "but you do sound a lot like my fourth-grade schoolteacher."

"Alright, you," he said angrily, "come over here."

I stood up and turned to face him. I could tell by his red face that he wasn't going to put up with any insubordination. He was about my height, but overweight by at least fifty pounds, and he was beginning to breathe heavily. He told me to stand at attention in the middle of the room.

"Alright, soldier," he said, "get down and give me ten pushups."

I got down and started doing pushups. When I was almost done, I felt his boot on my back, and he was pushing me to the floor.

"Are you going to tell me who was laughing at me?" he asked.

I had to restrain myself from telling him what I really thought of him, so I kept silent, hoping that he would stop this mini persecution. Just then, I heard somebody tell him to stop, but he just kept on pushing until I was totally prone on the floor.

Finally, he took his foot off my back and asked the others if there was anyone else willing to join me. As I had hoped, no one took up his offer, thus denying his search for the offender.

"Stand up," he said.

We now stood face to face, and I could see that his face had turned a deeper red, as he began to shout at me.

"It's people like you that are tearing this country apart. If it were up to me, I'd put you in front of a firing squad, and have you shot for treason!"

As I listened to him rant, I began feeling sorry for him. I knew that he had probably just come back from the war, and that his patriotic values were at an all-time high. I then thought of a religious parable, *Please forgive him Lord, for he knows not what he is doing.* I kept staring at his Adam's apple, and thought, *please stop this senseless tirade, and choke on your words of hatred and violence.* I repeated these words to myself over and over again, and noticed that he was beginning to have trouble speaking. Just as I had hoped, he started to cough, and he simply walked away. He then turned and made a motion with his hand for me to go back to my seat.

The MP was still having problems with his breathing, so he left the room and did not return. Another MP came in and sat down in a chair next to the door. One by one, we were called in for our interviews, which each lasted about fifteen minutes. When I went in, I saw a captain sitting at a desk, surrounded by a mound of paperwork.

He pulled out a folder and opened it.

"Sit down," he said. "Are you Private Allan Glass?"

"Yes, sir, I am."

"Are you having any problems," he asked, "either personal or family?"

"No, sir, I am not."

"It says here that you recently spent three months in the Reno County jail for possession of marijuana. Is that correct?"

"Yes, sir, it is."

"Not guilty," he said. "The case was thrown out for lack of evidence, is that true?"

"Yes, sir, that's true."

"Do you still want to smoke marijuana?"

I thought about his question, and I flashed back to Reno, and having to answer the prosecutor's questions. He's trying to trick me into answering yes or no. If I said no, it would mean that I had smoke pot once before.

"Sir," I said, "I have never smoked marijuana and I don't intend to start."

"Good answer," he said, "most guys usually fall for that question."

He wrote something down, then he asked me another question.

"Now that you have had time to think about your actions of June 10, when you went AWOL, are you ready to serve your country in the manner you were trained for?"

I seized the opportunity to inform him of the outrageous change of my MO, from being trained as an anti-tank crew member to that of an infantry soldier.

"Yes, I know," he said, "it's all here in your records."

"So, does that mean I'll be going back to Fort Jackson to receive proper training?" I asked.

"No, son," he said. "I'm sorry about your change of MO, but you're not the first one who has had this happen to them. The Army has given you basic training, and because we need to use our forces effectively, you will be used accordingly, in order to win this war."

That's a load of B.S., I thought, but I nodded in agreement with him.

"You will be placed in a regular barracks building here at the Presidio," the captain said, "and put on a work detail while you await further orders. If you decide to go AWOL again, I assure you that when you are caught, you will be placed in the stockade."

He stood up and shook my hand.

"Good luck," he said. "You may leave now."

I left the room feeling lucky to know that I wasn't going back to a jail cell. I spotted Ron, and gave him the thumbs up sign. I was then told to go over to the building next door where I would be fitted for some new fatigues. After changing into them, I ceremoniously threw my old jacket into the garbage can.

I was then told to go to the mess hall, as it was getting close to 5:00 p.m. I met Ron as he was coming in for his new clothes, and he told me that he was being placed in a barracks building also. When I got to the mess hall, I saw that there were at least fifty others waiting. I took my place at the end of the line and joined in on the conversations.

"Welcome to the Presidio," one of them said. "You're one of the new guys, right?"

"Yes," I said, "I just got in this afternoon."

"Did anyone else come in with you?" he asked.

"Yeah," I said, "there were eleven more. Why do you ask?"

"I'm looking for a friend of mine who was here for a couple of months," he said. "After he received his new orders, he went AWOL again. If he's caught, there are three things could happen to him. The first one is he gets sent back here and goes directly to the Presidio stockade. The second one is he gets sent to Leavenworth, Kansas, for two years, but that's usually reserved for the hard-core guys. The third one is that he gets to come back here with us, the 'minor fuck-ups' of the US military."

After talking with a few others, it didn't take long to realize that most of us were being given a second chance to rethink our error in judgment for going AWOL. We were only here for a short time, so they could issue us new orders for Vietnam.

Our barracks was a large, two-story building, and we occupied the upper story. That night, Ron and I retold our stories of how we were drafted, and how we both objected to the war. My first night of not having to worry about the guy next to me was a welcome relief, and I slept soundly until the wake-up call at 6:00 a.m.

Ron and I followed everyone downstairs and over to the mess hall for breakfast. After we ate, we went outside and got into formation for a roll call. After our names were read aloud, we were given our orders of the day. Mine was to be part of a four-man crew that collected the garbage from around the base. Jerry, who was in charge, was a GI who, because of a clerical error, did not have to go to Vietnam.

We instantly became friends, as he too was against the war. Jerry told me he needed two more guys and he asked me if I had anyone in mind.

"I just met Ron and Mark," I said, pointing them out.

"Alright," Jerry said, "let's go over here and talk."

Jerry led us over to where nobody else could listen in.

"I've got two months left in this place," he began, "and I do not need anything screwing it up. We have to go off base and take the garbage to a remote area on the other side of the Golden Gate Bridge. Should one of you decide to leave, it will be on my record, and that is something I don't want."

We understood what he was getting at, so we shook hands and took off for the motor yard. Jerry found his truck and we hopped in, and started making our rounds.

We drove around the base, and soon we had collected a dozen bags of garbage.

"That's enough for one trip," Jerry said.

He drove straight through the gates of the Presidio, and soon we were on the Golden Gate Bridge. It was another beautiful day in San Francisco, although it was now a little bit cooler than when I was here in June, staying with Jim and Martha.

I was in the front seat as we drove across the bridge, and a feeling of déjà vu came over me. It was only three months ago that I was sitting in the back of a Buick convertible and looking up at this very same bridge. Once we got to the other side, Jerry pulled off onto a dirt road.

"Once we get to the top," Jerry said, "you'll like the view."

Slowly, Jerry started driving up the side of the mountain. Once we got to the top, the view was spectacular, as Jerry told us it would be. A fenced-off area with locked gates stood before us. The dump was a simple pit carved into the side of the mountain, and it was teeming with seagulls, crows, and even a few eagles.

Jerry handed me a key and told me to go and unlock the gate. As I hopped out of the truck, it was as if the birds knew what was going to happen. Their cries of anticipation were reaching a deafening crescendo.

As I opened the lock, I ducked as a few gulls swooped down, as if they were asking, "What have you got for us today?" Then I pushed the gates open, and Jerry drove in and turned the truck around.

He got out and yelled, "Hurry up and get these bags out!"

I then found out why he was in such a rush. The sky darkened as hundreds of birds hovered over us, their droppings raining down on us from above. After we were finished, we jumped back in and Jerry drove outside the gates.

He stopped the truck and said, "Now somebody has to go back and lock the gates."

"Don't look at me," I said, "I opened them."

The three of us looked at Mark, who reluctantly got out to lock the gate. Jerry then drove to a flat spot and stopped the truck.

"I almost forgot," he said, "there is one more thing we have to do."

He pulled a bag of marijuana out of his pocket, and asked us if we had any objections to smoking a joint.

The three of us didn't have any objections, so while we were admiring the view, Jerry rolled a joint. We were high enough to see the Presidio below, which was covered from time to time by fog and low clouds. One other landmark of the city, the top of Nob Hill, was also visible. It reminded me of a medieval castle, and created a mysterious illusion of good and evil. When we were finished with the joint, Jerry asked me to grab the package of gum out of the glove box.

"Everyone please chew a stick or two before we get back to the base," he said, "I don't want anyone smelling pot on your breath."

"Good idea," I said. "Is there a problem with the use of pot in the Presidio?"

"Not really," Jerry said, "and I'd like to keep it that way."

The ride down the mountain didn't take long, and Jerry told us it was time for lunch. Before we entered the mess hall, Jerry told us to be careful of what we say and to be aware of who is listening.

"There are informants inside our barracks," he said, "so make sure you don't talk about pot or anything else that can get you thrown into the stockade."

After my first week at the Presidio, my life began to get back to normal. I also realized that I had not called my mother; I had kept telling myself while I was in jail that either the Reno police department or the Army would have contacted her. Now, I was feeling guilty for not phoning her and letting her know that I was alright. I went straight for the phone booth and called.

"Hello," my mother answered.

"I have a collect call from Allan Glass," the operator said. "Will you accept the charges?"

At first there was complete silence, and then I heard her voice.

"Yes, I will, oh Allan, is that really you?"

"Yes, Mom, it's me. I'm alright and I'm in San Francisco."

"What happened to you?" she asked, her voice starting to crack. "We thought you were dead."

I quickly told her the story of leaving Jim and Martha's and spending three months in the Reno County jail.

"Now I'm in a place they call the Presidio, and I'm awaiting orders to go to Vietnam, but I've decided that I'm never going to go."

"Did you know that your father left Japan as soon as Jim called? He arrived in California, and spent a week looking for you."

"No, Mom, I didn't know that. I'm so sorry that I didn't call you."

"Well," she said, "I'm happy that you are alive and well. I'll call your father right away. You know that we support you in whatever decision you make, just keep us informed the next time you go missing."

"I will," I said, "I promise. Now, call Dad and let him know I'm alright, I love you; bye."

After I called, it felt as though a huge weight had been taken off my shoulders, and I told myself that I would never do this to my parents again.

The month of September saw the four of us keeping up our daily routine of playing garbage men. It was also a time to catch up on the latest news, which was provided at the entertainment centre, which had a bowling alley, Ping-Pong and pool tables, as well as a TV.

The top news story was that the Republican Party, on August 8, in Miami, Florida, had nominated Richard Nixon as their presidential candidate. He was being challenged by Nelson Rockefeller and Ronald Reagan. The Democrats, on August 26, in Chicago, Illinois, nominated Hubert Humphrey for president.

The Chicago convention saw a few peaceful demonstrations against the war, but the following nights saw an escalation of violence. Chicago police took action against crowds of demonstrators without provocation. The police beat some marchers unconscious and sent at least a hundred to the hospital, while arresting one hundred and seventy five. So much for free speech.

September, my first month at the Presidio, went by quickly, but October was a different story. A prisoner from the stockade, Jeff, was released and transferred into our barracks on October 10. Although he was happy to get out, he told us stories of mistreatment by the MPs toward the inmates of the stockade. He told Ron and me that there was a friend of his who was being constantly harassed and mentally tortured.

Hearing this, I told Jeff that he should tell Colonel Martin, who was in charge of the Presidio.

"I tried to get that message to the colonel while I was still inside the stockade," Jeff said, "but it obviously never got to him. My friend is in a very fragile and unstable state of mind, and needs psychological help."

On October 11, after the morning formation, all hell broke loose. As Ron, Mark, and I prepared for our work day, a rumour was spreading that one of the inmates had been shot by a stockade guard. I asked Jeff if he knew who it was.

"I don't know," Jeff said, "but I'm going over to the colonel's office to find out."

I found Jerry and asked him if he had found out anything.

"No," Jerry said, "but if it's true, there will be an uprising inside the stockade."

We got into the truck and drove slowly past the stockade. The yard was eerily empty.

"They might be under a lockdown," Jerry said. "I don't see anyone."

We kept on driving and began picking up the garbage.

That evening, everyone was talking about the shooting. I found Jeff and I could see that he wasn't looking happy.

"It was my friend who was shot," Jeff said. "He was murdered by one of the guards. He was part of a work detail, and they were on their way to the colonel's home to do some gardening. He broke from the line and started running. Without warning, the guard, who was packing a sawed-off shotgun, blew his head off. I knew something like that was going to happen and I couldn't stop it."

I tried my best to calm him down, but his sorrow soon turned to anger.

"I'm going off base to tell everyone," Jeff said. "They're not going to sweep this one under the rug."

I never saw Jeff again.

The next day, word arrived at our barracks that a massive demonstration was being held in the city. As many as ten thousand people were taking part, and both GIs and Vets were part of the protest. The colonel, worried about the growing protest, warned us not to go off base to participate. In spite of this warning, many left the Presidio to join in. A small group of them held a ceremony at the entrance to the Presidio, presumably for the slain inmate. They were quickly arrested and placed in the stockade, which fanned the flames of unrest even further.

On Sunday, everyone was talking about the shooting, as well as the demonstrations. There was talk of starting up a protest inside the Presidio, but that idea was turned down. Instead, we decided to support the guys inside the stockade and send a message to the colonel regarding the inhumane treatment of the prisoners inside. It was sent anonymously, so that they could not act directly by putting another person in the stockade.

The morning of October 14, Monday, was a cool but clear day. During the morning formation, we were told that everything was back to normal, and that all work crews would be going back to their normal routine.

The four of us got in our truck and took off. We were curious to find out if there was anything happening at the stockade, so we headed in that direction. We stopped at a place where we had a perfect view of the yard, and saw the usual group of inmates. I had a feeling something wasn't right, so I asked Jerry to wait a few minutes.

"Sure," he said, "I even brought my camera, just in case."

It didn't take long before something did happen. Some of the inmates, who had been standing in formation, started walking over to another part of the yard. We could hear them singing, "We Shall Overcome," and after a few lines, they sat down. Jerry and I got out of the truck to get closer. They had linked their arms together, forming a chain, and continued to sing. One of the guards yelled at them to return to the formation, but they remained steadfast. Jerry took a few pictures, and we waited to see what was going to happen next. Soon the colonel arrived, and he too tried to order them back inside. Every time he spoke, the inmates started to sing louder, drowning him out. Then, complete silence took over, as one inmate stood up. He started to read something from a piece of paper, but we couldn't hear what it was.

"It's probably a list of grievances or demands," Jerry said.

Once he was finished reading, he handed the paper to the colonel, and sat down.

The colonel started talking but the group began singing. The colonel, seeing that he wasn't going to be heard, walked away. Just then we saw a group of MPs, wearing full riot gear, come out of the stockade. They marched right up to the group and stopped. After a few minutes, the MPs started to pick the inmates up, and drag them back to the stockade.

"That's it for today," Jerry said, "let's get to work."

We spent the day talking about the protest at the stockade, and wondered if they would get into trouble for doing it.

"They'll probably just get some more time tacked on," Jerry said, "or, hopefully, nothing will be done."

That night, we heard that the twenty-seven inmates who took part in the protest were being charged with mutiny, the most serious military offense. The image of these guys, facing the electric chair for singing "We Shall Overcome," sent shock waves throughout the community.[1]

The Summer Olympics started on October 12, in Mexico City. The games were boycotted by thirty-two African nations in protest of South Africa's participation.

On the eighteenth, US athletes Tommie Smith and John Carlos disrupted the games by performing the black power salute during the playing of "The Star Spangled Banner" at their medal ceremony.

After the Presidio 27 incident of October 11–14, thing quieted down at the base. I continued to work with Jerry, Ron, and Mark, and had met others who knew people living outside the base. Eventually, I made my way off base on the weekends, and found one house a virtual beehive of anti-war activity. These people were devoting their time and energy to stopping the war, by organizing protests and rallies. It was the first time since I had been drafted that I was meeting face-to-face with the people who thought like I did, and were doing

---

1   Author's note: The outcome of the trial saw several of these men receive sentences of fourteen, fifteen, and sixteen years each, to be served at Leavenworth, Kansas. They were eventually released in the spring of 1970, after serving a year and a half. They were released because of constant pressure by the public as well as the media.

something about it. Soon, I was helping out by answering calls and relaying messages within the city.

On October 31, President Johnson announced a total halt of US bombing raids in North Vietnam. On November 5, Richard Nixon won the presidential election by defeating Hubert Humphrey by a slim margin. A couple of weeks later, on November 14, a nation-wide "Turn In Your Draft Card Day" was declared, with rallies and protests on many college campuses.

Jerry, with whom I had worked since September, was finally discharged from the Army. His replacement was another GI who had been injured in Vietnam, and was now serving out the rest of his term at the Presidio. Ron and Mark were still here, and the weather was rapidly changing, with cooler, foggier evenings.

One weekend, while staying at one of the anti-war houses, I was given an unexpected gift. It was a stack of blank leave papers, the official document used by GIs when they are on leave, and each one was good for thirty days. I was given enough for five years.

"It's a reward for helping us out," they said. "All you have to do is type in the name and rank of an officer and sign it. Then, when you are asked to produce a draft card, give them one of these."

I could not believe my eyes, as the relevance of the gift began to slowly sink in.

I could now go anywhere and know that I was safe from being arrested for not producing a draft card. Since my time at the Presidio was nearing three months, I realized that my name was going to be called any day now. On December 10, I decided it was time to make plans for going back to Miami. I phoned my mother and asked her to send me the money to pay for a plane ticket home.

"Are they letting you come home for Christmas?" she asked. "Or are you running away?"

I wanted to tell her the truth, but I thought it was best to tell her that I was being given a month's leave because of Christmas. She accepted my story and told me that she would send the money.

I planned everything so that I would spend the weekend off base, get my money on Monday, and leave on Tuesday. I decided not to tell anyone about my leaving, since I had no way of knowing who the informants were.

Everything went as planned, and on Tuesday I said goodbye to the anti-war house, and took a taxi to the airport.

Chapter 5

GOING HOME TO MIAMI

I arrived at Miami International Airport at 6:00 p.m. As I got off the plane, the warm Florida weather was a welcome change from the cool, damp air of San Francisco. Instead of calling my mother to come and get me, I decided to walk for a while. When I arrived at my house, I knocked on the door, and my mother opened it slightly.

"Who is it?" she asked.

"It's me, Mom. I'm home."

She opened the door and told me to hurry and get inside. I gave her a hug and I could tell that she was worried about something.

"What's the problem?" I asked.

"They're here," she said, "they've been watching the house since yesterday."

"Who's here?" I asked.

"The FBI," she said, her voice trembling. "They were here last night."

"How do you know it was the FBI?" I asked.

"Because I went out and asked them for some ID," she said. "I told them if they didn't show me any, I'd call the police."

She opened the blinds a bit and peered out.

"They're not here now," she said. "I thought you said that you were on official leave?"

I told her the truth about my going AWOL, and she started to cry.

"You can't stay here tonight," she said. "They could show up anytime."

"I'll call Keith, and see if I can stay at his place tonight," I said.

After explaining my situation to Keith, he told me to come over right away. I gave my mother another hug and left.

I went out the back door and walked to Keith's. When I arrived, Keith's mom gave me a hug and I began telling them about the last six months, as well as the FBI watching my house.

"Why, yes," Maria said, "you can stay here, but you must know that Johnny is also staying here with us, so it's either the couch or outside in the shed."

"Let's throw Johnny's stuff out in the shed and give Al the spare room," Keith said.

"I'd like to do that too," Maria said, smiling, "but you know that we can't."

"It's alright," I said, "the shed will be fine."

It was getting late, so Keith and I carried a cot out to the shed. We talked for a while, and after I showed Keith my official leave paper, we agreed to tell Johnny that this was the reason I was home.

"I'm very tired," I said to Keith. "I'll see you in the morning."

The next day, I awoke to Keith's voice outside the shed.

"Hey Al, wake up, coffee's ready." .

I dragged myself out of bed and the two of us went inside. Maria greeted me with her ever-present smile, and poured my coffee.

"Johnny never came home last night," she said. "I wish he would get his own place again."

Just then, Johnny came in and looked at me.

"Hey Al," he said, "I thought you'd be over in 'Nam, killing those gooks by now."

"No," I said, "they screwed up my paper work and gave me a month's leave."

"That's too bad," Johnny said. "I wish I could go."

"He didn't pass their tests," Keith said, laughing, "so they gave him a deferment."

Johnny went over to Keith and threatened to punch him.

"Enough," Maria told him. "Do you want some breakfast?"

"No," Johnny replied, "I'm going to grab a sandwich and go back to my friend's house."

Johnny left and I told Keith and Maria about my plan to call my sisters, starting with the oldest, Ann.

I called and explained my situation to her and asked if I could stay with them.

"Well," she said, "I'd have to ask Norman; he's at work."

"Okay," I said, "but please let me know as soon as possible."

A few minutes later, Ann called back and told me that Norman agreed to let me stay there.

"You'll have to find a ride," she said. "Norm has the car and is working till 5:00 p.m."

"That's alright," I said, "I'll get a ride with Keith. See you soon."

We arrived at Ann's around noon, and Keith decided to come in and meet her.

Ann told me that although she was willing to help me out, she felt uneasy about letting me stay there.

"Do you think the FBI will come here?" she asked.

"I don't think so," I said. "Your last name isn't Glass anymore, so there is no connection there."

After Keith left, I spent the afternoon talking with Ann. She assured me that Norman was against the war, and that I should not feel guilty for doing what I felt was right.

Finally, Norm came home and I told him why I was there. He understood my situation, but reminded me that I would soon have to make a very important decision.

"We can't keep you here forever," he said dryly.

While Ann was preparing dinner, Norm and I drank beer and watched the six o'clock news and learned that the South Vietnamese government, after stalling for months, had finally agreed to join in on the Paris Peace Talks.

During dinner, we talked about the war and how it was affecting the nation. I let them know that they were now helping to end the war, by helping me, and I was truly grateful.

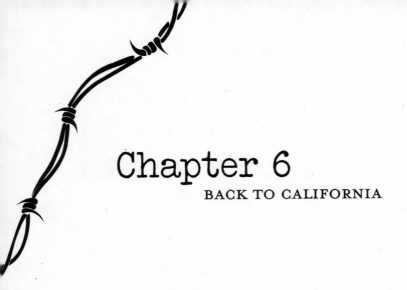

Chapter 6

BACK TO CALIFORNIA

I ended up staying with Ann and Norm for two months, and they finally told me that it was time to think about moving on. I had been talking to Keith about going to the West Coast, so we decided to look into it.

"Just like last time," Keith said, "we will need a better vehicle than my old VW to travel across the country."

We searched the newspaper want ads, for people who wanted their vehicles driven to other cities, and found one that looked promising.

Need driver for transporting 1968 Chrysler station wagon to Sacramento, California. Will pay gas and expenses.

We phoned and arranged to meet with the owner, and by the day's end, had signed all of the necessary papers. It was the perfect car, as it was large enough for one person to sleep in while the other one drove. I called my mother and told her about our plans, and the next day, Keith and I left.

It was February, and Mardi Gras was being held in New Orleans. Leaving Miami, Keith and I decided to drive nonstop to be able to see what it was all about. When we arrived, the streets were full of people drinking and celebrating. We watched as the floats drove slowly by, with people throwing candy and beads to the waiting partygoers. I looked at Keith and told him I had seen enough, so we took off. It was midnight as we drove into the state of Texas. Passing through Beaumont, we ended up on a stretch of road and we were going 100 mph. A few minutes later, a police car raced up behind us, his lights and siren signaling us to pull over.

The cop asked us the usual questions, and then proceeded to tell us that we were speeding and that he was going to write us a ticket. He asked to see some ID, and I produced my driver's license. When he asked for my draft card, I showed him my leave paper.

"So," he said, "you're in the Army."

"Yes, sir, I'm on my way to California, and then possibly to Vietnam."

"Well then," he said, smiling, "give me that ticket back."

He tore it up and said, "Keep the speed down; you'll live longer. Now get out of here."

We thanked him and sped off.

"Wow," I said, these papers have already proven to be useful."

We drove nonstop through the states of New Mexico and Arizona. Then we headed straight for Los Angeles, to where Mike, a friend of ours from Florida, had recently moved. After driving for three days, we needed a place to rest. Since we didn't have his phone number, we called information to get it. Keith called Mike and was told that we could not stay there, because Mike was having marital problems. We decided to keep on going to San Francisco.

It was getting late when we arrived in San Francisco, so we kept going to Sacramento. We got there at 6:00 a.m., too early to call the car's owner, so we found an all-night café and went in to get some much-needed nourishment and coffee.

At 8:00 a.m., I called the owner of the vehicle and told him that we were here. He couldn't believe that it only took us three days to get from Miami to Sacramento.

"I wasn't expecting it for another day or two," he said. "Where are you now?"

We gave him the name of the café, and he told us we were about twenty minutes away from his house. We got the directions and left.

After the owner looked over the car, he brought us into his house and added up our expenses. He paid in cash, and gave us each an extra $50.

"Where are you boys heading to now?" he asked.

"We are going back to San Francisco," Keith said, "so we need to get to the bus depot."

"Oh, I see," he said, "well then get back into the car and I'll take you there."

Soon, we were on the bus heading back to San Francisco.

It was nearly 11:00 a.m. when we got to the bus station. I flashed back to the time I had left Jim and Martha's house and had arrived at this very same station, eight months ago.

We started walking up the same street, and I was trying to remember which direction to go to get to the anti-war house, where I got my leave papers.

Just then, I spotted someone across the street that I thought I had met at the house.

"Come on," I said to Keith, "I think I see a friend over there."

We ran to greet him, and when he saw me he smiled.

"Hi," he said, "how have you been?"

"I'm sorry," I said, "but I don't remember your name."

"That's okay," he said, "I don't remember yours either. I'm John."

Once we had introduced ourselves, I asked him if the house was still going strong.

"They aren't there anymore," he said. "It broke up after Christmas."

"That's too bad," I said, "we are looking for a place to crash until we can find a place of our own."

"I'm staying with some friends," John said, "and you are welcome to come and meet them."

We arrived at an old, three-story house, and from the outside it looked like it could hold two more people, but I was wrong.

"I'm sorry," the owner said, "but we don't really have any more rooms to spare. If you need a place just for tonight, you can have the couches, but that's it."

We thanked him and took him up on his offer to spend the one night. In the morning, we went to a nearby café for breakfast, and started looking in the newspaper for a place to rent. We were informed that cheap rental houses were scarce, and from what we saw in the paper, they were right. Still, we decided that we had to walk around and ask. After an hour of going door to door, we came to the conclusion that we weren't going to find one that was in our budget.

Chapter 7
THE RED-LIGHT DISTRICT

Tired and frustrated, we ended up in the red-light district where there were hookers and drug dealers on every corner, and found a motel that advertised cheap rooms by the day, week, or month. We went in and asked how much for a room by the week. The manager asked us a few questions, and gave us the key. A few elderly people were sitting in the lobby, watching us intently. Keith and I felt terribly out of place, but we had no other choice. As we walked up to the second floor, a few of the motel tenants opened their doors and peeked out at us.

"This is really weird," I said to Keith, "let's hope we don't have to stay here very long."

The room was clean, with two beds and a bathroom. For cooking, there was one electric element, but no oven.

"Looks like we'll be eating out a lot," Keith said.

We were starting to get low on money, and Keith thought of a friend who might be able to help us, Tony, who was attending the University of Alabama.

"I'll call him right now," Keith said.

When he came back from using the one telephone that was located in the hallway, he told me that Tony was going to wire us $500 tomorrow.

"He wants us to send him some marijuana," Keith said. "They can't get anything good to smoke on campus."

"That sounds good," I said. "Let's go find John, and see if he knows anyone who will get us some pot."

We left the motel and went straight for Golden Gate Park. On our way there, I spotted another friend from the Presidio, Lee. We caught up with him and asked him about the marijuana.

"Sure," Lee said, "I can get you a kilo of Mexican for $150. Do you have the money?"

Keith and I counted out the remaining cash we had between us, and gave him the money.

"Meet me back here in the park in one hour," Lee said.

Lee took off in one direction, while Keith and I went to get something to eat.

After an hour, we went back to the park. Lee came back and handed us a package.

"If you want more," Lee said, "it's no problem."

"We'll probably take another one in a few days," Keith said.

"Alright," Lee said, "I'll see you two later."

Keith and I took the kilo back to the motel room and opened it up. To our surprise, someone had hollowed out the middle, and filled it with marijuana seeds.

"I don't believe this!" Keith said. "Your friend ripped us off!"

"No, I don't think so," I said. "It's the people that Lee got it from, or even whom they got it from. Anyway, let's roll a joint and head back to the park to find Lee." After reaching the park, we smoked the joint and waited for Lee to show up. I finally spotted him and we made our way over to show him what we had discovered.

"That's incredible," Lee said, staring at the pot. "I'll take it back right away and get you another one."

In twenty minutes, Lee came back with a new kilo.

"Here," he said, "this one is okay. I opened it up in front of them because they were quite surprised also."

After seeing that this kilo was indeed alright, we thanked Lee and took off.

The next day, we mailed the kilo to Alabama, and called Tony to tell him what we had done. Tony was happy to hear that his supply of pot was starting, and that he could use one a week, maybe more.

When we returned to the motel, and the manager asked us if we had any luck in finding a place.

"No," I said, "but we are going to keep trying."

After our first week was up, we began to realize that we were never going to find a house to rent that was in our budget, so we paid for another week at the motel.

One evening, there was a knock on the door. A tall man, clean-cut and well dressed, stood before me. He introduced himself as Jack, a friend of Professor Richard Adams of Miami, and that he was here looking for Keith.

Keith came out of the bathroom and asked who I was talking to.

"There's some guy here that claims he knows you," I said.

Keith came to the door and Jack introduced himself all over again. After thinking for a moment, Keith remembered Professor Adams, and told Jack to come in.

"I've flown here from Miami to score some hash and LSD," Jack explained, "and I was told that you might be able to help me out."

"We sure can," Keith said, "how much money are you talking about?"

"Three thousand dollars," Jack said.

"Wow," I said, "that might take a while."

"I'd like to get it as soon as possible," Jack said. "I'll give you the address and phone number of the hotel I'm staying at. Call me as soon as you can arrange to do the deal, alright? Preferably here."

After he left, Keith and I sat there, totally stunned.

"We have to find Lee and tell him that we also need some acid and hash," I said.

We found Lee, who told us his contact was for pot only.

We thanked him and reminded him that his supply of pot was still needed.

After this, we spent a few more hours in the park asking complete strangers if they could help us out.

"I don't like this," I said to Keith. "This is too big of a deal to ask of anybody, especially here in the park."

"I agree," Keith said. "We're not going to find anybody here. Let's go back to the motel and see if Jack has left any messages."

There wasn't anything from Jack, so we decided to go back to the park for one last try. It was getting late in the day, and not one person we asked had anything close to what we needed. We decided to call it a day and went to the steak house for dinner.

After dinner, we went back to the motel, and this time the manager handed us a note. It was from Jack, asking us to meet him at a certain restaurant at 7:30. We went directly there, and saw Jack waiting for us at the entrance.

"Hi there," Jack said, "can I buy you guys some dinner?"

"No, thanks," I said, "we've already had dinner."

"Well then, come on in and I'll buy you a beer. Have you been able to get the stuff?"

"No," I said, "we could only get about half."

"That's alright," he said with a smile, "I found a couple of dealers last night who can produce the required amount."

"How did you do that?" Keith asked. "You just got here."

"You just have to look in the right place," Jack said. "I'd like to close the deal tonight, at your motel, say around ten."

Keith and I looked at each other, dumbfounded.

"Yeah, sure," I said, "but don't make it too late or the manager will think that something isn't right."

"Okay, I'll be there around 9:30," Jack said. "Want another beer?"

When Keith and I left the restaurant, we went straight back to our motel room.

An hour later, Jack knocked on our door. He came in and sat on the bed and started explaining how it was all going to happen.

"When the two of them come in," he began, "I want you two to be sitting in those chairs over there, which will leave the other bed for them to sit on. They will take the drugs out of their briefcase and place them on the bed. Since there will be a few hundred hits of LSD, I would like you both to try one, is that okay with you?"

"I guess so," I said nervously, "it is the only way to tell if it's any good or not."

"Okay," Jack said, "once you have started to get off on the acid, simply let me know. I'll be checking out the weight of the hash, and when I'm satisfied, I'll close the deal by giving them the money. They'll count it, and then go. Are you sure you're both up to this?"

"We understand," I said. "This shouldn't take too long; I hope it's good acid."

It was 9:45 when we heard a knock on the door. Keith got up and let them in. Two men, wearing complete leather outfits, walked in. They went over to the bed and placed their briefcase on it and without saying a word, opened it.

Bags full of colored pills were tossed onto the bed, and saran-wrapped bricks of hash followed.

Jack looked at Keith and me and motioned us to take a hit each. We went over and grabbed a bag of pills and took one out. After swallowing them, we sat back on our bed and waited. Within fifteen minutes, Keith and I agreed that it was indeed acid, and gave Jack the thumbs up.

Jack smiled and opened his briefcase. He took out a wad of bills and handed it to one of the dealers, who quickly counted it. Then they stood up and went to the door.

"It's been a pleasure doing business with you," one of them said, "have a good evening."

It was all over in less than a half hour, and by this time, Keith and I were getting higher and higher.

Jack was most appreciative as he took two $50 bills out of his wallet and gave us each one. He then reached for a bag of acid and took out ten hits of acid, and placed them on the table. Next, he unwrapped one of the bricks of hash and broke a chunk off.

"Here you are," he said, "this is for helping me out. I'll tell the professor that you did all of the work in arranging this deal. Take care, thank you, and I'll see you later."

After Jack left, we grabbed the pills and hid them in the closet. We looked at the hash, and agreed to go outside and try it. The manager smiled as we made our way through the lobby. Once we were in a safe spot, we took out our homemade pipe and began inhaling the pungent and wonderful-tasting hash. We ended up going to the park, and didn't get back to the motel until 3:00 a.m. Thoroughly exhausted from our ordeal, we hid the hash and then fell fast asleep.

It was 7:00 a.m. when I was awoken by loud knocking on our door. Still in a daze, I got up, and without asking who it was, opened the door.

I was grabbed and thrown back down onto the bed. There were five of them, two in police uniforms and three in plain clothes. They handcuffed Keith and me, and began to search our room.

"Where are the drugs?" asked the one in charge.

"I don't know what you are talking about," I said.

They kept up their search and then one of them found the seeds from the first kilo of pot. When one of the policemen looked in my suitcase, he found my stack of leave papers and held them up.

"Hey Sarge," he said, "look what I found."

The sergeant, in plain clothes, came over and looked at the papers.

"Which one of you owns these?" he asked.

Keith and I played dumb and didn't say a word.

"You're both under arrest," the sergeant said. "Come on, let's get out of here."

They took us downstairs and through the lobby, which by now was full of curious onlookers. I saw the manager, who was watching us from behind the front desk, and this time he wasn't smiling.

Keith and I were escorted to the city jail. They separated us into different rooms and began asking me about what went on the night before.

"We have word that some people came up to your room last night," the sergeant said, "and I want you to tell me what happened."

"I don't know what you are talking about," I said. "What are we being arrested for?"

He then held up the stack of leave papers, as well as the one that was found in my wallet.

"Are you in the military?" he asked.

"No. sir, I'm not in the military."

"Well then," he said, "we have a problem. Just being in possession of these papers is a federal offense, so why don't you tell me how they ended up in your suitcase?"

"I don't know anything about those papers," I said.

The sergeant, frustrated by my lack of cooperation, left the room. When he returned, he told me that I was going to be taken to another holding cell. I asked to make a phone call, but my request was denied.

Once inside the cell, I saw the sergeant talking with two military policemen. They were wearing the same type of uniform as the ones who took me from the Reno, Nevada county jail to the Presidio wore. They came over to my cell and informed me that I was to go with them. They handcuffed me, and led me outside to their van. We arrived at another building that had various military branch insignias painted on the outside. Once inside, they put me in a wire cage with one bench.

"Sit down," they said.

One of the MPs stood in front of the cage and asked me a few questions. He was looking at my Florida driver's license and asked me if it was indeed mine.

"Yes, it is," I said.

"Well then," he said, "why don't we start at the beginning? At the motel, the police found you in possession of some interesting papers, one of which was filled out with your name on it. Tell me now, what outfit are you in, and are you AWOL?"

"No, sir," I said as politely as possible, "I'm not in the military, and you have no reason to hold me."

"Alright," he said, "if you want to play hardball, then we'll just keep you until you are ready to tell the truth."

He opened the door and told me to come with him. We went through a narrow hallway, down to a room that had a door with a small opening with bars on it. He took the handcuffs off and opened the door.

"Get in," he snarled, "and when you are ready to tell us the truth about your status, give me a call," and he slammed the door shut.

Once he was gone, I went to the opening to try to hear what they were saying, but I could hear nothing. I turned around and saw that my new home was a four-by-eight dungeon, and the smell from its previous inhabitants was overwhelming. There wasn't a toilet or source of water, and I was beginning to feel desperate. I called out to the MPs, and one of them came to the door.

"Are you ready to talk?" he asked.

"No," I said, "but I have to go to the bathroom, and I could also use a drink of water."

He just laughed and told me to use the drain, like everyone else before me. It had been

used a lot and it was making me feel sick to my stomach. It gave me the idea that if I told them I needed medical attention, they would have to take me to the hospital. Then, once I was outside, I could make a run for it. I flashed back to the Presidio stockade incident, where the inmate was shot when he tried to run away, and quickly dismissed that idea.

By now, I was feeling like my whole world was falling apart again. I sat down on the cleanest part of the floor and realized that I would probably end up back in the Presidio, only this time it would be the stockade. A couple of hours passed, then I heard both of the MPs coming down the hallway.

"Hey you," one of them said, opening up the door, "we're getting tired of waiting."

I looked up at them, trying to invoke some sense of pity from them, but all I got was the two of them tapping their batons on their thighs.

"Tell us the truth," they said, "or we'll get it out of you one way or another."

At this point, I could tell that they were not bluffing, so I decided to tell them the truth.

"Alright, I'll tell you everything," I said, "just get me out of this cell."

They laughed at their success and told me to come with them. They put me back into the wire cage and started asking questions. After they were convinced of my story, they told me that I would be taken to the Presidio as soon as possible.

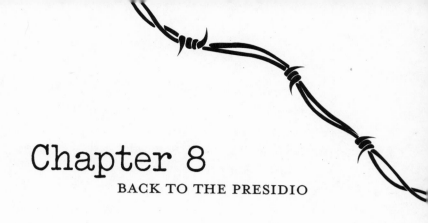

Chapter 8
BACK TO THE PRESIDIO

After three hours of waiting, two more MPs came and led me out in handcuffs to their van. It was now the beginning of March, 1969, seven months since my first visit to the Presidio, and the feeling of déjà vu was overwhelming. I was put in the same room as before, while my paperwork was processed. After an hour, I was told to go into another room, and I found myself standing in front of the same captain who interviewed me the first time.

"So," the captain said, "I see that you were here from September to December, 1968, is that correct?"

"Yes, sir," I said, "it is."

"Why did you leave?"

"I did not want to go to Vietnam, sir."

"You didn't want to go," the captain repeated. "Do you think that is up to you to decide?"

"Yes, sir," I said, "it's definitely my decision."

"So, you don't want to serve your country?" he asked.

"I'd love to serve my country, sir, but not in this war. I can't see any reason for being there."

The captain then proceeded to give me a lecture on the values of freedom, and how each American is responsible for fighting for those freedoms. I responded by telling him what I thought about the war.

"Sir, we cannot defeat communism, because it's an ideology, and it's also not like Hitler trying to take over the world. Personally, I think we are doing more harm than good. It has been going on for over three years now, so why haven't our superior forces won this war?"

The captain sat back in his chair and smiled.

"You remind me of the protestors and intellectuals who don't know anything," he said.

I sighed and stood there, knowing I was never going to convince him otherwise.

He went back to looking at my records, and then he stood up.

"I'm going to give you one more chance to come to your senses and realize that your country needs you now, more than ever," he said. "You are hereby confined to the regular barracks to await your new orders. Should you go AWOL again, you will be placed in the stockade. Do you understand?"

"Yes, sir," I said solemnly, while trying to keep my enthusiasm hidden.

I walked out of his room, totally stunned by his decision. The sergeant told me to report to the supply building, and get my new set of fatigues. Afterward, I headed for the barracks. It was like a homecoming, and soon I spotted Ron, my buddy from the cleanup crew.

"Hey, Ron," I yelled, "how's it going?"

"Hey, Al," he said, "where have you been?"

We spent the next hour telling each other our stories, and they were eerily similar. After this, I began thinking of Keith, and decided to call the city jail and ask if he was there. He wasn't, so I decided to call the motel and ask the manager if he knew anything. The manager acted as though he had never heard of us, and hung up. I didn't know who else to call, so I went back to focusing my energy on being back at the same place I started.

Life at the Presidio was the same as before, only this time I wasn't put on a work crew. I also found out that after the shooting of the inmate on October 11, things had quieted down, but the population of the stockade had reached its maximum number of inmates.

Maybe that's why the captain didn't put me in there, I thought to myself.

The morning formations were the same, and every day a couple of names were called out. The month of March went by quickly, and I was kept busy doing small chores, like working in the kitchen, and keeping the barracks clean.

April and May flew by, and I sensed the tension on the base was increasing. This was due to the fact that they weren't calling out names during the morning formations any more. Previously, the Army would call out your name, and give you two weeks of leave before you had to report. Now they realized that in those two weeks, guys were going AWOL. Sometimes, a couple of MPs would come just before lights out, serve someone their new orders, and take him away immediately. One guy resisted so strongly that they called up a few more MPs, who dragged him downstairs and placed him into a waiting van. I never saw him again.

By now, Ron and I were constantly aware of the possibility of an informant. Someone was planted inside our barracks to obtain information about anyone planning to leave the Presidio. One evening as I was washing dishes, one of the new guys, Tom, asked me a question that I will never forget.

"Do you want to go to Canada?" he asked.

I stopped washing and looked at him.

"Are you an informant?" I asked.

"No way," he said, laughing, "I'm not an informant."

"Canada," I said. "Why do you want to go there?"

"I heard that they are letting guys who are objecting to the war come and stay there," Tom said.

"I've never heard that before," I said, "but then again I don't know anything about Canada."

Tom and I agreed to talk more about his idea, but only when we were sure that no one was listening. We finished washing the dishes, and went back to the barracks. I told Tom that since he was new to the Presidio, he did not really know about the situation with an informant inside the barracks.

By this time, Ron came over to where we were and joined in on the conversation.

"Do you know who this informant is?" Tom asked.

"I have an idea," I said, "but I'm not a hundred percent sure."

Just then, the person I suspected showed up. He came right up to us and introduced himself.

"Hi," he said, "I'm Bob, from Oregon. Where are you guys from?"

The three of us obliged him with our answers, and Bob told us that he had just arrived. He told us the story of how he ended up in the Presidio, but it didn't make much sense. I was now sure that his guy was indeed put in here to get information regarding anyone's plans for leaving. The whole time he was acting a bit nervous, and he eventually left to go over to the bowling alley. The three of us joked about his behaviour, and we felt sorry for him being put in this situation.

Over the next few days, the more Tom and I talked, the more I began to trust him. Tom's reason for being at the Presidio was both amazing and unbelievable.

"I'm from Utah, where I enlisted in the Army," Tom said. "I decided that after my basic training, I would try out for the Special Forces, like the Green Berets. Things were going smoothly until my wife, who was almost eight months pregnant, began showing signs of giving birth prematurely. When I asked for some time off, they refused, saying they had a schedule to keep, and that my training should continue with no interruptions. After I found out that my wife had gone into the hospital, I left on the weekend without telling my instructors, and I was planning to be back on Monday. When they found out I had left, they called my parents and asked them if I was there. My parents, thinking that I was on a planned leave, told them the truth. They came on Sunday and arrested me for being AWOL. They handcuffed me, in front of my parents, and brought me here to the Presidio."

"That's incredible," I said. "So now you have had a change of mind and want to leave?"

"Yes," Tom said, "I cannot fight for a country that treats its citizens like they treated me. Ever since the war started, my parents kept telling me that we were there to stop communism, but now that I've had time to think about everything, I can see that it is a futile war, and I don't want any part of it."

"What do you know about Canada?" I asked.

"When I was a kid, my father, who was in the mining business in Utah, was asked to go up to Saskatchewan to help start a potash mine. We ended up moving there, and I went to school there for three years."

"Interesting," I said. "All I know about Canada is from a TV show that I watched as a kid. It was about a Canadian policeman and his dog, riding around in a sled in ten feet of snow."

"Oh, yes," Tom said, laughing, "it was called 'Sergeant Preston of the Yukon;' I remember that one."

Over the next few days, Tom and I talked more about leaving the Presidio.

We came to the conclusion that we would need a ride off base, as well as someplace safe to stay. I talked to Ron about coming with us, but he declined.

"If you guys need a ride off base," Ron said, "I think I can help with that."

"How would you do that?" I asked.

"My girlfriend comes to visit me when she has time off from work," Ron said, so when you are ready to go, I'll get her to come here."

"Sounds good to me," I said, "now we just have to figure out where we are going to stay off base."

I thought about Keith and wondered if he was still here in San Francisco. I decided to call his mother in Florida to see if she had heard anything from him. She told me that he was still in San Fransisco, and she gave me his address. I then headed over to the bowling alley to tell Tom the good news. When I got there, the informant was there, talking to Tom. I went up to them and asked to speak to Tom privately.

"Tom," I said, "I just found out that my good friend Keith is still in San Fransisco. I haven't talked to him yet, but I know we can stay with him until we figure out a way to get to Canada."

It was now June 12, and the weather wasn't the only thing heating up in the Presidio. The MPs were still waking guys up at night and taking them away. I called Keith and explained our situation.

"Wow, man," Keith said, "it's good to hear your voice. When are you planning to come here?"

"As soon as possible," I said. "I'll call you and let you know."

Tom and I found Ron and asked him about his girlfriend.

"I just talked to her, she's coming tomorrow night," he said.

"That's good to hear," I said, "can you let her know what we are planning to do?"

"Sure," Ron said, "I'll call her now."

With the informant hanging around us like a lost puppy, we had to make sure that he wouldn't be around the barracks when it came time to leave. We asked a couple of friends to keep him busy while we made our escape.

The next day, I called Keith and told him that we would be there that night.

Ron's girlfriend showed up just after 7:00 p.m., and after an hour or so, we grabbed our belongings and went to her car. The informant was kept busy at the bowling alley, so we had no problem leaving. As we drove outside the gates of the Presidio, I prayed that I would never see that place again.

Chapter 9
LEAVING THE PRESIDIO

We arrived at Keith's apartment at 9:00 p.m., and when he opened the door, I gave him a hug and started to cry tears of joy.

"Hey, man," Keith said, "why are you crying?"

"I'm okay," I said. "It's been really tense this past week, and I'm so glad to see you."

I introduced Tom and the three of us went into the kitchen.

"I knew you were coming," Keith said, "so I rolled a joint."

I looked at Tom, and asked him if he had ever smoked pot.

"No," Tom said, "I've never tried it, but I would like to."

While the three of us passed the joint around, Keith began to explain what had happened to him after we were busted in the motel room.

"Since they only found the seeds," Keith said, "they had to release me."

"What about the ten hits of acid and the hash?" I asked.

"That's a mystery," Keith said. "Apparently they never found it. I went back to the motel to search our room, but the manager told me that it had already been cleaned and rented out. Anyway, I've already scored some more pot and acid. This town really rocks."

We talked for another hour or so, and then we all started yawning.

"I'll get you guys some blankets," Keith said. "See you in the morning."

The next day, we talked about our plan to go to Canada. Keith got a map of North America and spread it out on the kitchen table. Canada was a huge country, and Tom showed us approximately where he and his parents had lived in Saskatchewan. After looking at the US cities on the border, Tom mentioned the fact that even though his immigration status was still good, I did not have any valid reason for going across the border.

"It would be terrible if they let me through, but stopped you and returned you to the Army," Tom said.

"Well then," I said, "that means that we can't go across where there is a legal border crossing with immigration agents."

We kept looking at the map, and I pointed to a place in northern Idaho.

"How about here?" I asked. "There's a lake and a river that goes into Canada; we could use that as our guide."

"You won't see anybody there," Keith joked, "and you better get ready for a long walk."

"Yes," Tom agreed, "who knows what kind of terrain is there."

"We need a better map," I said, "one that shows us if there are any roads."

Keith went to the nearest gas station and came back with another map.

"Here," he said, "this one shows all of the roads that are close to where you are thinking of going."

"There's Highway 3," I said, pointing, " it's just on the other side of the border, close to where this river ends in Canada."

We spent the day tossing around other ideas, and came to the conclusion that we would sleep on it.

Tom suggested that if we were going to hike our way into Canada, that we would need sleeping bags and a tent.

"I can probably get them from a friend in Salt Lake City, my hometown."

Keith made some phone calls regarding transportation to that part of the US.

"There aren't any airports that far north in Idaho," he said. "They suggested taking a Greyhound bus from Salt Lake City, which goes to Helena, Montana, and then westward to Coeur d'Alene, Idaho."

We found Coeur d'Alene on the map, and agreed that we would then have to hitchhike or take another bus to Sandpoint, Idaho.

"What a trip," I said. "There's got to be an easier way."

Tom sat back and looked at me.

"It's the only way that we can ensure our getting in without getting caught," he said. "On the other hand, we could take our chances and try to go through customs the regular way."

"No," I said, "I like the idea of going up through northern Idaho. We can do it."

"Alright then," Tom said, "I'll make the call to my friend and get the camping gear together."

"What about our plane trip to Salt Lake City?" I asked. "We don't have any money."

"Relax," Keith said, "I found out how much it costs, and I can cover it."

The three of us spent the rest of the day listening to music and watching TV. One song by the Chambers Brothers, "Time Has Come Today," became our appropriate theme song. I was also interested in seeing the six o'clock news, to find out what was happening with the war. President Nixon was telling the people that the US was continuing its peace talks with the North Vietnamese, and he announced his plan to withdraw US ground forces, eventually handing over control to the South Vietnamese forces. On the other hand, the number of anti-war protests was also growing, saying the Nixon administration was planning to escalate the bombing of North Vietnam.

It was now June 16, ten days before my twenty-second birthday. One final thing that was needed was some decent clothes, so we headed to the nearest thrift store and found a couple of suits and ties. We were now ready to leave San Francisco and our flight to Salt Lake City was booked for the following day.

"Hey Tom, where are we going to stay in Salt Lake City?" I asked.

"That's a good question," Tom said. "We might have to get a motel room for a few days, depending on how long it takes to get our camping gear from my friend."

Again, Keith came up with enough cash to keep us going.

The next morning, we called a cab and waited. Keith then handed me a couple of hits of acid.

"You can do these whenever you like," he said, "and call me when you get to Salt Lake City."

The cab arrived and we took off. On the way to the airport, I showed the acid to Tom, who just smiled.

Just as we got to the airport, I decided to ingest one of the LSD tablets. Tom watched me and I offered the other one to him. He took it, and to my surprise, put it in his mouth and swallowed it.

"This is going to be one hell of trip," he said, smiling.

We made it onto the plane, and began one of the most interesting "trips" of my life.

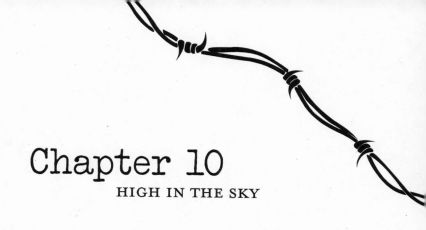

Chapter 10

HIGH IN THE SKY

We found our seats on the plane and I looked at my watch. A short, one-hour flight and we would be in Salt Lake City, Tom's hometown. I could feel the LSD taking effect as we taxied down the runway. I smiled as we raced along, feeling the anxiety of taking off. Once we were airborne, I told Tom I was going to the washroom.

I made my way to the rear of the plane, and entered the tiny room. My senses were now working overtime as the drug made its way through my system. I did my thing and got up to leave. I decided to look at the mirror, and I fell into a deep state of hypnosis. My face began talking to me, and as I stood there, motionless, I started talking back to the face in the mirror. Suddenly, I heard loud knocking on the door. I realized what had happened, and opened the door. The flight attendant was standing there, and she asked me if everything was okay.

"Yes," I said, my face red with embarrassment, "everything's fine."

As I left the washroom, I could see that there were a few people waiting in line. I made my way back to my seat, where Tom was, and sat down.

"What were you doing in there?" Tom asked.

I looked at my watch and saw that I must have been in there for at least fifteen minutes.

"Wow," I said, "that was weird. How are you doing?"

"I feel hot and sweaty," Tom said, "and I feel overdressed."

"I know what you mean," I said, "but don't worry, we'll be there soon."

We tried talking about what we were going to do once we got to the airport, but it was obvious that Tom could not think straight. I gave up and began listening to the people, who were seated behind us, laughing hysterically. I turned my head and saw that it was a young couple in their twenties. I listened for a while, and then I decided to ask them a question.

"Excuse me, are you two going to Salt Lake City?"

"Yes," the guy said. "We're just coming back from our honeymoon in San Francisco. Why do you ask?"

"I couldn't help but hear you guys laughing," I said, "and it sounds as though you are high on something."

They looked at each other and then started laughing again.

"You're right about that," he said. "It's just some Seconal that we got in San Francisco. We were told it would calm us down for our flight home."

"Alright," I said, "I'm sorry to bother you."

I turned back and looked at Tom. He was looking at me like I was an alien or something.

"I thought you were going to ask them for a ride," Tom said.

I thought about what Tom had just said, and realized that was exactly why I started the conversation in the first place. I got up my courage and turned around to face the newlyweds.

"I'm sorry to bother you again," I said, "but my friend and I are both stoned on LSD, and we need a place to stay tonight."

They looked at me strangely, and started laughing.

"I'm Steve," he said, "and this is my wife, Sally. I have a friend who is coming to the airport to pick us up. If he brings a van, then you can come with us."

I sensed that Steve was someone I could trust, even in our predicament.

"Steve," I said, "I'm going to tell you something that I hope won't offend you."

"What's that?" Steve asked.

"Tom and I are in the Army, and we are on our way up to Canada. We are deserting the military to avoid going to Vietnam."

"Wow," Steve said, "that's incredible. Yes, we will gladly help you out."

I thanked them and turned back around.

"Did you hear that?" I asked Tom.

Tom just smiled and asked me how much longer was his trip going to last.

"Maybe an hour or so, I said trying to ease his anxiety, not much longer."

I looked at my watch and saw that we were going to land in twenty minutes.

We landed at 1:15, and Steve told us to follow him.

"My friend owns a car dealership," Steve said. "There he is now, in the white van."

I nudged Tom and whispered, "How does it feel to be home?"

Tom just smiled and didn't say a word, as we piled into the van. Steve explained to us that they lived in a group home shared by a dozen college students. As we arrived at their house, which was in a well-to-do neighbourhood, Tom kept looking around, like he knew where we were. The five of us got out and went in. After Steve checked the place out, he told us that he and Sally had to go over to Sally's parents' house.

"Make yourself at home," Steve said, "and if anyone else comes in, just tell them that Sally and I are back and that we've gone over to her parents' home."

"Okay," I said, "thanks for everything."

I looked at Tom, who was sitting in the living room. Because we had the whole place to ourselves, Tom and I changed clothes and put on some music.

"This is great," Tom said. "I'm glad you asked them for a ride, because I couldn't speak a word."

We were relaxing in the front room when I heard someone open the front door. I tensed up, and looked at Tom. Three people came in and glanced at us on their way to the kitchen.

"Hey Tom," I whispered, "do you remember the names of the newlyweds?"

"No," Tom said, "that's funny that I can't remember them, it must be this damn drug."

The more I tried to remember the names, the more confused I got. I could hear the three people talking, and realized that they were trying to figure out who we were.

I got up and went into the kitchen and introduced myself.

"I'm sorry," I stammered, "but my friend and I were brought here by ... I can't remember their names ... but we were on the same flight from San Francisco as they were, and they told us that we could stay here ... and they just went over to her parents' place ... yes, they're at her parents' place ... please call them if you don't believe me."

The three looked at each other and one of them asked, "Do you mean Steve and Sally?"

"Yes!" I shouted, "That's exactly who I mean."

He called Sally's parents to confirm my story, and after hearing her voice, he hung up and welcomed us into their house. Then, the three of them took off, saying they were going over to another friend's house.

Tom and I were getting hungry, so we decided to check out the refrigerator. It reminded me of Keith's—empty—so we decided to call for a delivery of Chinese food.

Just then, Steve and Sally returned.

"Hi," Steve said, "how's it going?"

"Fine," I said. "We have just ordered some Chinese food. Won't you join us?"

"No, thanks," Steve said. "We just came back to change clothes and then we are going out to dinner with Sally's parents. We might not get back until late, so Sally will get your bedding together before we go. Hope you don't mind the couches."

Tom and I thanked them for helping us out. The food arrived and we finished it off in record time. A couple more people came in and they introduced themselves to Tom and me.

"Hi, I'm Gary, and this is Joe. Steve told us about you guys," Gary said, "and that you are heading up to Canada."

"Yes, we are," I said, "but first we have to get some camping gear together."

"Well then," Joe said, pulling out a joint, "I guess you'll have time to share this with us."

I stared in amazement, thinking that I would never see one again for a long time.

"Perfect," I said. "We're just coming down off an acid trip."

"Do you have any more?" Gary asked.

"I'm sorry," I said, "but I don't."

We went into the kitchen to light up the joint, and soon we were sharing stories about our lives.

"We're in college right now," Joe said, "and hoping that the war will end soon."

"I too was in college for a year and a half," I said, "right at the beginning of the war in 1965. I ended up getting drafted because my grades slipped below a C average."

After sharing the joint, Joe and Gary left to visit some of their friends.

Steve phoned to tell us that they were going to stay at Sally's parents' house for the night, and that we should make ourselves comfortable.

"Hey Tom, are you going to call your friend about the camping gear?" I asked.

"Not tonight," Tom said. "I'll do it tomorrow."

The next day, Tom called his friend, Jeff.

"Jeff," Tom said, "did you get the gear I was asking for?"

"Yes," Jeff said, "it's at my girlfriend's parents' house. You remember Nancy."

"Oh yes, of course I do," Tom said. "Can we get the gear tonight?"

"Yes, you can, but what's the rush?" Jeff asked.

"We are planning to go to Canada as soon as possible," Tom said. "There's no reason to stay here any longer. One more thing, please don't mention any of this to my parents."

"I won't," Jeff said. "I'll call Nancy and let her know you're coming tonight."

"Thanks, Jeff," Tom said. "I'll let you know when I'm in Canada."

I could tell that this was the moment of truth for Tom. His decision to leave his country, his parents, and his wife, were all coming to a head. After he hung up, he went into the living room to be by himself.

I went in and asked him if he was still into going to Canada.

"Yes, I've made my decision to go," he said, "and I'm going to help you get there too."

"I don't think I could make this trip by myself," I said, "and I'm really glad that I met you in the Presidio. I also believe that we are making the right decision."

After talking with Tom, I called the bus depot and got the departure times for leaving Salt Lake City, as well as the connecting routes for our destination of Coeur d'Alene, Idaho. It was going to be a fifteen-hour trip that would see us leave at 5:00 p.m. and arrive in Idaho at 8:00 a.m. the next day.

That night we walked to Nancy's parents' house and grabbed the gear: two sleeping bags, two backpacks, and one two-person tent. Then we went back to Steve's house.

Steve called and I told him about our plans. He told me that he was happy to have been of some help, and he wished us all the luck in the world.

We left the next day.

Chapter 11
GOING TO IDAHO

June 19, 1969

We boarded the bus for the fifteen-hour trip to Idaho. I watched nervously as Tom was about to leave his home state of Utah. If he was ever going to back out of going to Canada, this would be the time to do it. The bus driver closed the door, and slowly drove away.

Tom stared out the window. I knew that he was thinking about his wife and his parents, and I tried to imagine what he was going through. The driver informed us that our first stop would be Ogden, Utah. Tom turned away from the window and looked at me.

"That's where my grandparents live," he said solemnly. "I wish I could call them."

"We'll be in Canada in a few days," I said, "then you can call them, and I'll call my parents."

"Yeah," Tom said, "I guess your right about that."

He took out the paperback that he had taken from Steve's place, and began reading. I could tell that it was his way taking his mind off of what we were doing.

Soon, we arrived in Ogden and Tom looked around the depot, hoping to see his grandparents there. I kept quiet, not wanting to upset him. We picked up a few more people, and the bus took off for Logan, which was just below the Idaho border.

"Too bad we aren't going straight up to Coeur d'Alene," I said, looking at my map, "it would sure be quicker."

Tom ignored me and kept reading his book. I took this as a signal to leave him alone. Meanwhile, I was able to accept our trip as the final step of protesting the war. *If everybody did the same thing*, I thought, *the war would surely come to a halt*. I knew this would never happen, but it was a dream that I would always hope for.

After stopping in Logan for a few minutes, we crossed into southeastern Idaho, making stops in Pocatello and Idaho Falls, where we stopped to have supper at the local diner. Then we took off for Helena, Montana. We awoke to the sound of the driver's voice, telling us that we were in Helena, and that we would be here for about twenty minutes.

I looked at my watch and saw that it was exactly 3:00 a.m. I immediately flashed back to the time that I had left Jim and Martha's house in Belmont, California, as it had also been 3:00 a.m. Tom and I got off the bus to stretch our legs, and the cold night air was a definite wake-up call.

"We're in the Rocky Mountains," Tom said, "that's why it's so much colder here."

"I hope we don't have to go over any mountains to get into Canada," I said jokingly.

Tom just smiled and told me that we should be ready to accept any kind of terrain or weather conditions.

"Come on," I said, let's get back into the warm bus."

A few more passengers got on and soon we were on our way to Missoula, Montana.

We arrived in Missoula at 5:00 a.m, and were told our next stop would be the last,

Coeur d'Alene, Idaho. As we made our way into northern Idaho, the morning sun was beginning to shine, and I could now see the rugged land that was all around us.

Coeur d'Alene was a town with a population of about twelve thousand people, and as the bus rolled into the depot, we saw a grocery store.

"We'll have to go there and get a few things for our hike into Canada," Tom said.

We got off the bus and headed straight for the store. Once inside, Tom and I made different suggestions as to what we thought we were going to need for our hike.

"It's going to take at least a few days," Tom said, "so we had better get something that doesn't weigh too much, but will give us enough energy to make it all the way."

"How about we start with breakfast?" I said, smiling, "like bacon and eggs."

"Okay," Tom said, "now lunch and dinner, and also some matches."

For lunch, we decided on getting four cans of soup, two cans of meat, one jar of peanut butter, and one loaf of bread.

"There," I said, "now we need dinner."

Since we didn't have any way of keeping large pieces of meat fresh, or cooking them for that matter, we decided to get things that were already cooked and ready to eat. Once we were finished shopping we stuffed our backpacks with the items and left.

We started walking and asked a man for directions to Sandpoint.

"It's that way," he said, pointing, about forty or fifty miles due north."

We thanked him and started walking again.

"We had better stick out our thumbs," Tom said. "The faster we get there, the better."

Just then, we spotted a police car coming from the opposite direction.

He stared at us as he went by, and I was beginning to feel a bit paranoid.

An old pickup truck came by and stopped. The driver, an elderly man, rolled the passenger-side window down, and told us to throw our backpacks into the back.

"Hurry up," he said, "before the sheriff comes back to check you out."

We got in and he asked us where we were headed.

"Sandpoint," Tom said. "We hear it's good camping up there."

"That's where I'm heading too," the man said. "What are you planning on doing there?"

"We're on summer holidays from college in Utah," Tom said.

"I never made it to college," the man said, "but I do remember when I used to take off for parts unknown myself."

When we arrived at the small town of Dover on the western tip of Lake Pend Oreille, approximately five miles from Sandpoint, Tom said it was where we wanted to get out.

"Okay boys," the man said, "if this is where you want out, then I wish you all the best. Goodbye."

We thanked him and got our things out of the back of the truck. It was now after 10:00 a.m., and we prepared to walk the twenty miles to Coolin, which was at the southern tip of Priest Lake. After walking for nearly an hour, we heard, then saw a vehicle coming toward us.

It was another pickup truck, with a mom and dad and one little girl inside.

"You boys heading for Coolin?" the mother asked.

"Yes," Tom said, "we're going camping there."

Without blinking an eye, the father told us to hop in the back of the truck.

"This is going to save us a few hours of walking," Tom said, smiling.

Once we arrived in Coolin, we asked the father which side of the lake was best for camping.

"The west side," he said, "there are still some areas with picnic tables, and beaches that are great for swimming. Have fun. Oh, and one more thing, you might run into some black bears, so just keep your distance, especially if you see cubs."

Again, we thanked them for their help and took off.

Chapter 12

THE PRIEST LAKE HIKE

Day 1 June 20

"These people don't have a clue as to what we are doing," I said.

"I know," Tom said, "and neither do we."

It made me feel good to know that Tom still had a sense of humour. It was now 11:00 a.m., and we started on our journey into the wilderness, not knowing what lay ahead.

"I'm hungry," I said, "let's eat."

"Not now," Tom said, "let's follow the lake some, and then we'll stop."

We started up the lake, which was about twenty miles long, and made jokes about how we didn't have any weapons for fighting off bears or whatever.

"I know something that we forgot to bring," Tom said.

"What's that?" I asked.

"A container for water," Tom said.

"We don't need a container," I said. "We've got a whole lake to drink from."

"I know that, but it might be difficult to get through all of that bush to get close enough to get a drink.

"Anyway," Tom said, looking at the map, "there's supposed to be a town called Nordman about halfway up the lake, maybe we can pick up a container there."

Tom was right about the thick underbrush on the edge of the lake. Walking along the lake wasn't as easy as we had hoped. The area closest to the lake was also swampy, so we decided to head west until we got to higher and drier ground, but always keeping the lake in sight.

Once we made our way up to where the trees were larger, the walking got easier. There were small hills that kept us going up and down, like a roller coaster, and soon we were getting to the point where we needed some rest and nourishment.

"Alright," Tom said, "let's take a break."

We made sandwiches with the canned meat and then Tom gave me a look.

"I told you we would need a container of water."

We started the walk down to the lake, but as we neared the edge, the ground became wetter and softer. Soon, we were losing our shoes in the mud. I took them off and continued onward. Tom watched as I struggled to keep from sinking into what was now feeling like quicksand. I looked back and he had a big grin on his face.

"What?" I screamed, "Why are you laughing?"

"Come on back, before you get stuck and I have to come in and rescue you," he said.

I was sweating and completely out of breath, so I turned around and headed back.

"We'll just have to keep going until we find a better place to get a drink from," Tom said.

Eventually, we saw an area that was clear enough to try. The ground was still mucky, but there wasn't any thick underbrush. We got our drink and then headed back up to higher ground. It was now 2:00 p.m., and the sun was really taking its toll on us.

"I'd like to go for a swim," I said, wiping the sweat from my brow, "too bad there isn't a dock around here."

Tom ignored my wish and told me to keep walking.

We kept going for another hour and then I spotted a clearing near the edge of the lake.

"Okay," Tom said, "we'll go down there and try to get in your swim."

I raced down to the edge and dove in.

"Come on down!" I yelled. "The water's fine."

Tom came down and dove in.

After washing off the black muck, and feeling recharged, we decided to start our walk again, only this time, we stayed closer to the lake.

"It would be great if someone was to come by with a boat," I said.

"Yes," Tom agreed, "that would be great."

As we walked, we couldn't help but admire the area for its peacefulness and tranquility. We knew that there wasn't going to be anybody showing up, much less in a boat, but still, we had to keep up our spirits somehow. We walked for a few more miles, and soon, it was 5:00 p.m.

"I'm getting hungry," Tom said. "Let's get to the top of this hill and make dinner there."

We made our way to the top, and from there we could see clear across to the other side of the lake. We started to gather some dry twigs for a fire.

All of a sudden, I grabbed Tom's arm.

"Do you hear that?" I asked.

"Hear what?"

"I think I hear a boat," I said.

We both sat in silence, and then Tom heard it too.

"Yes," he said, "I can hear something that sounds like a motor."

We looked in both directions, and then I spotted a boat coming from the north end of the lake.

"There it is!" I shrieked. "And it's heading south."

Tom and I started racing to the edge of the lake.

"That large rock! I shouted. "We have to get out to it!"

I made it down first and thrashed my way through the muck. The rock was large enough so that I could climb up onto it. The boat was in the middle of the lake, and fast approaching. I started screaming and waving my arms frantically. Just as the boat was getting to the point where I thought it was going to pass us, it slowed down and swerved over toward the rock. Tom had made his way over to the rock and I told him the good news. An elderly couple, in a sixteen-foot fiberglass speedboat, slowly approached the rock.

"Hello," the man said cautiously, "are you in trouble?"

"Me and my friend are from Canada," I said, "and now we are heading back."

Tom eventually crawled up onto the rock and the couple looked at each other. They whispered something to each other, and then asked us if we would like a ride to the north end of the lake.

"That would be great," Tom said, "as long as you don't mind a little mud."

They inched the boat closer to the rock, and we jumped in.

"You don't sound Canadian," the man said, looking at me.

I replied that I was tired and that I didn't sound like myself.

"Are you boys hungry?" the woman asked.

"We were just going to make something to eat," Tom said, "when we heard your boat."

The woman then reached into a cooler and grabbed two sandwiches and two colas.

"You boys still have a long hike ahead of you," the man said. "You're lucky we came along."

"We are using the lake and river as our guide," Tom said. "Our map isn't that good."

The man reached into a compartment and took out a map and handed it to Tom.

"You can take this with you," he said. "You'll it need more than I ever will."

Then the man turned the boat around and hit the throttle. It took about thirty minutes to reach the north end of the lake. We made our way to an old dock that was still usable.

"There you go," the man said. "Sorry we can't take you any farther."

"Thank you very much," Tom said. "You've saved us at least a day or two of walking."

We waved goodbye as they sped off.

"Can you believe that?" I said. "And we now have a better map of the area."

Tom scanned the map and pinpointed the spot where we now stood.

"This is definitely the end of Priest Lake," Tom said, "and the river that feeds it goes directly north for a few miles, then a small lake or pond is next. After that, it looks like another river that goes up into Canada. Depending on the terrain, I'd say two more days to get into Canada."

"Sounds good to me," I said. "Let's get going. We've got a few more hours before it gets dark."

We followed the river, and it wasn't long before we spotted a couple of deer. Tom mentioned that he had been taught how to hunt by his father. I told him about my first time with guns in the Florida Everglades.

"Too bad we don't have a rifle now," Tom said. "Venison is truly delicious."

"I've never had venison," I said. "I've only gone hunting once, if you can call it that. I went with a couple of high school friends to the

Everglades, just to shoot at birds, snakes, maybe a rabbit. It all started out with the three of us walking into an area that had tall, over-your-head grass. We had one shotgun, which they gave to me, one Winchester 30-30, and one 357 Magnum handgun. They had warned me to watch out for rattlesnakes and even wild boar. We spread out, keeping each other in sight, and after a while, I got ahead of them. I decided to stop and wait for them, so I made my way over to a small clearing. When I got to the edge of the clearing, I heard the distinct sound of a rattler. I yelled out to the other two and told them what I had heard. They asked me if I could see the snake, and after taking a closer look, I replied, yes, he's right in front of me! 'Shoot him!' was their frantic reply. I lowered the shotgun, pointed it at the snake, and pulled the trigger. When the dust had settled, the snake was totally gone. By that time, my two friends had caught up to me. I looked again at the spot where the snake had been, but didn't see anything."

"You're lucky you didn't get bit," Tom said. "He was warning you by making that rattling sound."

"Yeah, I know that now," I said.

Tom and I kept trading stories while we walked, and after a couple of hours, we reached the small lake. Darkness was coming on fast, so we found a suitable spot for pitching the tent.

As Tom opened up the tent, something sent him reeling backwards.

"What's the matter?" I asked.

"Smell that," he said, pointing to the tent.

As I got closer, the musty odour of a tent that hadn't been used in years sent me back, coughing and choking.

"That is awful," I said. "I think we'll be sleeping under the stars tonight."

"You got that right," Tom said, as he threw the tent on top of a small bush to air it out.

"What about the sleeping bags?" I asked.

Tom opened them and gave me the thumbs up.

"They're okay," he said.

"We're lucky that we have good weather," I said, "otherwise ..."

We got a fire started and agreed to heat some soup. Tom had a small but adequate Swiss Army knife, which he used to open the cans.

"Now, if we only had some spoons," Tom said.

"No problem," I said, as I produced two plastic spoons that I had taken from the general store in Sandpoint.

"Alright," Tom said, "I think the soup is ready."

He slowly lifted the steaming cans of soup from the edge of the fire, using two sticks.

"You act as though you've done this before," I said.

"Oh yes," Tom replied, "I've been on a lot of camping trips in Utah."

We sat around the fire, eating our soup, and telling stories of what it was like to grow up in Florida and Utah.

"I remember going on one trip when I was fifteen, to the Great Smokey National Mountains on the North Carolina-Tennessee border with Donny, a friend of mine, and his parents. It was my first time away from home and we had a great time going down the river in giant inner tubes," I told Tom.

"I was also fifteen when a couple of friends asked me to go camping and skiing," Tom said. "It was great skiing until the last day."

"What happened?" I asked. "Did you break your leg?"

"No," Tom said, "we almost died getting caught in an avalanche. After setting up our tents at the bottom of the mountain, we snowshoed up the mountain, with our skis tied to our backs. Once we got up high enough, we started skiing down, and that's when the mountain started to crumble. There wasn't much we could do except try to outrun it. Luckily for us, we were on the edge of the slide, and we escaped getting totally buried."

As we lay in our sleeping bags, our conversation turned back to our trip.

"We've got enough food for two more days," Tom said.

"I wish we there was some way of knowing where we are," I said.

"Oh well," Tom said, "don't worry about that. Let's just get some sleep so we can get an early start tomorrow."

The Priest Lake Hike
Day 2 June 21

Day two of our hike started out with the sun rising over the mountains. It was 6:00 a.m., and I could tell that it was going to be another hot one. I looked at Tom, who was still sleeping

I wish we had some coffee, I thought to myself, as I got up to look for some wood to start a fire for our bacon and eggs. When I returned with some wood, Tom asked if breakfast was ready.

"Good morning, Tom," I said, "perhaps while I'm getting a fire together, you can figure out how we're supposed to cook, since we don't have a frying pan."

Tom thought about it for a few seconds.

"I know," he said, tossing me his Swiss Army knife. "Take the two soup cans we had last night and remove the ends. Then cut them and flatten them out."

"You know," I said, "that just might work."

After getting the fire started, I found the soup cans and began making frying pans out of them.

Once the fire had built up enough, I let it die down a bit and placed the flattened tins on top. The bacon was next and the strips began sizzling almost immediately. Next, I carefully broke the eggs and placed them between the bacon, which acted like a fence to keep the eggs from running off the sides of the tins.

"This is actually working," I said, feeling proud at my outdoor cuisine skills.

"You remembered spoons," Tom said, smiling, "how about forks?"

"Oh yes," I said, and I went into my pack and found two plastic forks.

Tom and I ate our bacon and eggs without saying a word.

"That was delicious," I said.

"We might as well cook the rest of the bacon now," Tom said. "It isn't going to keep in this weather."

I placed the rest of the bacon on the tin cans, and while we waited for it to cook, we got our things ready for the next leg of our journey. Once Tom was ready he took out the map and looked at it.

"According to our map," Tom said, "this lake is about three to five miles long."

"That's what the people with the boat told us," I said.

"So, it should only take us an hour or so to reach the end of the lake," Tom said. "Then there are two rivers that feed into the lake, and we have to take the one that goes to the right."

The terrain at first was flat, but soon began to turn hilly, with more underbrush and trees. After a half hour of walking, we were both sweating as the temperature kept rising. We made our way upward and once we got to the top, we could see the end of the lake. Larger trees now dotted the landscape, along with mountain ranges with snow-capped peaks.

"I'm hungry," I said, "let's stop for a sandwich."

Tom gave me that look as if to say, "C'mon Allan, we'll eat after we reach the end of the lake."

We were catching our breath, when I saw something that looked like a black bear.

"Tom," I said, pointing off into the distance ahead, "does that look like a black bear to you?"

Tom looked to where I was pointing, and at first he said he couldn't see anything. Then he grabbed my arm and pointed.

"There it is," he said, "yes, it's a black bear alright, and it's a big one."

We stood there, watching the bear, which was about a hundred yards away, when Tom pointed again.

"Look to the left," he said, "I see a couple of cubs."

Tom and I watched the mother as she made her way toward the edge of the lake, her cubs following behind her.

"Let's get going," Tom said. "As long as we keep her to our right, with the wind blowing toward us, she won't catch our scent."

I followed Tom as we started out, keeping a watchful eye on momma bear.

It wasn't long before we were even with her, and it looked like she was in no hurry to leave the spot she was in. Soon, we were at the end of the lake where the two rivers emptied into it.

"We'll have to wade across one river to get over to the one we want to follow," Tom said.

"I'm ready for that," I said. "It'll feel good to cool off."

As we made our way across, we joked about the idea of having to do this in Vietnam, and were both thankful of where we were and what we were doing.

Once we made it to the other side, we sat down for a rest and to dry off. While we rested, we each made a peanut butter sandwich, and I wondered if there were any more bears around. Tom assured me that they wouldn't bother us if we didn't get in their way.

We were now on the east side of the river, the terrain was again flat and we made good time.

"The map shows that this river runs true northward," Tom said, "so we have to stay close to it."

What the map also showed us was that the river was now leading us upward into the surrounding mountains. The closest mountain on the map was Mount Pend Oreille, at 6,785 feet, which is part of the Cabinet Mountain range. Just north of that range were the Purcell Mountains. The ground continued its gentle upward trend, and was also definitely getting rockier and it was harder to walk. As we made our way, the thick canopy of trees were now blotting out the sun. It helped as it made it cooler, giving us more energy for the uphill climb. It was now getting close to 5:00.

"I sure hope this flattens out soon," I said. "I hate walking uphill."

"I don't think we're going to find any flat ground up here," Tom said.

As my pace slowed down, Tom's seemed to speed up, and he was soon way ahead of me. When he reached the top, he looked back down at me and yelled out words of encouragement.

"Come on, Al! you can do it."

As I approached the top, Tom was excited about something. I figured it was more bears, so when I reached his side, I asked him what he was so excited about.

"Look down there," he said, pointing down to a clearing that was near the river.

"What is it?" I asked.

"I don't know," Tom said, "it's a big pile of something, and it sure looks interesting."

He took off running, and I followed him as best I could.

What we found made us shake our heads in amazement. It was a huge mound of dark green tin cans, about six feet in diameter and three feet high. Tom grabbed one of the cans and started laughing.

"Would you believe this is an Army C-ration can?" he said.

I picked one up and noticed that it was marked "fruitcake."

"I've got fruitcake," I said. "What do you have?"

"I've got fruitcake also," Tom said.

As we began going through the pile we realized that they were all fruitcake.

"There's got to be something else besides fruitcake," Tom said, as he frantically rummaged through the pile.

After we went through most of them, we came to the sad conclusion that we were looking at a couple hundred pounds of fruitcake. We started laughing and joked about how the Army might be close by.

We stopped laughing and started looking around for other signs of military presence. We found nothing else that would suggest that the Army was nearby.

"This is too weird," I said. "Nobody is going to believe this one."

"I don't even believe it," Tom said. "They haven't been here for very long; there's no rust whatsoever."

After our paranoia died down, we opened up a couple of cans to see if they were edible. They were delicious, and soon we had devoured three cans each.

"We might as well take some with us. Who knew we would run into a 'grocery store' way out here?" I said, laughing.

I looked at the time and it was getting near 6:00 p.m. We decided to go forward for another hour.

"Since we now know that the Army is or was here," Tom said, "we shouldn't leave any evidence behind. They might be coming back."

"Yeah," I said, "you never know when the 101st Airborne is going to drop in on us."

We took our empty tin cans with us and left.

After an hour or so, we decided to stop on top of a small hill. From there we could see around us in every direction, still mindful of the Army's possible presence.

We got a small fire going and we heated our last two tins of soup.

After eating, we got comfortable in our sleeping bags, leaving the tent for another day, when the weather required it. Tom was looking at the map, trying to pinpoint our progress, when he let out an "oh no."

"That doesn't sound good," I said. "What is it?"

"Well, I'm following the river we are on alright, but it sort of ends with no explanation," Tom said.

"What the hell does that mean?" I asked.

"Either it's a misprint or the river dries up or something," Tom said. "I'm not sure."

"What comes after that?" I asked. "How are we going to keep our bearings for heading north?"

"Also," Tom added, "the elevation seems to be rising drastically, but there's no mention of any mountains. I guess we'll find out tomorrow afternoon."

"Right now, I'm just hoping that we don't get awakened in the middle of the night by the Army," I said.

"Or by a bear," Tom said, laughing.

For the next hour, I couldn't get to sleep. Tom's mention of a bear kept me up, and I kept hearing things in the bushes. Tom, on the other hand, was soon fast asleep, his snoring a tell-tale sign.

Suddenly, I awoke; it was 3:00 a.m. I calmed myself down and went back to sleep.

A couple of hours later, the morning sun woke me up. I heard something, and peered out of my sleeping bag. It was Tom, and he was making a fire.

"It's my turn to cook breakfast," he said.

After breakfast, I talked about how exciting this whole trip was, and that someday I would write a book about it.

"Let's just get to Canada before we make any plans to do such a thing," Tom said. "Besides, we don't know the first thing about writing any book."

"That's true," I said, "but it's worth dreaming about."

The Priest Lake Hike
Day 3 June 22

June 22, 1969, started out to be another beautiful day. Tom and I took inventory of our food supply. Two eggs, a few pieces of bacon, half a jar of peanut butter, four pieces of bread, popcorn and candy, and two tins of fruitcake.

The terrain along the river was still fairly flat, and we made good time. Tom kept mentioning a break in the river, which was only a few hours away by his calculations.

After an hour of not saying a word, I asked Tom what he was thinking about.

"I've been thinking about my wife," he said. "She must be worried; and mad at me."

"Once we get to Canada, are you going to phone her?"

·"I guess so," Tom said. "It's the only part of this trip that I am uncomfortable with."

"She'll understand," I said, trying to relieve the tension that would always be on his mind.

Tom didn't respond, so I decided to change the subject and asked him about the border.

"How much farther to the border?" I asked.

"I don't care about the border," Tom snapped, "it's that break in the river that's got me worried."

With that little outburst, I knew it wasn't time for jokes, so I kept my mouth shut. The river that we were following kept changing in size, but we were able to keep it as our guide. It was now getting close to noon, and at times it felt as if we were walking around in circles. I was beginning to feel a little weak, so I stopped.

"Hey Tom, how about we stop for something to eat?" I asked.

"No!" he said abruptly, "not now!"

He was obviously irritated about something, either the trip or worrying about his wife. I stayed back a few paces and followed him.

After another hour went by, and I caught up to him and demanded that we stop for lunch.

"If we keep on stopping, we'll never get to the border!" he shouted.

"And if we don't stop and eat," I said angrily, "I'm not going to make it to the border!"

"Well then," he shouted back, "you'll just have to stay here, won't you?"

He began to walk away, but after a few yards, he stopped and turned around.

With his head hanging down, he slowly came back toward me. He looked up at me and smiled.

"I'm sorry, Al," he said. "I don't know what got into me."

"I think I do," I said reassuringly. "Come on, let's rest here and I'll make you a peanut butter sandwich. And oh yes, for dessert, some extraordinary fruitcake."

That made Tom laugh, and I knew right away that he was back to his old self.

After we ate, we realized that our peanut butter was almost gone, and that we had also finished the bacon. That left two tins of fruitcake and some popcorn. This bit of information did nothing to improve our outlook on things, but it was the truth. We had calculated that it would take three or four days to reach the border, and now it was looking like it would take longer. With our food supply almost gone, it was going to be a battle of mind over matter.

We pushed on, and we kept our spirits up by telling each other that we would be in Canada before sunset. Tom and I had nothing to lose now, knowing we were getting close.

We kept going on what seemed to be a never-ending upward climb. It was getting close to 4:00, and Tom kept telling me that the break in the river, according to the map, should be just around the bend.

As we approached, Tom stopped and said, "Listen, do you hear that?"

"Yes," I said, "it sounds like the river, or like water rushing."

We increased our pace, intrigued by the sound that was obviously getting louder. We were still going upward for another couple hundred yards when the ground started to level off. We also noticed that the river was beginning to spread out and that the ground under our feet was getting softer. Soon, we were walking in moss covered muck, and had to stay on the edges. The weather had been getting noticeably cooler as we went along, and the noise of rushing water was also getting louder.

"I have a bad feeling about this," Tom said.

Then, what we had seen on the map suddenly made sense.

We now stood a hundred yards away from a huge waterfall, which was coming down off the side of a mountain. A virtual rock wall was now standing in our way.

"That's what the map was showing," Tom said. "Too bad it wasn't more descriptive."

We stood there, admiring its beauty, and then we realized that we weren't going to be able to go straight up.

"We'll have to walk around this waterfall," I said.

Tom started to walk to one side, and I followed him.

"Where are you going?" I asked.

"There's got to be a spot where we can climb up," he said, "otherwise it's going to be at least a few more hours if we have to go around."

"That's true," I said, "but it's steep on both sides."

We spent almost an hour looking on both sides of the falls for a way to go up instead of going around.

After a while, Tom pointed to the right side and said, "There, this is where we are going to go up."

"You're kidding," I said, "everything is so wet and slippery; we'll die trying."

Tom just gave me that look and told me that we had to try it.

I felt my paranoia coming back, and felt very intimidated by the task that lay before us.

"Have you ever rock-climbed before?" I asked Tom.

"Yes," he said, "many times in Utah, but of course it wasn't wet like this is."

"Well we don't have mountains in Florida," I said, "so this is all very new to me."

Tom and I went over our choices. Finally, Tom was eager to try it so he made his way over to a spot and started climbing. After going up a mere fifteen feet, the rocks he was stepping on became loose and he came sliding back down on his belly.

"Are you alright?" I asked.

"Yes, yes, I'm okay," Tom said, brushing the mud and dirt from his clothes.

After that failed attempt, we agreed to spend the night there, and give it a try first thing in the morning. We finished off the small amount of peanut butter, and made the most out of the last two tins of fruitcake.

"I guess my idea to bring popcorn was pretty stupid," I said, "since we don't have any way to pop it."

Tom was ignoring me, as he was again studying the map.

"We are only ten miles from the border," he said, "and about another twenty miles to the first Canadian highway."

"As long as we don't come up against any more water falls," I said.

"Tomorrow will be our last day," Tom said. By tomorrow night we'll be sleeping in a motel room."

"Sounds good to me," I said. "I can't wait to have a hot shower."

The Priest Lake Hike
Day 4 June 23

I woke to the sounds of birds chirping and crows cackling. This time the sun had yet to clear the tall mountains to the east, and I thought about having no food for breakfast.

I called to Tom and he opened one eye.

"It's time to get going my friend, the sooner we leave the sooner we'll get to Canada."

Tom got up and I watched as he took his backpack, sleeping bag, and tent and stashed them behind some bushes.

He turned around and told me to do the same.

"We won't need these anymore," Tom said, "and we'll make better time without them."

I agreed and threw my stuff in with his.

"It would be great if someday we could come back here to see if they are still here," I said.

Tom just smiled and started walking to one side of the falls.

"We'll go this way," he said, "and take the first available road going north."

I was glad to hear him make a joke out of our situation, and it made me feel confident that we were going to make it.

After about an hour of walking away from the falls, we picked a spot to start our climb, which looked to be about a distance of seventy-five to a hundred feet, straight up. We stayed even with one another at first, and made the first twenty feet in record time. The next fifty feet got harder, with Tom telling me to take my time and avoid slipping all the way back down. We took ten-minute rest stops and eventually Tom was the first to reach the top. He came over to where I was coming up and shouted words of encouragement. When I made it to the top, we hugged each other and then fell to the ground, thoroughly exhausted from the climb.

"Alright," Tom said, "now we have to head back to the river, and hope that it leads us to the border."

We made good time without the backpacks and sleeping bags. We found the river and it showed us the way north. After a couple of hours, Tom mentioned that we should be close to the border, and the possibility that we might actually be standing on Canadian soil.

"That would be incredible if we ran into a border marker," I said jokingly.

"I don't think so," Tom said, "but you never know."

We kept up our brisk pace, feeling rejuvenated at the thought of entering Canada, but at the same time feeling confused as to where exactly we were.

We came to a spot that overlooked a valley, and suddenly Tom stopped and grabbed my arm.

"What's the matter, Tom?" I asked.

"Look down there," he said, "do you see what I see?"

I peered through the trees down to a clearing and saw what looked like cabins.

"It's a bunch of cabins!" I shouted. "Let's go."

"Wait just a minute," Tom said, "we can't go down there until we know what they are."

"Okay," I said, "you're right."

We found a spot to sit and watch the cabins, to see if there was anybody there. There weren't any vehicles around, and after fifteen minutes we decided to go down. There were six cabins, each a different size, so we went directly to the largest one. There was a large padlock on the front door. We looked through the windows to see if there were any clues, like pictures or signs on the walls, to tell us where we were.

"I can't see anything," Tom said. "We'll have to try and break the lock so we can go inside."

We searched the immediate area and I found a steel bar.

"This should do it," I said, as I started hitting the lock.

After giving it a few good whacks, the lock popped open.

We went inside and started going through the paperwork that was on the desk.

"It's a logging camp," Tom said, "but I can't tell if it's a Canadian or American camp."

Just then, we heard a vehicle coming. We ran outside and placed the lock back on, then ran around to the back of the cabin.

A large pickup pulled up and stopped. A man with a cowboy hat got out and stood outside his truck, opening a briefcase that was on the front seat. We watched as he stayed there for a while. Tom whispered to me that we should go and talk to him.

"Let me do the talking," Tom said. "I'll tell him that we are Canadians and that we got lost, and that we are trying to make it back to the highway."

I was about to add my two cents to his plan, when he started walking out from behind the cabin. I followed him, and noticed the truck was equipped with a gun rack that had two rifles prominently displayed.

Oh God, he's going to shoot us right here, and nobody will ever know, I thought.

We got about ten feet from the man, who still had his back to us, when Tom started to speak.

"Excuse me, sir," Tom began.

The man quickly turned around to see who was talking.

"Jesus Christ!" he exclaimed. "You almost gave me a heart attack. What are you boys doing here?"

"We're Canadian," Tom said, "and we have been on a week-long camping trip. We got lost and now we're trying to find our way back to the highway."

After catching his breath, the man looked at us and asked us why we didn't have any camping equipment.

Tom could see that he was getting suspicious so he told him that we had to ditch our equipment in order to make better time.

The man just laughed at our misfortune, and told us that he was in charge of this logging camp, and that they were shut down for the summer by the Forest Service.

"Is that the US or the Canadian Forest Service?" Tom asked.

"The Canadian Forest Service," the man said. "You see, even though this is an American-owned logging camp, it's on Canadian land."

When I heard him say this, I realized that I was standing on Canadian soil for the first time. I wanted to scream and jump up and down, but I remembered that we were supposed to be Canadians, as far as this logger was concerned.

Tom then asked him if it was possible to reach the highway from here.

"Oh yes," the man said, smiling, "but to go directly from here, you'll have to go back over this mountain which will have about ten feet of snow on the top. I would gladly drive you boys up to the top, it's not really that far, but with all that snow, even my 4X4 wouldn't get very far. Besides, I'm just here to pick up some papers and then I'm due back in Spokane, our company headquarters."

"That's okay," Tom said. "How do we know which roads we should take?"

The man then went on to explain the roads were marked with numbers.

"Stay on Number 5 until you come to a fork, and then take Number 8. That will take you to the top. From there you should be able to see the highway, and then it's all downhill from there."

We thanked him and took off.

Once we got around the first bend, I asked Tom if we should have told him about the lock.

"I don't think he would do anything," Tom said, "he doesn't seem like the type."

We started going uphill and it didn't take long to notice the first small patches of snow. As we walked, I kept looking back, to see if the logger was coming to ask us about the lock. He didn't, so I soon forgot about him.

After a couple of hours, we came to the fork in the road and took the Number 8 road. It too kept on going straight up, and the snow started getting deeper.

"It looks as though he wasn't lying about the snow," I said.

My Army dress shoes were finally beginning to fall apart, and I noticed that one heel was coming loose.

"These shoes are useless up here," I said. "My feet are wet and cold."

"Well, there's nothing we can do about it now," Tom said, laughing, "just be glad they got you this far."

The snow was now getting deeper, and Tom told me to make sure I stayed on the road and not go off to the side. I didn't know why he told me this but it was one piece of advice I wished I had listened to.

I was beginning to slow down, and I felt a little bit dizzy. No food for twelve hours and this uphill walk was taking its toll on me. Tom was ahead of me when I decided to take a break. Without thinking, I made my way off to the side, in order to sit up against a tree. As soon as I went off the road, I sank into the soft snow up to my waist. I began screaming at Tom, who by now was at least fifty yards ahead. Finally, he heard me and came running back down.

"I told you not to go there," he said, standing there with his hands on his hips.

He got down on his belly and crawled over to where I was, and grabbed my hand. Slowly he pulled as I struggled to free myself from the hole I was in. Once out, we both crawled back to the road. I was exhausted, so we both took the time to rest.

"I told you not to go there," Tom said. "Now you know why."

"Skip the sermon," I said. "I'm feeling very weak and dizzy."

"Alright," Tom said, "we can't stay here too long, we'll freeze; so let's get going."

Tom helped me up and we restarted our uphill climb. Again, Tom got way ahead of me, and then I heard him yell. I knew we were getting close to the top, but I couldn't tell what he was yelling about.

When I got closer, I heard him call with excitement, "I can hear cars!"

As I reached him, I started to hear the sound of vehicles down below, and then I spotted them.

"There's the highway!" I yelled. "We made it! Come on, let's get down there."

I tore off both heels from my shoes and went sliding down the mountain, with Tom right behind me.

We made our way down to the road, and soon we were both standing on the edge of the road, in the middle nowhere. We were both excited, as well as shivering from being wet and cold, but thankful that we had made it.

A few trucks and cars went whizzing by us, as we got our bearings as to which direction was east.

Tom and I had talked about this part of our trip, and had decided to head to Saskatchewan, where Tom and his parents had once spent three years. We stuck out our thumbs and it didn't take long for a car to stop. A black four-door sedan slowed down, and then pulled off the road. The driver yelled at us to get in.

"Where are you boys going?" the driver asked.

"We're going to Saskatchewan," Tom said.

"Saskatchewan," the driver said. "We're going all the way to Toronto. I'm Jerry and this is Mack. We're Civil Service workers for the government."

Tom explained to them that we were college students from the University of Saskatchewan, that we were on summer break, and that we had been hiking and got lost.

Meanwhile, I was sitting there shivering and my teeth were chattering. Mack turned and noticed my condition.

"Are you alright?" he asked.

"Yes," I said, "but I could use a hot shower and some food."

"Well," Jerry said, "we did pass a motel just before picking you guys up, and there's a restaurant just up ahead, so, what will it be, food or a hot shower?"

"Food, please," I mumbled.

"Me too," Tom said.

"Alright," Jerry said, "to the restaurant it is."

"Here's an apple," Mack said, handing it to me.

I took the apple and quickly gobbled it down. A few seconds later, I could feel myself getting sick, and I knew I wasn't going to be able to keep it down. Tom noticed so he asked Jerry, the driver, to pull off the road.

"He's going to get sick," Tom said, "please stop."

Jerry found a safe place to pull over and stopped. I quickly opened the door and stuck my head out. After I finished throwing up, I closed the door and assured them I would be alright.

Arriving at the restaurant, Jerry asked Mack if he wanted to stop for a bite to eat.

"Sure," Mack said, "might as well since we're here."

"After we eat, we'll take you boys back to the motel," Jerry said, "is that okay with you?"

The four of us went in and although it was a hot summer day, Tom and I thought it best that we start off with some soup.

Jerry and Mack had some soup too, and then they told us to order anything we wanted, and they would pay for it.

"If you prefer to eat it later, Mack said, you can get it to go, and then we'll take you to the motel."

"We can get something to eat at the motel," I said, "you've already done a lot for us."

"No, you can't," Mack said, "it's just a small motel; no restaurant."

"Oh," I said, "I'm glad we found that out."

Tom and I each ordered the largest cheeseburger combo on the menu to go.

Jerry and Mack finished their soup, and then they drove us back to the motel.

It was getting near 5:00 p.m. when we arrived at the motel. We thanked Jerry and Mack for their generosity and went into the office.

An elderly man in his late seventies came out and looked at us.

"What can I do for you boys?"

We would like a room with two beds," Tom said.

"Just for the night?" he asked.

"Yes," Tom answered, "just the one night."

"That will be $20," the man said.

"Each?" Tom asked.

"Nope, just $20 for the two of you."

Tom handed him an American twenty-dollar bill, and the man just stood there and stared at it.

"Darn it," he said, looking confused, "I can never figure out the exchange rate on this stuff."

"Never mind about that," Tom said, "just keep it."

The man handed Tom the key and asked if we came in a vehicle.

"No," Tom said, "we have been hitchhiking the last few days."

Then he told us, "No partying or loud stuff, you hear?"

"No problem," Tom said. "Oh yes, there is one more thing, is there a washing machine that we could use?"

"You do look as though you've been through hell and back," the man said, looking at our clothes. "There's a small room with a washer and dryer at the back; I'll unlock it so you can use it."

We thanked him and took off for the room.

As soon as we got in, I quickly undressed and headed for the bathroom.

"Sure, go ahead and have the first hot shower in a week, just don't use all of the hot water," Tom said.

"While I'm in here, could you please take my dirty clothes to the washing machine?" I asked. "I'll do the same for you after I'm done."

After we finished getting everything clean, we heated up our cheeseburger combos and turned on the TV.

The local news was on first, and then the news turned to the Vietnam War. President Nixon was giving a speech about how he had given the North Vietnamese communists a deadline of October 30 to bring the war to an end. He then went on to describe the anti-war movement as a negative force, which only served to prolong the war.

"Wow," I said, "he still isn't telling the truth about the war."

Tom just nodded in agreement, but kept his attention on the news. After Nixon was done, the media covering the war presented a totally different slant on things. The critics of Nixon's policies were now saying that while he was negotiating for peace on one hand, he was escalating the bombing on the other. The American public, through its continuing protests and marches, kept up its demand for ending the war.

Once the news ended we were both too tired to watch any more TV, so we turned it off and got comfortable in our beds.

"Good night, Tom," I said. "We made it."

PART IV:

Stay,
Stay,
Stay

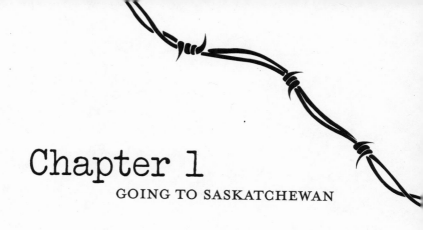

Chapter 1
GOING TO SASKATCHEWAN

Our first night in Canada was spent in the province of British Columbia, in a one room motel somewhere on Highway 3, on June 23, 1969.

Tom and I had achieved our objective of making it across the border without getting caught. We had just gone through an incredible journey that took us from the Presidio Army base in San Francisco to Salt Lake City, Utah, and finally, crossing the US-Canada border from Idaho. We also realized that it was not the end of our journey, but the beginning of another quest, one that would eventually have us become permanent citizens of Canada.

Since we did not have any knowledge of what was going on with Canada's immigration policies, Tom and I were playing it safe. The plan was to head for Saskatchewan, where Tom's parents had come to work at one of the first potash mines. Tom had gone to school there for three years, when he was eleven years old. That was ten years ago.

Looking at the map, Tom searched for the small town.

"Here it is," Tom said. "Allan, Saskatchewan."

I heard him say it but I didn't believe him.

"Did you just say Allan, Saskatchewan?" I asked.

"Yes, I did," Tom said, smiling. "I was going to tell you sooner, but without a map showing the actual town, I knew you wouldn't believe me."

I stared at the map and saw that the name of the town was indeed spelled the same way as mine.

"Well," I said, "it looks as though we're only three hundred miles from there."

"It should take less than a week to hitchhike there," Tom said.

"Why don't we find out how much it would cost us to fly to say, Saskatoon? It's close to Allan."

"I'd rather not ask my grandparents for more money right now," Tom said, "besides, hitchhiking will give us a better understanding of how the Canadians feel about the war."

"I guess you're right about that," I said.

The evening was spent lying in our beds and talking about our trip to Saskatchewan.

"What happens if we get stopped by the police?" I asked Tom.

"Nothing," Tom said. "Remember, we're just a couple of Canadian college kids on summer break."

"Right. We don't need to show a damn draft card to them. What happens if you don't find anyone you know or who remembers you in Saskatchewan?" I asked.

"That I don't know the answer to," Tom said.

"I'd like to come back here," I said, "and go to the West Coast, to Vancouver. It seems to be the place everyone is heading for."

Tom didn't say whether or not he agreed with my plan, and soon the two of us were fast asleep.

The next day, I awoke to see that Tom was already up and drinking coffee.

"Where did you get that?" I asked.

"From that coffee maker," Tom said, pointing. "I went and asked the manager if he knew where we could get some coffee, and he let me use his machine."

"Alright," I said, "now all we need is breakfast."

We then heard someone knocking on our door. It was an elderly woman, and she was holding a basket.

"Good morning," she said, "I'm the manager's wife, and I thought you boys would like some freshly baked blueberry muffins."

"Wow," I exclaimed, "this is unbelievable; thank you!"

While we looked at the map again, Tom and I ate the muffins.

"Can you believe this?" I said. "These Canadians are very nice people."

After we were finished, we returned the coffee maker and the muffin basket and bid our farewells.

We began our trip to Saskatchewan on the Trans-Canada Highway, and it didn't take long to get a ride. A large camper van pulled over and stopped.

A family of four was heading to Calgary, Alberta. We told them that we were from Ontario, and that we were heading home.

When we arrived at Fort Macleod, Alberta, the family dropped us off and told us to stay on Highway 3, which went to Lethbridge and then to Medicine Hat.

It was now noon, and since we were standing in front of a small restaurant, we decided to have lunch.

Tom mentioned the fact that we were going to need some more money, so we asked the waitress for a map, and if she knew where the closest Western Union office was.

"It isn't around here," she said, laughing. "There's nothing much around here. I'll ask my manager if he knows."

She came back with our order and told us the closest office was in Regina, Saskatchewan.

We looked at the map and saw that Regina was at least four hundred miles away.

"It's going to take us a day or two to get there," Tom said. "We had better call now so that the money will be there when we arrive."

I called my mom, and she was overjoyed to hear my voice.

"Oh, son," she said, "I'm so glad you called. I've been praying for you."

"Listen Mom, we are in Canada, and everything is alright, but we need some money to be sent to Regina, Saskatchewan."

"I have no idea where that place is," she said, "but I'll give the information to the office here. They're getting to know me quite well."

"Thank you, Mom, I'll call you when I get the money. I love you; goodbye."

Tom called his grandparents, and they agreed to do the same.

We finished our lunch and went back to find another ride. The first car stopped. A single man, driving a large station wagon, pulled over and motioned for us to get in.

"Hi, I'm Pete," he said, "where are you boys heading to?"

"Regina," Tom said.

"You're in luck," he said, "that's where I'm going."

"We're from Ontario," Tom began to explain, "and we're actually going to visit some friends who live in a small town just east of Saskatoon. Maybe you've heard of it—Allan, Saskatchewan?"

"I've heard of it," he said, "but I've never been there."

As we passed through Lethbridge, I began noticing that a lot of long-haired hippies were going in the opposite direction. Pete noticed me staring at them and he chuckled.

"There are a lot of those people in Vancouver," Pete said. "They like smoking that weed."

I just smiled and nodded my head in agreement.

For the next two hours, we exchanged stories to pass the time.

Soon, we were entering to town of Medicine Hat, and Pete decided it was time for a quick pit stop.

When we got out of his air-conditioned car, the heat almost knocked me over. It was now in the high eighties, and we still had a long way to go.

Once we resumed our trip, Pete looked at his watch and told us that we should be in Regina by 8:00 p.m.

The Rocky Mountains were now a distant memory, and we were now into the flatlands of Alberta, and entering the province of Saskatchewan.

"It'll sure feel good to get home," Pete said, "but first we'll get some dinner in Swift Current, if that's alright with you boys."

We arrived there at 5:30, and Pete knew exactly where he was going. He stopped in front of a small diner, and told us he would treat us to the best chicken salad sandwich in the world.

After we finished eating, we took off again, and arrived at the outskirts of Regina at about 8:00. Pete dropped us off at a motel, and we thanked him for his hospitality.

After paying for the room, Tom and I had just enough money left for breakfast. Tom got the first shower this time, and I looked through the phone book for the address of the Western Union office.

There wasn't anything worth watching on TV, so we talked about our impending trip to Saskatoon, and then to Allan.

"I'm hoping that after ten years, someone will still remember me, and will give us jobs," Tom said. "I know it's a long shot, but what else can we do?"

I could only agree with him as I didn't have a clue as to where we could find work. A chance of beginning a new life in a new country was not going to be easy.

It was now June 25, one day before my twenty-second birthday, and it was going to be another hot one in Regina, Saskatchewan.

After breakfast, we went to the Western Union office, which was a few blocks away. We showed the clerk our ID and asked if our money had been sent.

"It just came in this morning," he said. "Please sign here."

My mom had sent me $200, and Tom's grandparents had sent him $100. We thanked the clerk and headed out to begin our trip to Saskatoon.

While we stood on the road with our thumbs out, I couldn't help but notice the number of long-haired hippies going in the opposite direction.

"Hold on, Tom," I said, "I've got to go over there and talk to them."

Me, with my short hair, went over and asked them where they were heading.

"Vancouver," was their unanimous answer.

I told them what Tom and I were doing, and they told me that the people in Vancouver would be very supportive. I thanked them for the information and went back to where Tom was. Just then, a car stopped and we got in.

A young couple, just returning from a trip to BC, was now heading home to Saskatoon. After the usual introductions, they asked us where we were going.

"We're actually going to Toronto," Tom said, "but I want to visit Allan on the way; have you ever been there?"

"I've heard of it," the driver said. "It's a very small town. Why are you going there?"

"Ten years ago I spent some time there while my dad helped to start up a potash mine," Tom replied. "I just want to see if there is anyone there that would remember me."

"Probably everyone," joked the woman. "Those small towns don't change much."

We arrived in Saskatoon at 11:00 a.m., and we asked them to drop us off at the visitor's bureau. Tom and I went in to get directions to Allan.

"You take the Yellowhead Highway," the woman said. "Trans Canada 16; it begins down the road at the first traffic light, just look for the signs."

Tom was getting excited at the thought of returning to the place where he spent three years as a kid. I, on the other hand, was beginning to feel like a fish out of water.

We made it to the signs marking the beginning of Highway 16, and it didn't take long to get a ride from an elderly couple.

"We're going to Elstow," they said, "but we'll take you to Allan, it's not far from Elstow."

Tom went through his explanation of why we were going there, and soon we were arriving in Allan.

They dropped us off at the train depot. We went in and asked the clerk for directions to the general store. Tom was slowly getting his memory back, and after thanking the clerk, we left the depot.

As we started walking, we came upon a group of kids playing nearby. Tom asked them where the store was. The kids were afraid to talk to us, but finally, one of the older kids pointed down the road.

"It's that way," he said.

We thanked him and took off.

"This place hasn't changed very much," Tom said.

Suddenly he stopped walking and stared at one of the houses.

"I think I remember this house," Tom said. "Come on, let's go and see if they remember me."

It was now close to noon, and the heat was beginning to get unbearable. I decided to wait while Tom went and knocked on the door. A woman opened the door and they talked for a few minutes. Tom came back and told me that although he remembered her, she did not remember him.

We kept walking and soon arrived at the store. Tom asked the cashier if the manager was there.

"He's at the back," she said, "at the meat counter."

Tom and I proceeded to the rear of the store to look for him.

"Hello boys," he said, "what can I do for you?"

"Hi, Mr. Stevens," Tom said, "you probably don't remember me, but I'm Tommy, Mr. Rogers's son."

The manager looked confused at first, and then his eyes lit up.

"Little Tommy Rogers, is it really you?"

Mr. Stevens came out from behind the meat counter and stood there looking at Tom.

"It's been about ten years or so, hasn't it?" he asked.

"Yes, it has," Tom said. "I'm glad to see that you remember me."

While Tom was engaged with the manager, I returned to the front to grab a bag of potato chips. A few minutes later, Tom came to the front and his facial expression told me everything.

"What's wrong?" I asked.

"Oh, he remembers me," Tom said, "but he told me that things aren't so good around here. We might have better luck in Saskatoon, but for now, there's nothing for us here. I guess it was a mistake to come."

I immediately wanted to turn around and head to Vancouver, but I could see that Tom was feeling depressed about what he had just found out.

"We should at least find a place to stay for tonight," I said. "It's hot and I'm tired."

Tom went back and asked the manager about a place to stay.

"The manager called a place," Tom said. "We can have it for a month if we want."

We met with the people who were renting the house, and explained to them that we were undecided about how long we would need it. We agreed to pay them for a week, and I knew that we wouldn't be staying longer.

The next day, my twenty-second birthday, was spent in a town where the children were afraid of us and the adults didn't want to have anything to do with us.

It felt as though Tom and I were not only in a different country, but on a different planet. After a couple of days, it didn't take much to convince Tom to leave and head back to the West Coast, to Vancouver.

One day before July 1, Canada Day, we left the town of Allan, Saskatchewan, and never looked back.

Chapter 2

BACK TO WEST VANCOUVER

As we made our way back to Saskatoon to start our journey to the West Coast, I couldn't help but feel sorry for Tom, as his plan to find work had failed. I kept telling him that we would find work either in Vancouver or somewhere close to there. I also reminded him that once we got to Vancouver, we could see an immigration lawyer and find out if Tom would be able to legally stay in Canada.

The hitchhiking was good and it only took us a few days to get back to BC, our last ride taking us into a town called Hope.

After getting a room at a motel, Tom and I were again getting low on money. We made the usual calls and asked that the money be sent to Vancouver.

"I'm so thankful that we have someone to keep us going," I said.

"Yeah," Tom said, "I just hope we can find some work soon, so I don't have to keep asking my grandparents for money."

"I feel confident that we can find some kind of work here," I said.

Leaving Hope, we were picked up by a long-haired hippy driving a VW van. As we got in, I couldn't help but smell marijuana.

After going through the usual questions and answers, I told the driver exactly what Tom and I were doing.

"I'm cool with that," he said. "I hear there's a lot of you guys coming here. Have you got a place to stay?"

"Not yet," I said. "We're looking for work, you know, the kind that doesn't require working visas or immigration papers."

"I understand that," he said. "Hey, you should check out the Georgia Straight newspaper guys, I hear you can buy them for a dime and sell them for a quarter."

"Hmm, yes, we'll check it out; thanks," I said. "But right now we're looking for the Western Union telegraph office in Vancouver, where my parents are sending money to us."

"That's cool," he said, "we'll find it."

He went on to talk about how he had grown up in the interior of BC, but had moved to Vancouver recently.

"I really like the people here," he said, "not like those idiots back east. Where are you guys from?"

"I'm from Florida," I said, and "Tom is from Utah."

"Wow," he said, "how in the hell did you guys meet up?"

"It's a long story," I said, "someday you'll have to read the book."

"No shit," he said, laughing, "that's a good one."

He drove us into the downtown part of Vancouver, and pulled into a gas station.

We got the address of the Western Union office, and was told that it was just a few blocks away. We thanked the hippy for the ride and started walking toward the Western Union office.

We found the office and went in. After showing our IDs, we asked the clerk if our money had been sent. Roy, the clerk, looked at his watch and said, "No, nothing yet. I'm closing for lunch, but I'll be back here around one."

"Okay," I said, "we'll come back then."

We spent the next hour walking around downtown Vancouver, and noticed that there were a lot of hippies and people of Asian descent.

There was an atmosphere of activity on every street we went on, with the smell of incense and marijuana everywhere. An area known as Gastown had an especially high concentration of small shops and restaurants.

"I like this city already," I said, "it reminds me of San Francisco."

Even though we both had short hair, everyone we walked by was smiling and flashing the ever-popular peace sign. The peace symbol was also hanging in just about every store window we passed.

Brought on by the war in Vietnam, the peace slogans and symbols were part of Canada's way of showing the world that they did not agree with the war. Since we had yet to meet other deserters face-to-face, Tom and I began to look for any organizations that could help us out.

Soon, it was time to go back to see if our money had arrived.

"Nothing yet," Roy said.

"This is terrible, I said, "if we don't get our money today, we won't be able to get a motel room for the night."

"You should check out the hostels," Roy said, "they don't cost anything."

"Thanks a lot for that info," Tom said, "but we don't really want to spend the night with a bunch of strangers."

The afternoon dragged on as we made ourselves comfortable in the lobby of the Western Union office.

At six o'clock, Roy told us that even though he was open till ten, he was shutting down for an hour for dinner.

Tom and I decided to go to a Chinese restaurant for dinner.

"Why do you think it's taking so long?" Tom asked.

"I don't know," I said, "but if it doesn't come, we just might have to stay in that hostel."

At seven, we went back to the office. Roy was just getting back and was opening the doors. He went over to see if our money had arrived.

"Sorry" he said, "nothing yet."

"Damn it," I said, slamming my fist on the table. "Your equipment must not be working properly."

"I'll check again," Roy said, as he sensed that I was becoming irritated.

"No," he said, "nothing here, and I assure you, the equipment is working."

I looked at the time and realized that we still had a couple of hours to wait. I apologized to Roy for my little outburst, and began reading every newspaper and magazine twice.

A story in the *Vancouver Sun* caught my attention.

"Hey Tom," I said, "it says that there is a major construction boom going on in a place called Whistler. Something about it becoming a major skiing destination to rival Vale and Aspen."

"That's nice," Tom said, "if you're a construction worker."

"Well," I said, "at least it's a possibility, right, Roy?"

"Yes," Roy said, "from what I've heard about Whistler, a lot of money is being spent there to develop the place. They're going to be building houses, condos, chalets, everything that the big skiing resorts in the states have."

It was now getting close to ten o'clock, and Roy checked to see if our money had come in. He walked over to where we were sitting, and saw that Tom had fallen asleep.

He looked at me and whispered, "Nothing has come in, but I'm going to trust you boys, and let you spend the night in the back room. There's a cot and a couch, and some bedding. Come on, I'll show you. Oh yes, one more thing, here's the coffee maker, and there's coffee and milk in the fridge."

I went with Roy into the back room, and found everything he had mentioned.

"I'll be here at 7:00 a.m., Roy said. "We open at 8:00. See you boys then." Roy left, locking the doors behind him.

Roy had told us to stay in the back room and not come out, because the police patrolled the area all night.

"Tom," I said, "wake up. We're spending the night here."

"What? Where are we?" Tom said.

"We're still here at the western Union office," I said, "Roy is letting us stay here tonight in the back room; come on."

Tom and I went into the back room and I offered him the couch. It didn't take long for Tom to go back to sleep.

Meanwhile, I sat on the cot, and thought about all of the Canadians we had met during our first week in Canada. Even though they had never met us before, they always showed us that they were kind and understanding. I now realized that this country, because of their non-involvement in the war, was a peace-loving country, and it felt good to want to be a part of it forever.

I lay down on the cot and didn't wake till 6:15. Tom was still sleeping, so I stayed on the cot until 7:00 and then got up and started making coffee.

The noise of the coffee percolating woke Tom.

"That smells so good," Tom said, "what time is it?"

"It's around seven," I said. "Roy should be here any moment."

Just then, Roy arrived, and he came into the back room carrying a box of something.

"Oh good," Roy said, "I'm glad you started the coffee, because I've brought some donuts for us to share. So, how was it last night? I hope it wasn't too noisy."

"No," I said, "it was pretty quiet."

We finished the donuts and coffee, and then Roy looked at his watch.

"Well," he said, "I'd better go and put the open sign out, and see if anything has come in."

"I wonder how much longer we're going to have to wait for our money," Tom said.

"If it doesn't get here by noon, we'll have to call and see what the problem is," I told him.

Just then, Roy called us to come out.

"Good news," he said, "your money has come in."

"How much?" I asked.

"Two hundred dollars each," he said, "one from Florida and one from Utah. I thought you two were from the States."

Tom and I looked at each other, and realized that we hadn't been fooling anyone by telling them that we were from Ontario.

"It don't matter to me where you're from," Roy said. "Just sign here, and the money is yours."

After we signed, Roy asked us if we were still going to Whistler to look for work.

"Yes," Tom said, "now all we need is directions to get there."

Roy took us out to the street and pointed.

"Walk down to the lights and you'll see a sign that says North Vancouver. Once you get there, then it's West Vancouver, Squamish, and finally Whistler."

We thanked Roy for being so understanding, and left.

Chapter 3
WHISTLER

It was a cool but sunny beginning to the day, and it didn't take long to get a ride to North Vancouver. From there, we got a ride all the way to Squamish.

As we waited on the road in Squamish, I couldn't help but admire the area. Lush green forests surrounded us, and we were only minutes away from the city.

Again, it didn't take long to get a ride, this time from a young man in his twenties driving an old station wagon.

"Hi," he said, "where you guys going?"

"Whistler," Tom said.

"I'm not going that far," he said, "but I can take you about halfway. Hop in."

The man introduced himself as Rollie, from New Westminster.

"I'm Tom, and this is Al," Tom said.

"Why are you going to Whistler?" Rollie asked.

"To look for work," I said.

"Oh yes," Rollie said, "I hear they're building a huge ski resort."

"That's what we've been told," I said, "but so far we haven't talked to anyone who has been there."

"I've never been that far either. Right now, I'm going back to my tent," Rollie said.

Tom and I looked at each other, and then Tom asked him what he meant.

"Oh," Rollie laughed, "I don't live in a tent all the time; I'm just camping out for a couple of weeks. It's in a nice spot, beside the Cheakamus River, just off the highway."

Rollie could tell by our reaction that we weren't from the area, and that we didn't have a clue as to where he was talking about.

"Where are you guys from?" he asked.

"We're from Ontario," Tom said.

Rollie just chuckled and said, "Well, forgive me if I'm wrong, but your accents don't sound to me like you're from Ontario. Am I right?"

"Yes, you're definitely right," I said, "I'm from Florida and Tom is from Utah."

"I knew it," Rollie said, "I could especially tell by your accent, Al, being from Florida. So, are you draft dodgers, or what?"

"We're actually deserters," I said. "We just came up a week ago."

"Oh, right on," Rollie said, "I've never met deserters, but I have met draft dodgers."

Rollie was another understanding Canadian, and he assured us that he knew what was going on with the war and the US political scene, but when we asked him about the Canadian government, and what was being done to help people like us, he just shrugged his shoulders and replied, "I haven't got a clue. Your best bet would be to go and see an immigration lawyer. For now though, would you like to visit with me in my humble abode?"

"Sure," we said, "but we don't have anything to contribute."

"No problem," he said." I just picked up some more food in Squamish, and I make the best campfire coffee in the world."

We arrived at a point on the highway, and turned down a dirt road.

Rollie's tent was big enough for four people, and once inside, we found everything arranged in a neat and tidy manner. He started the coffee and then brought out some cheese and bread.

"Help yourself," he said. "I'm not a very good cook, so this will have to do."

Rollie told us that he worked for a printing business in New Westminster, and that he lived in the basement suite of his parents' house.

"I have a girlfriend," he said, "but she doesn't like camping. It's also my way of getting out of the city for a while."

"It's beautiful out here," I said. "I prefer this to living in the city any day."

We spent about an hour there, and then decided we should get going.

"Feel free to stop in here again," Rollie said. "I'll be here for another week."

"Thank you for everything, Rollie," I said, "goodbye."

As we walked back to the highway, I said to Tom, "I like him, and I have a feeling we're going to be seeing him again."

We got a ride from a young couple who were on their way to Pemberton, the next town after Whistler. After answering the usual questions, we asked Ted, the driver, if he knew anyone who might be interested in hiring us. He told us about some people he had met, who had just purchased a large chunk of property and were in the process of clearing their land.

"They could use some help, if you're into that kind of work," he said.

"That would be a start," Tom said. "Do you know where it is?"

"Yes, Ted said, they marked the road that leads into their property with a sign, now we just have to look for it; it's about ten miles from here."

Eventually, we found the sign and Ted dropped us off.

"It's down this road about a half a mile," he said. "Good luck."

We found a large trailer, and knocked on the door.

A man opened the door and asked us what we wanted.

"We're looking for work," Tom said, "and we were told that you might need some help clearing this land."

"I'm Gerry," the man said, "wait here and I'll get my boots."

Gerry came out and pointed to a backhoe and a bulldozer and asked us if we had any experience with heavy machinery.

"No, sir," Tom said, "we've never operated anything like that."

"Well then," Gerry said, smiling, "the only work I can offer you is to clear this area here of all the rocks. I'll pay you two bucks an hour, each."

He looked at us and waited for our reaction to his offer. Tom and I looked at each other, and then we agreed to his offer.

"There is one more thing," Tom said, "we don't have a place to stay."

"You're welcome to stay in the electrical shed over there; it's clean."

We went over and had a look inside. I pulled Tom aside and whispered, "It's not the accommodations I was hoping for, and there aren't any beds in there."

Gerry heard me say this, and he told us that he had a couple of cots that we could use.

"What about food?" I asked.

"You boys are welcome to eat with me and my wife, Sarah," Gerry said. "Come on in, I'll introduce you to her."

It was getting close to noon, and after meeting Sarah, we all sat down to have lunch.

"So," Gerry said, "where are you boys from?"

I looked at Tom to see if he was going to tell them the truth, or keep with the "we're from Ontario" version.

"We're from the States," Tom said. "I'm from Utah, and Al is from Florida."

"I thought you were from the States," Gerry said, "but I wasn't sure."

I looked at Tom again, and then started telling Gerry and Sarah the whole story.

Gerry and Sarah listened intently as I poured out my feelings on the "what and why" we were doing such a drastic thing.

"Wow," Gerry said, "that's quite an ordeal you two just went through."

Sarah then told us that they were both against the war, and that she and Gerry would do anything to help us out.

"Thank you," I said. "Since we have been in Canada, everyone we have met has told us the same thing."

"I've heard that there are some Canadian kids who are actually going down and joining the US military," Gerry said. "Why they would do that I haven't a clue."

Then Gerry said, "Are you two ready to go to work?"

"Yes, we are," Tom said. "Let's go."

After Gerry showed us what he wanted done, he left to go to town.

We began the chore of picking up rocks and putting them in the wheelbarrow, and then dumping them at a prescribed spot. We were not used to this sort of work, and it didn't take long to feel our muscles tightening up and getting sore.

I stopped working and looked around in awe at the undeveloped land that stretched for miles in every direction,

"What's the matter?" Tom asked. "Is this work too hard for you?"

"This is sure beautiful land," I said. "I hope we can afford to own a piece of it someday."

"We'd have to talk to Gerry," Tom said, "since he is into real estate."

After a couple of hours had passed, Gerry returned from his trip into town.

"Here you go," he said, tossing Tom and me a couple of chocolate bars each. "I thought you might like these."

"Thank you," I said, "it's been awhile since we've had chocolate."

"How's it going?" Gerry asked.

"It's okay," I said, "but it's very boring and back-breaking."

Gerry just laughed and agreed with my remark.

"It's too bad you've never operated heavy machinery," Gerry said, heading into his trailer, "then you wouldn't be so sore."

"He could teach us," Tom suggested. "I'm into learning, how about you?"

"Sure," I said, "I don't want to be picking up rocks by hand for the rest of my life."

Gerry came out and we asked him about teaching us.

"Yes, I could teach you," Gerry said, "but I couldn't let you run it without you being covered by liability insurance. If you got hurt, I'd be on the hook for damages."

"Oh," Tom said, "I forgot about that. Anyway, Al and I are interested in finding out more about buying or leasing land around here."

"Sure," Gerry said, "we can talk about it over dinner."

At 5:00, Gerry told us to quit working and go and have a shower.

Sarah told us that she had placed some of Gerry's old clothes on the bed for us to change into.

While Tom showered first, I sat with Gerry and Sarah and enjoyed a cold beer. They proceeded to tell me about their life, and how everything changed when Gerry got hurt in a logging accident.

"We were going to buy a place in Vancouver and start a family," Sarah said. "We had saved up enough for a good down payment on a house when Gerry got hurt and had to spend a year on compensation. Everything was put on hold, and we ended up renting. While Gerry was waiting to go back to work, he took a course in real estate."

"When I got out of rehab," Gerry added, "I was told by the doctor that I shouldn't go back to logging, because I would have trouble with my legs. The real estate course was the beginning of my new career, with the pay being just as good, and it was not as dangerous. That's when we decided to move out of the city and purchase this piece of property, before everything is gone. This area is booming."

Tom came out of the bathroom and I went for my shower. After I was finished, we sat down to a meal of roast beef, mashed potatoes and gravy, and fresh garden beans.

"This is like being treated like celebrities in a five-star restaurant," I said.

"I'm sure that after all the work you guys did today, you won't feel like that in the morning," Gerry quipped.

We assured them that this was the best meal we had in a long time, and that we would be willing to work as long as our bodies did not give out.

"I can agree with that," Gerry said.

After dinner, Tom and I volunteered to do the dishes, and Sarah gladly accepted our offer. Then Gerry got out his maps, and the four of us had fun looking at the areas, with Gerry pointing out the centre of activity for the resort.

"Everything within a three- mile radius of this area here has been bought up, so you're looking at the surrounding areas here, and here. This is where we are right now."

"Well, now for the bad news. How much is an acre going for?" Tom asked.

"We paid $30,000 for five acres," Gerry said, "and the word is that it's going to keep going up."

"There is government land that I think is available through the Homestead Act," Sarah said. "It provides 640 acres of land for a minimal fee, provided you work the land and live on it."

"That sounds good," I said, "where is this land?"

Gerry pointed out the areas between Whistler and Pemberton, and also north of the Mount Currie Indian Band reservation, at a place known as D'Arcy.

"It's mostly desolate land," Gerry said, "and you have to make sure there is a water source all year round."

We talked about the responsibilities of owning land, the pros and the cons, and then Gerry told us that if we wanted to leave and check it out, that he wouldn't have a problem with it.

Then Gerry yawned and said, "I think it's time to hit the hay. See you tomorrow around seven."

That night, while we were getting ready to go to sleep in the shed, I asked Tom if he was interested in going farther north to look at the land in question.

"Don't you think that we should finish the job we've started here first?" he asked.

"I don't think this job will ever be finished," I said, "at least not by hand. I think they are just helping us out because of the situation we're in."

"Alright," Tom said, "let's work for another four hours tomorrow, and then we'll go up there. If we don't like what we see, then we can always come back down here."

In the morning, I heard a knock on the shed door. It was Sarah, telling us that breakfast was ready. It was another super meal, with bacon and eggs served on a real plate, instead of on a flattened tin can. We told Gerry about our plan to work for four hours, and then we wanted to go farther north to look at the land that was available.

After we were finished, Gerry paid us in cash for the work we had done, and told us that after we got cleaned up, to join him and Sarah for lunch.

During lunch, Gerry handed us a couple of maps which showed where there was government land available, known as Crown Land.

"Take these maps," he said. "They'll show you where to look, and don't worry about the clothes, you need them more than I do."

Chapter 4

GOING TO D'ARCY

After lunch, Gerry drove us to the northern part of Whistler to begin our journey to D'Arcy.

"Take care," he said, "and good luck."

"Thank you for everything," I said. "Goodbye."

It didn't take long to get a ride to Pemberton.

"There isn't much up there," the driver said, "except a lot of land that nobody wants."

"That's okay," I said, "the cheaper the better."

He dropped us off in front of signs that read Mount Currie and Birken. Soon we were picked up by a young man who was a member of the Mount Currie Indian band.

"Where are you guys heading to?" he asked.

"D'Arcy," Tom said, "to look at Crown Land."

The man laughed and then became serious, and with a stern voice he told us, "It all belongs to us, you know. The government has no business in selling that land; they don't own it!"

Tom and I sat in silence, stunned at his outburst.

The young driver relaxed and started laughing.

"I'm just kidding," he said, "I do that to all of the white people who pass through here. You guys don't look or sound like you're from around here, am I right?"

"You're right," I said, "we're from the States."

"Oh, a couple of Yankees," he said. "Well, good luck on getting anything from this government."

He took us to the far end of the reservation and told us that we still had about thirty miles to go to get to D'Arcy. Tom and I got out and checked the maps that Gerry had given us.

This time, we had to wait an hour for the next ride. It was a station wagon with a middle-aged couple inside, and I could tell that they were equipped for camping and fishing.

"We're going to D'Arcy," I said.

"Well, we'll get you halfway there," they said. "We're going fishing up at Birken."

When we got to a fork in the road, the driver stopped and pointed us in the right direction.

This time, after waiting for another hour, we began wondering if anyone was going to come by.

We decided to start walking when we heard a vehicle coming. A pickup truck, with a woman driving, stopped.

"Where are you two boys going?" she asked.

"D'Arcy," I said. "It's not too far from here, is it?"

"No, it isn't," she said, smiling. "It's where my family and I live."

"Oh, you live there," we said. "That's great, maybe you can help us out."

We quickly explained to her what we were hoping to do, and she told us to hop into the truck. We asked her if she had horses for rent. She told us that she did, and soon we arrived at a beautiful farm house, with chickens running freely around the house.

"I'm Doreen," she said, "and my husband's name is Jack."

Just then, three children came running out of the house.

They were obviously excited about their mom being home, but when they saw us, they stopped and started walking in a polite manner. They went over to the truck as Doreen was beginning to grab bags of groceries that were in the back, and on the front seat. Everyone pitched in, grabbing a bag or two, and then we all went into the house.

Her husband Jack was sitting at a large dining room table, sipping a cup of coffee.

"Hello," he said, and gave his wife a peck on the cheek. "How did everything go?"

"Fine," Doreen said. "I picked up these two boys just outside of Birken, and they are here to rent horses so they can look at some Crown Land that they were told about."

"We me a real estate person in Whistler who gave us these maps of where to look," I said.

I placed the maps in front of Jack, and he looked them over and then told us that the land we were looking at was practically useless.

"Why?" I asked.

"Because there is simply a lack of water," he said. "If I were you, I'd go over here, to this side of Anderson Lake."

Doreen came back with some sandwiches and more coffee.

"Here you are," she said politely, "I hope you like ham and cheese."

"Oh, thank you," I replied, "ham and cheese is great."

After eating and talking about the land in question, I could tell that Jack wanted to ask us a personal question or two.

"I hope you don't mind me asking," he said, "but are you two from the States?"

"Yes, we are." Tom said. "I guess our accents gave us away, right?"

"Yes indeed," Jack said, smiling. "I thought you weren't from around here. One more question. Are you by any chance a couple of draft dodgers we've been hearing about lately?"

"Yes, sir," Tom said. "It's a long story, but the two of us did not want to go to Vietnam."

"Well, you can relax; Doreen and I are also against the war," Jack said.

"I'm so glad to hear that," I said. "In the one week that Tom and I have been here, we've not met one Canadian who is in favour of the war."

While the kids, Toby, Mark, and Shane, left to do some chores, we went back to looking at the maps.

"It's almost 5:00 now," Jack said, looked at his watch, "and it will take you about half an hour to ride out to the property I've marked on the map. You can spend the night here with us, and then get an early start in the morning. Shane will get your horses ready for you after breakfast. How does that sound?"

"That sounds good to me," I said. "It'll be cooler in the morning."

The next day, we were up early for breakfast and afterward, Shane, the oldest, went and saddled up two of their horses.

We spent the next hour heading out to Anderson Lake, the area that Jack had pointed out. Along the way, Tom and I debated the pros and cons of what we were doing.

"We've only been here ten days," Tom said, "and already we're looking to buy land. I think we're rushing into something we know nothing about."

"Still," I said, "I feel really fortunate to be out here riding horses, and at least be given the time to think about what we want to do next."

"True," Tom said. "After what we've just been through, this is a nice way to slow down and get a plan together that works for both of us."

After finding the lake, we stopped to let our horses get a drink, and we really soaked up the atmosphere of the land.

The morning sun was getting hotter by the minute. I made a reference to about the hot weather, without an ocean breeze.

"Look," Tom said, "I know you'd prefer living close to the ocean, but please do not keep reminding me of it."

"I'm sorry," I said, "I won't mention it again."

We rode around part of the lake, and found the parcels of land that were available for homesteading.

"It's okay," I said, "but I for one would never live here."

"Yeah, I guess I couldn't live here either," Tom said, "but only because it's so remote."

We agreed to enjoy riding for another hour, and then headed back to Jack's farm. When we arrived, Shane came out and took our horses back to the barn.

"They're waiting for you," Shane said. "Dinner is almost ready."

The aroma of another delicious meal greeted us as we went inside.

"Hello, boys," Doreen said, "Jack is watching TV. Go wash up for dinner."

After we washed our hands, we joined Jack and noticed he was watching the news.

"I don't watch too much TV," Jack said. "We only get one channel out here, the CBC."

The newscast began with a story about the planned moon landing.

"In the US, NASA is reporting the scheduled lunar landing flight will go ahead for July 16. They hope to put a lunar landing module on the surface of the moon, where the astronauts will leave their module for a walk on the moon."

"That is really something," Jack said." "The Americans want to be the first ones to walk on the moon."

"I wish they would take care of the problems here on earth first," I said.

"They should be spending that money on the citizens of the US," Tom added.

"Now, back to local news, the Canadian government is now recognizing both French and English as Canada's official languages."

Just then, Doreen came in and told us that dinner was ready. Jack turned off the TV, and we went into the dining room.

"So, after having a look at the land, are you still interested in buying it?" Jack asked.

"We've decided to keep on looking," I said. "Our first priority of course is to find out what the Canadian government is doing about guys like us, and whether or not we can stay."

"Oh Jack," Doreen said, "did you tell them about the hippy commune down the road?"

"No, I didn't," Jack said. "You may have missed the sign, but there are about twenty or thirty people living on a piece of land that they bought, and apparently they are starting some kind of commune."

"We didn't see the sign," I said, "but doing something like that would be great."

"Yeah," Tom added, "I don't like the idea of staying here illegally."

With that, we dined on a delicious meal of pork tenderloin, potato salad, and fresh vegetables. Dessert was not to be left behind as the kids proudly served their own homemade ice cream with fresh strawberries.

"So," Jack said, "does that mean that you're going back to Vancouver?"

"Yes," I said, "we must see a lawyer who specializes in immigration matters, and also to try and get some work."

"Well, if you ever want to come back here, you're more than welcome," Jack said.

"Thank you very much," Tom said, "we just might do that."

That night, Tom and I talked about going back to Vancouver.

"I'd like to stop in at Rollie's place," I said. "I think he can help us out one way or another."

"Sure," Tom said. "Good night."

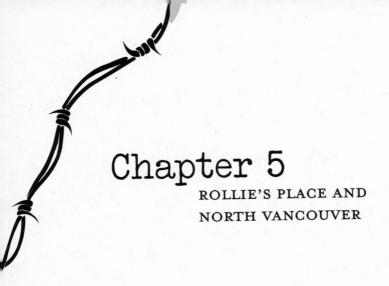

Chapter 5

ROLLIE'S PLACE AND
NORTH VANCOUVER

Sunrise came around 5:30 a.m., and I woke to the sound of the kids going out for their morning chores. Tom and I got dressed and went into the kitchen, where Doreen was busy making breakfast.

"Pancakes or omelet?" she asked.

"I'll have an omelet," I said, and Tom opted for the pancakes.

Jack came in and told us that he had to go to Pemberton today to get animal feed, so we had a ride all the way into Pemberton.

We said our goodbyes to Doreen and the kids, and left.

It was July 5, 1969, twenty days after leaving the Presidio army base in San Francisco, California. Tom and I were now traveling around Canada, having been in three provinces. It was truly an astonishing change of environment. We were in a country whose future was based on peace, not war.

Soon, we arrived in Pemberton and after thanking Jack, we started hitchhiking toward Rollie's place. Our next ride was from a man who was going to Vancouver.

"We're going to visit a friend, who is camping out on the river about ten miles south of Whistler," I said, "if we can remember where the road is."

"Okay," the man said, "just let me know where you want out."

It took about an hour to get to the road, and then I shouted, "Stop! This is it."

We thanked him and got out, and started walking down the road to Rollie's tent.

"Hello!" I shouted. "Rollie, are you there?"

I heard him moving around inside, and then he stuck his head out.

"Hi," he said, smiling, "it's the Yanks. I knew you'd be back. Come on in."

We went in and sat down, and the smell of coffee and pipe tobacco filled the tent.

After explaining everything, we asked him if he knew of anyone that could help us find work or a place to stay. He thought for a moment, and then he told us that he had a friend, whose mother, Marie, was the owner of an apartment complex in North Vancouver.

"As for work," Rollie said, "you two don't have work visas or any papers, so I can't help you out there."

"Well, just getting a place of our own would be a big help, then we could look for work," I said.

"I was thinking of going into Vancouver today or tomorrow," Rollie said. "I'll see if I have my friend's phone number in my wallet."

Rollie found the number, and asked us if we wanted to go and check out the apartment.

"We sure do," I said. "Our own place is just what we need."

We closed up Rollie's tent and he fired up the old station wagon.

"So Rollie," I asked, "do you know how much one of these apartments cost?"

"Not exactly," Rollie answered, "but they should be in the range of two-fifty to three hundred a month."

Tom and I counted the money we had, which came to just over four hundred dollars.

"Well," I said, "hopefully we can get it for two-fifty or three hundred a month. That will leave us between a hundred and a hundred-fifty for food."

We arrive in North Vancouver, and Rollie drove to a gas station to phone his friend about the apartment.

"I've got the address of the apartment," he said. "It's just off Lonsdale and Fourth Street."

When we arrived, Rollie told us to wait in his car, while he went to see if there were any vacancies.

He came back with a big smile on his face.

"You're in luck," he said, "Marie has one vacancy. It's only got one bedroom, but it has a couch that can pull out to be a bed, for three hundred a month. She's gone there to make sure everything is working."

I was feeling very excited as we followed Rollie to the apartment.

We went in and found Marie scurrying around the place, turning on different appliances. When she saw us, she stopped and came over.

"Everything is working," she said. "I do hope you like it."

It didn't take long for me to like what I saw.

We sat down at the dining room table and talked about the rent.

"It's three hundred a month," she said, "but because Rollie has told me that you are here because of the Vietnam War, I'll let you have it for the rest of the month for one-fifty. Is that okay with you?"

"Oh yes," I said, "thank you very much."

We quickly counted out the money and gave it to her.

"Well, I guess you two would like to go and get some groceries," Rollie said.

"Oh," I said, still in shock over our newly acquired place, "yes, that would be great."

"All right then," Rollie said, "thank you Marie, I'll see you later."

Tom and I again thanked Marie as she handed us the key.

"If there's anything you need, boys," Marie said, just ask. "I'm in number 101. Now go and get some groceries, and I'll finish cleaning up here."

We drove to a supermarket, and while we were inside, I flashed back to the day that Tom and I were in the small store in Idaho, getting things for our hike through the wilderness.

Tom grabbed a cart and I started following him around the store.

"Wait a minute," I said aloud, "we don't have to share the same cart anymore," and I went to get my own.

After that outburst, the two of us began racing around the store like children in a candy store.

Meanwhile, Rollie, who had finished his shopping, came back into the store to see what the holdup was. He spotted us in the check-out line looked at our selection of food and laughed.

"You guys are going to have to find some women to cook for you," he said.

"That sound good to me," I said.

After paying for our groceries, we loaded them into Rollie's car and took off for the apartment.

"Rollie," I said, "since you've been so helpful, you must come back here after your camping trip is finished."

"I'll do that," Rollie said with a smile. "See you guys later."

After we put our groceries away, I grabbed a bag of potato chips and sat on the couch. Looking southward, I could see the skyline of Vancouver.

"Well Tom," I said, "we are now sitting in our own apartment and looking at the city of Vancouver. Did you ever think that it would end up this way?"

"No," Tom said, holding a bag of candy. "We have been fortunate to have met people who are sympathetic to our reasons for coming here. I don't think we could have made it without their help and generosity."

"I agree with that, my friend," I said. "These people have proven to me that we came to the right place."

Tom sat down beside me with his candy, and the two of us sat there, staring out at the city.

I realized that even though we had just gone through an incredible journey together, we still had our own individual plans for the future.

Just then, we heard a knock on the door.

"Who is it?" I asked, opening the door.

"It's me," Marie said, "I forgot to ask you if you wanted the telephone hooked up."

We agreed that it would be good to have a telephone, so Marie went over to the closet, grabbed the phone, and hooked it up.

"It's included in the rent," she said, "except of course for long distance calls. Also, I have a spare TV if you want; it's down in my apartment."

"Yes indeed," I said, "I'll come down with you now and get it."

It was 3:00 p.m. when I turned on the TV. There were three American channels and two Canadian channels.

"There's only soap operas," I said. "Are you interested?"

"No way," Tom said. "Turn that crap off."

I turned off the TV and went back to the couch.

"I wonder what's happening at the Presidio," I said.

"Wouldn't it be funny if there wasn't anybody left there? You know, like everybody went AWOL at the Presidio?"

"Please," Tom said, "don't mention that place again."

Tom was into one of his serious moods, so I decided to change the subject.

"I wonder what's happening with the war," I said.

"I don't want to talk about that either," Tom said.

"Well then, Tom," I said, "just what in the hell do you want to talk about?"

"Right now," he said emphatically, "nothing."

"What's wrong with you?" I asked, "Am I missing something or what?"

"No, Al," Tom said, "it's not you. It's just that I miss my family and my wife, but you wouldn't understand."

"Well," I said, "why don't you call them?"

Tom got up from the couch and went into the bathroom, slamming the door shut.

It was the first time that Tom had gotten so emotional, and I figured that he had been keeping it inside the whole time we were travelling together, and it had to come out sooner or later.

A few minutes later, Tom came out and apologized for slamming the door.

"I'm sorry, Al, it's just that I feel guilty about what I did to them. Knowing that my parents are mad at me for leaving, plus the fact that my wife was ready to give birth soon. I just don't know what to say to them."

"Maybe your grandparents have convinced them that what you did, and why you did it, was for the better," I said. "I'd call them first and tell them that we have made it into Canada, and see what they suggest."

While Tom was thinking about what I had just said, I sat there thinking about my priorities. Now that Tom and I had a place of our own, the next step would be to see an immigration lawyer and find out the Canadian government's position, and what steps I should be taking in order to stay here.

"Don't you have anyone that makes you wish you hadn't left?" Tom asked.

"Not really," I said, "but if I did, I'd definitely want them to come to Canada."

"I'd like to think my wife would be willing to come and join me," Tom said, getting up from the couch, but I won't know that until I talk to my parents."

Tom went over to the telephone.

"Do you want me to leave?" I asked.

"Please," Tom said. "It will be easier to talk to them without you here."

"Alright, I'll go out for a walk around the block," I said.

When I came back, Tom told me that his parents were softening their stance on his leaving the way he did, and his wife hadn't had the baby yet.

"They say she has another month to go," Tom said. "She's doing fine, and living with her parents."

"That's good to hear," I said. "I'm sure they will support you in whatever you decide to do."

I could tell that Tom was feeling better, now that he had talked to his parents, and I took the chance to thank him again for helping me out.

"I'm very grateful, and lucky to have met you at the Presidio," I began. "If it weren't for you, I'd probably be in jail. By leaving, you have not only made a great sacrifice, but you have also made a statement as loud as anyone could make. Now, you must believe in yourself, and get on with your life here in Canada. If the Canadian government would allow it, I'm sure it would be easy for your wife to come and have the baby here, as a Canadian."

Tom looked at me and smiled.

"You sure have a way of simplifying things," he said. "Yes, that would be the perfect ending to this whole trip."

After talking some more about what we had just gone through, I suggested we go for a walk and find a liquor store to get something with which to celebrate.

"Sounds good to me," Tom said.

We asked the first person we met for the location of a liquor store.

"So, my friend," I said when we got there, "what will it be, champagne, beer, or wine?"

"Let's do this right," Tom said, as he picked out the largest bottle of champagne that he could find.

I began to give him half of what it cost, but he held up his hand and said, "This is my treat, for setting me straight."

"Alright," I said, "if that's the way you want it, who am I to complain?"

We headed back to the apartment and Tom put the bottle in the fridge.

"They say 'fridge' up here," Tom said, smiling. "I remembered that from my years spent in Saskatchewan."

"I'll bet there are more of those Canadian words to learn," I said.

We gave the champagne a half hour to chill, and then proceeded to uncork it.

"Here's to the future," Tom said.

I nodded in agreement as we each drank our first glass in one gulp.

"That's good stuff," I said, "I'll have another."

Tom and I sat on the couch without saying another word, drinking glass after glass of champagne.

It didn't take very long for the two of us to finish the bottle, and soon I was drifting in and out of consciousness.

As I went into a deep, liquor-induced stupor, I realized that although I had just lost my country, I had indeed, kept my soul.

Epilogue

Tom and I found work at a car wash in Vancouver that paid us cash at the end of each day.

"No working papers required," the manager told us.

I found a couple of lawyers who specialized in immigration matters, and they told me that I could apply for landed immigrant status, but that the Canadian government had not yet publicly announced any policy regarding draft dodgers or deserters. Because of this uncertainty, I decided to wait for a more positive announcement from the government.

Eventually, I met a girl from Ontario, and we made plans to start a communal house in Burnaby. Tom's situation was more complex, and the two of us eventually parted ways.

After I left the job at the car wash, I never saw or heard from Tom again.

Starting my life in Canada was a new journey, but that's another story.

Printed in Canada